Clive Grinyer
Redesigning Thinking

Clive Grinyer

Redesigning Thinking

How Service Design is Solving Our
21st Century Challenges

DE GRUYTER

ISBN 978-3-11-139282-0
e-ISBN (PDF) 978-3-11-139796-2
e-ISBN (EPUB) 978-3-11-139916-4

Library of Congress Control Number: 2025932079

Bibliographic information published by the Deutsche Nationalbibliothek
The Deutsche Nationalbibliothek lists this publication in the Deutsche Nationalbibliografie;
detailed bibliographic data are available on the internet at http://dnb.dnb.de.

© 2025 Walter de Gruyter GmbH, Berlin/Boston, Genthiner Straße 13, 10785 Berlin
Cover image: Hybert Design
Typesetting: Integra Software Services Pvt. Ltd.
Printing and binding: CPI books GmbH, Leck

www.degruyter.com
Questions about General Product Safety Regulation:
productsafety@degruyterbrill.com

To Mr. Laney, my first design and technology teacher

Advance Praise for *Redesigning Thinking*

"We won't redesign everything we need to, unless we redesign our thinking. The need for creative problem solvers is greater than ever, so this book is right on time. It is full of examples, insights and tools for navigating the complexities and challenges of our lives today. Clive brings such humanity and warmth to this subject. It should not only be on all designers' reading lists, it should be part of the school curriculum."

– **Minnie Moll**, CEO of the Design Council

"Packed full of tips, tricks and insights. This book is an essential read for anyone who wants to redesign and rethink the world, and help us solve the big, complex societal challenges that we face. What impact will you create?"

– **Professor Alex Hill**, Co-founder and Director of the Centre for High Performance

"Clive Grinyer has pioneered design in business, public services and education, and here he is bang on target in arguing that what needs redesign is not just things and services, but rather how we think. This engaging and smart book shares many vivid examples of how new ways of thinking can help us understand and better grapple with the problems that surround us. I hope it will encourage a new generation of brilliant designers to use their skills where they're most needed."

– **Geoff Mulgan**, Professor of Collective Intelligence, Public Policy and Social Innovation at University College London

"*Redesigning Thinking* couldn't have arrived at a better time. I've worked with Clive over the years, both at the RCA and with clients, and his insights ring true. Design is at a crossroads. Organisations urgently need design to shape the future of their customers, services, and role in their communities—balancing well-being and sustainability with cost, growth, and risk. As AI takes on routine design tasks, Clive makes a compelling case for why the future needs designers who think differently—bringing human insight, powered by empathy, creativity, and ingenuity. Rather than fighting for a seat at the table, designers must redefine their role and scale their impact. Or, as Clive puts it, 'engineer design, don't design engineering.'"

– **Peter Neufeld**, Partner; Head of Customer, Innovation & Experience Design, EMEIA, FSO, EY Seren

Acknowledgements

This is less of a textbook and more of a discussion around the value and purpose of design, innovation and human advancement. It's been made possible by many conversations with the creative, inspirational and knowledgeable people I'm lucky to know, many of whom have contributed to this book. I would like to thank the team and all the students of the RCA Service Design course and tutors Judah Armani, Carolyn Runcie, Nick de Leon, Nicolas Reboleddo, John Makepeace, Richard Atkinson, Qian Sun, Andrea Edmunds, Hanna Kops, David Eveleigh, Alex Hill and graduate Allison Bajet, who told me to write this book.

I am grateful for the time given me by Tom Hardy, Ben Terret, Andrea Siodmok, Sarah Drummond, Sanjay Rain, Sophie Thomas, Camilla Buchannan, Stephen Bennet, Rama Gheerawo, Lin Hu, Sanjay Khana, J. Paul Neely, Alex Barclay, Sarah Corney, Geoff Mulgan, Justin Huang, Mark Wheelhouse and Robert Chatley, Aoran Sun and, of course, John Bird.

Steve Hardman at De Gruyter was instrumental in commissioning this book before moving on to look after his wife Samantha Whitaker. Please do all you can to support their work with the MND Association and buy her poetry book *Standing Tall*. Thank you to Jaya Dalal for her support after stepping into the role.

I'm incredibly grateful for the patience and support of my wife, Janis.

Foreword

Clive Grinyer invited me to speak to design students at the Royal College of Art.

We talked about design and social usefulness, of designing for the social good of society. Then Clive threw me a question that I did not hesitate to answer:

"If you were going to redesign one thing in society what would that be?"

The answer fell out of my mouth unaided by reflection.

"I would redesign thinking."

There was no thought or hesitation in my reply. I threw out my thought without thinking. I had been brought into an environment of designers and redesigners and it seemed natural to talk in their terms. In the same way if I had been brought into a group of police officers I would think in terms of law and order.

The expression "out of the mouths of babes oft times comes gems" springs to mind that afternoon when Clive made me think about thinking. I was the rather old babe who was forced to think by Clive. And by that make me think about thinking.

Having delivered my talk and answered Clive's question I went home and sitting on the train reflected on my useful piece of evangelising about the social intervention work that I am involved in. My work in parliament, and my work in the street movement I have built around a street paper. My decade after decade of work in and around the crisis of poverty. And of the impediments that held back the work that I was doing.

My parliamentary work was like pulling teeth. Trying to get the government to assign more of its assets to preventing people falling into poverty. That once someone inherits poverty from their parents then they are rarely able to break the cycle, without tremendous levels of help and investment. That if government could muster its own efforts, and the efforts of business, charities and the community into helping break the inheritance of poverty, then we would live in a different world.

According to the British Medical Association (BMA), 50%[1] of people suffering from cardiac related illnesses were suffering from food poverty. That our hospitals were full of people destroyed by poverty. That our prisons were full of those who were born into poverty and need. That our schools were often impeded in delivering on education because inherited poverty got in the way of educational delivery.

That no doctor, teacher or police officer was trained to get people out of poverty, yet they were left to clean up the damage done by poverty.

---

[1] "Health at price", British Medical Association, June 2017.

My throwaway comment, got out of me by a genius of a question, suddenly made me think about the thinking I had encountered in government, in society, and in charities as a design issue. It was the thinking that needed redesigning. The reflecting on what the evidence was presenting itself in the day-to-day crisis of poverty I waded through.

What had I to do in my own life to get out of crime and poverty and rough sleeping and prison?

I had to redesign my thinking, to recalibrate my life by moving away from the survivalist, self-harming thinking that had kept me in poverty.

What Clive had asked me to do was reflect on the obstacles to my work by approaching it as a design issue. As a poorly designed design issue. His question elicited a level of thoughtfulness that now informs my ask of government. That informs my ability to think my way beyond the crisis to the crisis' solution.

This book is an essential read because the author brings together evidence as to what is the greatest design crisis in the world today: that thinking itself needs redesigning. For it is the current thinking that holds back our ability to create in an ever-changing world.

I went to speak to design students and in the process, I was redesigned, by a simple and now seemingly obvious challenging piece of thinking. Clive Grinyer did me a great favour: by helping me to see what needs to be done in the struggle to end poverty in people's lives – to rethink thinking itself. To redesign thinking so that we recalibrate our thinking to provide the answers to the most pressing questions of our day.

**The Lord Bird MBE,
member of the House of Lords and founder of The Big Issue**

Contents

Acknowledgements —— IX

Foreword —— XI

Introduction —— 1

Chapter 1
The Burning Platform —— 7
    The Rise of Services —— 13

Chapter 2
The Need for Change —— 16
    A Sense of Purpose —— 17
    The Balancing Act —— 20
    But Things Are Changing . . . —— 23
    New Values —— 24
    Ethical Technology —— 25
    Sustainable Business —— 26
    The New Paradigm —— 29
        How Do We Redesign Thinking for Change? —— 30
        How Do We Design for Change? —— 32

Chapter 3
In Technology We Trust —— 34
    Fear of Tech —— 35
    The Transformation of Personal Technology —— 36
    Technology Solves Problems We Don't Have —— 40
    Heroic Failures – Segway —— 40
    Google Glasses —— 41
    Speech Recognition —— 42
    The Metaverse —— 44
    Invisible Enablers —— 45
    Data and AI —— 46
    Humanising Technology —— 48
        How Do We Redesign Thinking for Technology? —— 49
    An Anecdote on Designing for Technology —— 51
        How Do We Design for Technology? —— 52
    Always Start With Research —— 53
    Testing Ideas —— 55
    Storyboarding —— 55

Make the Advert —— 56
Next, Features —— 56
Design the Technology —— 57
Designing for Real People —— 58

Chapter 4
How to Make a Poor Decision —— 59
Doing the Right Thing —— 59
Good Design, Bad Decision —— 62
Data Will Tell Us What We Need to Know! —— 64
Trust —— 64
The Price, and Value, of Data —— 65
Affordance —— 68
The Value of Data —— 68
Surprising Data —— 69
Balancing Data —— 71
Listening with Our Eyes —— 72
Research Wisely and Carefully —— 74

Chapter 5
The Design Approach —— 76
The Double Diamond —— 79
Discover —— 81
Who Are We Designing For? —— 81
Why Don't We Just Ask People What They Want? —— 84
"If You Want to Experience Something, You Have to Experience it" —— 85
Research for Design —— 85
What's Really Going On? —— 86
Interviews —— 87
Experience the Experience —— 88
Co-creation, Co-design —— 89
Handing Over the Pen —— 90
Card Sorting —— 91
Epiphanies —— 91
Mapping Journeys —— 92
Good Journey Mapping —— 93
Other Design Methods —— 95

Chapter 6
What Is the Problem? —— 97
    The Value of Challenging the Brief —— 97
    Describe the Problem, Not the Solution —— 99
    How Might We? —— 100
    Why, Why, Why, Why, Why —— 100
    What Does a Good "How Might We?" Look Like? —— 101
    What Does Success Look Like? —— 103
        How Do You Redesign Thinking to Define a Problem? —— 103
        How to Redesign Design to Define a Problem —— 104

Chapter 7
Time for Creativity —— 105
    Creativity is Scary —— 108
    Permission to Have Ideas —— 109
    What About My Hunch? —— 110
    The Philosophy of Failure —— 112
    How to Be Creative —— 112
    Inclusivity —— 114
    Everyone Has a Good Idea —— 115
    Everyone Can Draw —— 116
    Rules of Collaborative Creativity —— 116
    Defer Judgement —— 117
    Encourage Wild Ideas —— 118
    Stay Focused on the Topic —— 118
    One Conversation at a Time —— 118
    Be Visual —— 119
    Go for Quantity —— 119
    Creativity Methods —— 119
    Sharing Ideas —— 122
    Brainstorming —— 123
    Co-Creativity —— 123
    Voting on Ideas —— 124
    Capturing Ideas —— 124
    What Next? —— 125
        How Do You Redesign Thinking to Be Creative? —— 125
        How Do You Design with Creativity? —— 125

Chapter 8
The Power of the Prototype —— 127
    Solving an Argument —— 129
    Stop Trying to Get it Right in One Go —— 129
    Understand Different Types of Prototyping —— 130
        Paper Prototypes —— 131
    3D Prototypes —— 131
    Advanced Digital Prototypes —— 132
    When to Prototype —— 132
    Who Are You Testing Prototypes With? —— 132
    The Three Stages of Prototyping: Stage 1 – the Proposition —— 133
    Make the Advert —— 134
    Tell the Story —— 135
    Artifacts —— 135
    Stage 2 – Features —— 137
    Usability —— 138
    Useful Exercises —— 139
    The Power of Prototypes —— 140
        How to Redesign Thinking to Prototype —— 140
        How to Use Prototypes as a Designer —— 141

Chapter 9
Visions and Stories —— 142
    What Do Stories Look Like? —— 143
    The Story of Frank —— 144
    Visions —— 147
    What Are Vision, Strategy and Execution? —— 147
    Weak Signals —— 150
    Target Visions —— 152
    Creating a Target Vision —— 154
    Engineering Emotion —— 154
    How to Use Stories —— 155
        Target Visions and Stories for Redesigning Thinkers —— 156
        Target Visions for Designers —— 157
    Examples of Design Principles —— 158
        "Getting to Know Me" —— 158
        "Attentive Service" —— 158
        "Celebrating Colleagues" —— 158
        Reasons to Love Us —— 159
    Dieter Rams' 10 Principles of Good Design —— 159
    Creating the Story —— 162

Chapter 10
The Blueprint for Change —— 164
- The Blueprint —— 165
- The Story —— 168
- The Front Stage —— 169
- Brand Behaviour and Design Principles —— 171
- On-Stage Actions —— 174
- Offstage Actions —— 175
- Support Systems and Processes —— 176
- Terrible Tech —— 176
- The Capability of the Organisation to Deliver the Service —— 177
    - Blueprints for Redesigning Your Thinking —— 178
    - Blueprints for Designers —— 178

Chapter 11
Making Change Happen —— 179
- Small Changes for Big Impact —— 180
- Change by Discovery —— 181
- Designing New Lives —— 183
- Designing Policy —— 185
- Policy Design Around the World —— 188
- Organisational Change —— 189
- Design as an Agitator —— 190
- Design Changing the World —— 191
- Designing Services in Emerging Economies —— 193
- Designing for a Sustainable World —— 193

Chapter 12
It's Not Easy —— 197
- Leadership from Within —— 197
- People and Change —— 200
- Behaviours —— 202
- Ambition —— 206
- A Case Study of a Strategic Approach to Design —— 208
    - How to Redesign Your Thinking to Bring Design Into Your Organisation —— 211
    - How to Design for Success —— 212

Chapter 13
Redesigning Thinking —— 213
    Stop Solutionising —— **217**
    Listen With Our Eyes —— **217**
    Share Your Ideas Early —— **217**
    Defer Judgement —— **217**
    Engineer Designs, Don't Design Engineering —— **218**
    The Manifesto for Redesigning Thinking —— **220**
    The Consequence of Not Redesigning Our Thinking? —— **221**

Chapter 14
The Future's Bright —— 223
    Speculative Design —— **224**
    Raising Our Ambition —— **226**
    Optimism, Vision and Pragmatism —— **227**
    The Future of Design —— **232**
    New Territories for Design —— **233**
    Enormous Change Is About to Happen —— **236**

Further Reading List —— 239

List of Figures —— 241

About the Author —— 243

Index —— 245

Introduction

I live in a house that is about 100 years old in a suburb of London. The house was designed by an unknown architect who was working for a developer keen to capture the financial opportunities from the growing the need for housing in the 1920s.

My house is like many others in suburban London. At an exhibition of Britain at War in the Imperial War Museum in London, I came across an exact facsimile of my house. It was a replica of every house that was built at this time with a hall and staircase, living room in the front, kitchen in the back with bedrooms and a bathroom upstairs.

The house is built of brick and is attached on one side to another home that is the mirror image of the one I live in. It does not have a garage but does have a front garden, which at some point became covered over to become a drive, as car ownership became more popular in the suburbs after the Second World War. It clearly once had a gate, but this would have been melted down during the Second World War to be used in creating ammunition.

The road I live on is wide and lined with magnificent male plane trees. I mention their gender as it was decided to plant male trees to reduce the quantity of seeds that would need to be cleared up each spring. The unintended consequence of that decision is that I and many other London residents suffer chronic hay fever caused by the male pollen that swirls around the air for much of the year.

The road has many speed bumps to limit the speed cars can travel, the type you can get your wheels either side of, so many are able to ignore the 20 mph speed limit. Today, the pavements are littered with Christmas trees sprawling like New Year's Eve drunks, trying to keep hold of various brown, black and blue bins full of festive rubbish, waiting for the local authority to take them away.

On the corner of the next street from mine are three charge points, available for people with electric cars to charge them if they need. They are not used much as many people charge their cars on their own driveways, but they send out a message that change is coming, something fundamental is happening.

The pavement outside my house was renewed about a decade ago but now looks messy and crumpled as various utilities have dug it up to lay down cables for accessing broadband internet, had water meters fitted or have been cracked and damaged by heavy vehicles delivering and taking away skips and materials from the many building extensions that have gone on in this road in recent years.

The cable into my house that delivers broadband internet meets various generations of other wires with forgotten purposes for telephones, alarms and power supplies to sockets used or unused. I have forgotten or never knew the purpose of many of them but am too scared to pull any out in case one of them is important. Once inside they find their way to a Wi-Fi box that in turn feeds numerous Wi-Fi points currently connected to ever increasing devices – interactive digital objects from televisions to sound systems to iPads and mobiles and lighting. In my front room I have eight remote controls that I juggle with to turn on TVs and various set top products, set volume levels, change channels or turn the fire on. I am the only person in the household who holds the secret knowledge for changing channels access the various platforms offered by the competing providers of entertainment, sport, news and information we consume.

Around the house heating systems click on and off, thermostats are set, ovens and microwaves go ping, for different reasons, one temperature, the other time, and twice a year, and sometimes more if there is a power cut, I have to reset their clocks, each one in an entirely different way, and during the seasons between changing them, I always forget how to do this. I then go and sit in my car for a long time whilst I find out how to change the clock on the dashboard, before driving to my parents to go through the same process for them.

When not mastering technology, I pay bills and people and buy things, usually through my mobile phone and try and sustain life as best I can. I buy tickets, and lose my password and try and register, to be told that my name has already been used. Yes, by me! Websites and mobile apps tell me to find things in settings that are now called something different and look for buttons that are not there. I'm asked to tick tiny buttons I always miss, that turn out to be the legal terms and conditions of the transaction.

In this description of what surrounds me, there lies a complex entanglement of physical material, infrastructure, utilities, systems, technology, historical and social change, economics, government policy and design decisions. Much of this world allows me to operate as a human, to have a roof over my head, to sleep securely and earn a living. Most of these interactions are not ones I have chosen by design; I may have little, or sometimes am offered too much choice, but I have never been asked for my opinion on most of these decisions. But, in the most part, they have been made in a way I can understand, though I have little or no agency over them.

This book is about how some of those decisions are made and how we design and shape the world around use. Where we live, our surroundings, the objects around us, the technology we use, the rules we abide by or break: All are the way they are because of decisions people make, perhaps with purpose and intent, or invisibly, even accidentally. Because it's about decisions, it's therefore about people: how they view other people and decide what's important and their assumptions and how we consider the future outcomes and impact of our decisions, or don't.

As a child I loved to spend time with my grandmother who owned a dress shop in the local village. She had a regal style and would emerge every day around ten o'clock to greet her adoring customers who would file into the shop to view, consider, try on and eventually buy new outfits. The shop was surprisingly high quality for its location in a small village and had copies of fashion magazines that would lie casually in the window below the same garment styled on an unnaturally but fashionably twisted and pouting mannequin.

My grandmother understood well the theatre of the shopping experience, brilliantly combining chat, local gossip and friendship with creating new identities for her customers who would leave happy and excited at the combination of personal reinvention and with reassured confidence in their new image. She, with some help from my mother, understood the economics and business model of the shop, balancing the local taste and demand with the reality of affordability and their own profitability. That understanding would put good food on their table and allow my grandfather to buy a new car every two years.

Once every three months or so my grandmother and mother would travel to London. London was a magical concept to my sisters and me. Two hours seemed a long way away and it was a place of intrigue, bustle and museums. It was a big occasion when they went to London, and they would leave with intent and much make-up and return in a flurry of bags of garments and magazines. They would talk excitedly of the fashion shows they had been to and displays at the dealers of next season's fashions, and they would speak with excitement as they confidently proclaimed that the following summer would be white and that the following spring would be blue. They knew this as fact and would be happy to share this knowledge with their customers who would lust after and crave their blue and white garments, confident that their good taste would be noticed and commented on by all.

To my young self, this seemed a magical knowledge to bring back. A message from the oracle at Delphi, the whisper of a high priestess in the confidential conversation with a god who could predict the future. To prove it, the sumptuous photos in the magazines *Vogue*, *Harper's Bazaar* and *Draper's Record* would proudly confirm the prediction to the delight and excitement of the prospective customers peering through the shop window.

Where did this knowledge come from? What wizard, magician, or prophet? My mother said they came from Paris, or "the designers" but this didn't mean much to me. Slowly it dawned on me that these decisions were made by people. Individuals who had the incredible job of deciding what people would want to wear. Somehow, they would decide, divine and design these objects of both desire and commerce – and then get people to change their minds and buy something different next summer. Amazing!

This was a big revelation for me. I began to look at the world differently after this epiphany. Why was a thing like that and not another way? Why was something made of a particular material, made in two halves and fastened together in that way? Why was something ugly and something else beautiful? This childish curiosity, it turns out, is an early sign of the kind of behaviour very common in people who go on to be creative and work in the world of design themselves.

This epiphany, and a curiosity into how the world was made, led me at the age of 16 to study a new course: design and technology. This seemed a magical topic combining analytics and decisions with the practical skills of working with materials to make things. I had found my vocation, as many others have since. Design as part of an education is an incredibly valuable and underappreciated thing for all, not just designers, but for me it pointed me in the direction of my future career.

Studying at the Central School of Art and Design (now Central St. Martins) where I could enjoy the luxury of spending 3 years practising how to be a designer, led me to my career, working with businesses small and large across product design, digital and finally service design, all over the world. And all because of my grandmother's dress shop.

For those who have not encountered design before or considered why it might be relevant to you and the way you think, design is probably something that is attached to a handbag, or responsible for creating fashion, that might have adorned my grandmother's shop window. You may understand it better in architecture, or perhaps as a garden, or home interior design, as many television shows have focused on, with stylish makeovers of our homes and gardens.

But this is not a book about that type of design. It's a book aimed at everyone who makes decisions and, more than that, is aiming to make things better. Better means many things to many people. It might mean sell more, or make more profit, or have a positive impact on a part of society, or keep something that is precious or reduce damage to our environment.

The decisions we make are increasingly likely to be in response to those challenges. But unfortunately, those decisions don't make a world work as well as it could. Unfortunately, our governments make ill-informed decisions without understanding the consequences. Our businesses create products and services without talking to the people who will use them. They create solutions that don't fit the people they are for and don't solve the problems they have.

This is largely because we make assumptions, have opinions and believe it is a good thing to jump to a solution and "just do it", and damn the consequences. We remain primitive in how we make rational decisions and, even in a world swimming in data and information, we make poor decisions that fail, usually at great expense.

There is a way to think more humanely, to create better business and navigate through complex systems to make things work. It's called design.

We "design" how hospitals work, how we get rid of our refuse, how we apply for passports. In every case, we desire things to be simple, to be beautiful and be affordable. But from handbags to hospitals, we must understand that humans are making decisions, and they are made against criteria they believe are correct. But if we choose inappropriate or myopic criteria, the consequence is that we rarely get beautiful or even usable hospitals; systems are designed without empathy for the people who use them; and we continue to develop technology that many cannot access or understand.

The premise of this book is to share an understanding of the way the world around us is designed, intentionally and unintentionally, and how we can use the methods that are used in design not to design a handbag, or the shape of a car or a mobile phone, but as a problem-solving tool that will help every one of us be better at making decisions.

This is design in a different way to anything you ever thought it was. Put aside your preconceptions about design: It's a successful activity with rigour, scientific method and effective outcomes that works.

This book is also for people who are designers or wish to become designers. Design has a habit of developing compartments for different types of design, graphics, product, user interface, service, operational and organisational design, interaction, interior, retail and landscape. Not all are helpful when we wish to use design to improve the experience of patients and nurses in hospital, or redesign conveyancing, or the law or a government policy. But that is where design is increasingly present as organisations, businesses and the public sector employ designers.

The book is also focused on an emerging type of design that's called service design. For many, this will be a new term, perhaps one that is puzzling, but one that is one of the fastest growing subjects to study and for employers to hire. Service design applies the methods of many design disciplines and practice to take a broader holistic look at what we are designing. A product, or a graphic communication is always part of a larger system. A pull-out queue barrier, video recognition system and a sign are integral parts of the airport experience that should service the purpose of the passenger getting to their plane. They need to be understood as part of a system and that understanding is a form of design, orchestrating the greater objective rather than the single object.

Service design is the architecture for systems in the way that architecture is the design of a complex building. You need to collaborate with engineers and building experts when you create a building and the same is true of services. As a result, service designers have an impact on orchestrating and facilitating collaboration and delivering against a vision. They are capable of changing the way organisations design their actions to be more effective, impactful and successful.

Service design is hot. Service designers are being employed in financial services, healthcare, local authorities, government departments, management consultancies and business big and small. In recent years, I have run courses in service design for the Bank of England, fire and rescue services, social housing organisations, TV companies, toy companies and consumer electronic brands. Service design is becoming established in Europe as is the use of design for broader social, as well as commercial impact around the world in the US, India, China and South America.

Service design is the art of designing services, as will be shown in this book. It is also the design of the experience around a product or the points of action in a service – the service aspect of anything we use, physical or digital. Nothing is in isolation: marketing, selling, subscribing, fulfilment, use, after use, are all connected when we, as consumers, customers or citizens, interact with any type of product or service. Service design is the consideration, the design and the orchestration of the before, during and after of everything we use.

And let's remind ourselves, the experience of the before, during and after is there anyway. Design is not an option, it's happening all the time, just usually accidentally and without consideration. Which is why the idea that thinking consciously, using the tools and methods that are used in design, makes sense to all of us when we make decisions. There is no such thing as no design. Everything is designed, just mostly badly.

We are frustrated when things are designed badly. When none of the Frequently Asked Questions on a website reflect the problem we have and we cannot find out how to contact a person to find the answer we are really looking for. Like a malfunctioning smoke alarm, or a website we can't log on to or a government system that is full of unacknowledged bugs with devastating consequences on their users who depend on it, we have to live with it every day until we are able, or have the chance, to change it.

So, whether you are a leader in business or in government, a practicing designer looking to use your skills to enhance your impact or a student keen to use your creativity to improve the prospects of the planet and society, this book aims to provide the inspiration and practical tools to change how we think and ensure we design a future that works for all. There are many brilliant books that will develop an academic, or much more detailed evaluation of the tools and methods of service design. But I hope this book explains the why: why design methods can solve important problems and should be integrated into every organisation and our decision-making processes.

Whether you are a decision maker or a designer, at the end of each chapter I give tips on how to redesign thinking to create better outcomes and how to apply design skills to help organisations succeed and the people who access their services thrive.

The subtitle of this book is *How Service Design is Solving the Challenges of the 21st Century* because this combination of a human-centred approach, design methods that shape the world and an understanding of the complexity of systems is making real change and solving real problems. From an ageing population to financial management, responsible technology and how we can reduce the damage to the planet, design is an essential ingredient in imagining, making tangible and delivering, a better future for us all. Here is how.

Chapter 1
The Burning Platform

> *You live the surprise result of old plans.*
> Jenny Holzer

In May 2020 the UK government announced that its response to the growing threat of the Covid-19 virus to the UK would be to develop a "world class" Test and Trace system. Using the power of geolocating software built into smartphones that over 99% of the population use, they would build a service that would notify people who had been near any person who had tested positive for the virus. The phone would "ping" a notification that there had been close contact and instruct each person to then isolate for a period of two weeks, regardless of whether you were showing any symptoms, to reduce the chance of further transmission to others. So far so good.

In June of 2020 the BBC radio programme "File on Four" ran a documentary piece about the failure of the system. People reported receiving messages from numbers they did not recognise and suspected they were from scammers trying to con them out of money. The army of people, often students, who were drafted as call centre agents, reported that they were left alone for weeks, untrained, with no communication or advice as to what they should be doing.

Some 18 months later the rapid development and roll-out to the UK population of vaccines against Covid-19 had reduced the numbers of patients, and the threat of transmission to vulnerable people was over. By this time, the "world class test and trace system" had consumed a lot of money – estimates range between £12 to £36 billion ($15–40 billion).

Around halfway through the crisis, the management consultants who were advising the UK government began to hire designers. The government had begun to realise that their systems were not effective and had not considered the human elements such as how to interact with the warnings and instructions they were sending to the public to nudge people to do the right thing. They weren't communicating clearly to citizens and the staff inside the service who were there to ensure it ran smoothly. They employed a new breed of designers called service designers – designers using the methods of design that are used to design products, websites and digital apps – to consider every aspect of the service to ensure it had the impact it was crucial it achieved in order to save the vulnerable from a potentially life-threatening virus and ensure that hospitals were not overrun with patients. Eventually the service began to have the impact it was intended to have, but by this time the emergency was over, the vaccine had huge uptake and was effective and normal life began to return.

I am sure that in the minds of policy makers and civil servants, they believed that they tried to do the right thing. They set up an organisation with a specific task. Brought in the big tech companies of Apple and Google along with national infrastructure partners. Set the ambition of creating a "world class" service. But it was a massive and very expensive failure.

Perhaps it didn't occur to them that the decisions they made might be deflected by such small details as people not recognising the number. Perhaps they thought that paying the people who made the telephone calls was sufficient, they didn't need to be kept in the picture or kept updated. I am sure that they didn't consider that the service needed to be "designed". Until it was too late.

Of course, the failure of the UK test and trace system was not because it wasn't designed. It was designed. Just accidently and unconsciously. The system delivered was the result of many decisions across many complex organisational structures and hierarchies working with people keen to do the right thing. But without the strategic realisation that the interface with the population, individuals receiving calls and messages that would have a profound impact on their lives, would need to consider their context and channel of that message and how it would be received, failure was highly likely. They needed to take care of the small details as well as the overall structure, to move beyond the functionality of the system and consider the receiver and their understanding and expectation, which was, it turns out, critical to the success of the massive investment. But that didn't happen, and it failed.

If we look at the organisational structure of the decision-making process for the UK Government Preparedness and Response unit in August 2019 (Figure 1.1), a few months before the pandemic hit, we can see the hopeless situation they were in. Design in this sorry story was completely arbitrary, accidental, a mish-mash of military-style command in an impossibly tangled infrastructure of organisational elements. The consequences were for some, tragic. As we look back and try to learn from what worked and what didn't work during this period of crisis, it's easy to blame one or many politicians, government departments or civil servants. Perhaps we are right to, for the one thing they didn't understand or consider was that they were designing a system and that in doing so there are methods and processes that allow you to design such a service to reduce the risk of failure and to achieve your objective. Unfortunately, for most, the word design does not connect with political decision making in a time of international crisis. But unfortunately, and without realising it, they were designers designing a critical response in a time of crisis. And their design skills were very poor.

Why should they have thought of design skills as important? Well, as the Nobel Prize winning economist Herbert Simon said, "Everyone designs who devises courses of action aimed at changing existing situations into preferred ones." This articulates an important concept – that we are all involved in the act of designing if we are trying to make something that is "preferred". I asked the Open

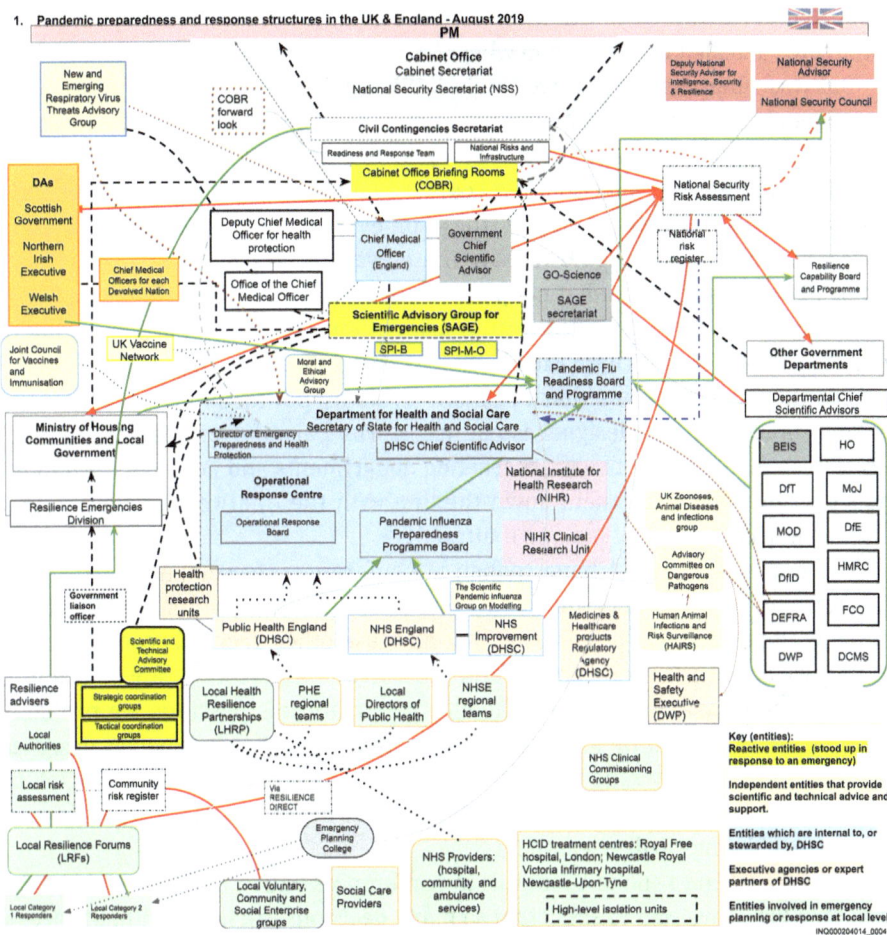

Figure 1.1: Pandemic Preparedness and Response Structures in the UK and England, August 2019 – National Archives, Crown Copyright, Covid19.Public-inquiry.uk.

AI program ChatGPT to simplify this convoluted sentence. The first attempt was still overly complex but when I asked it to simplify once more, it got it right. It said, "Anyone who plans to improve things by changing them is a designer."

I am pretty sure that everyone is in some way involved with changing existing situations into preferred ones. Either individually or together, we fix problems, make sure things work efficiently, keep up with the competition, make improvements in what we do, anticipate, and occasionally pre-empt and go further to satisfy people's needs or wishes. If Herbert Simon is right, then we are all designers, we just don't realise it.

My first boss and founder of the design company IDEO, Bill Moggridge, made a similar point that was a great epiphany for me. He said that "Few people think about it or are aware of it. But there is nothing made by human beings that does not involve a design decision somewhere."

Bill was referring to what we "make". When we build a house or make a car or a vacuum cleaner or a chair, we can understand that what Bill says must be true. So many decisions about the materials we will use, the processes required to make it for mass production, the cost we want to sell something for and the functional requirements of any of these objects are decisions we all need to make. In addition, we need to satisfy the emotional impact of the object: Is it beautiful and desirable so that people will buy and enjoy it in their home, showing off their car, having satisfaction in using their vacuum cleaner or sitting in comfort on their chair? These are all vital decisions that need to be well made.

But they are decisions that are made at many points along the process of making something. The designer is not necessarily part of every part of that process. Finance, factory managers, marketing departments and engineers will make their decisions and pass them down the line with the final requirement to prepare the object for sale by making it attractive.

For much of my life I have spoken at conferences, to companies, to senior managers, to governments and politicians about that last component of design and how important it is in ensuring that all those other decisions come together in a solution that is fit for purpose and attractive to a person to buy or use it. If our cars are ugly and built with the cheapest materials possible, we probably won't buy them even if their low cost is attractive. If our house is poorly designed and the rooms in the wrong place, or our vacuum cleaners work fine but can't be stored anywhere or our chair is strong but ugly, or the opposite, we, as emotional, proud, social beings, will reject them.

For many years I spoke about this in conferences with a talk that I titled "Lipstick on a Pig". I wanted to show that so many decisions are made without care or empathy, or in an unconscious and accidental way, that it is very difficult to make something attractive and desirable for customers. If something is poor value, unfit for purpose, designed without insights and empathy for customers, it will fail and that will impact on business success. So, design is not just a prettying up of something that has been engineered in a vacuum of knowledge or thought about what a customer wants, it's something more fundamental. It's something we can all use, gain value from and helps us make better decisions that will help us achieve our goals, make our business better, our policy more successful in its outcomes and our customers, users, citizens, happier and more appreciative of our decision. Which could make a lot of difference to our success.

But in the absence of design as part of our decision making, we are left with disasters.

When the crisis in Ukraine started, many refugees moved across Europe away from their homes that had now become war zones. The reaction of the UK immigration authorities was rapid but not helpful. As refugees with relatives in the UK sought to flee the violence, they travelled across Europe to the port of Calais, the nearest port to the UK, where they were greeted at a fold-up table by some UK civil servants with crisps and water and the news that the office was closed, and they had to return to Lille to be processed. They were then advised to use social media to try and find one of the many UK households who were volunteering to provide a home.

It's clear that there was no thought of the context, emotional turmoil, physical exhaustion or attempt to create a safe and secure way for families to support these tired and exhausted people, mostly women with children. There was no attempt to understand the context and use creativity to design a better system.

When Barack Obama won a tightly contested political battle to provide Medicare insurance to the vast majority of US citizens, opening up previously unavailable healthcare, it was declared a great victory. The Affordable Care Act had the objective to enrol over 48 million citizens but by 2016 had only achieved less than a quarter of that number.

Design was at the heart of the failure. Multiple contractors with incompatible systems had contrived to make signing on to Healthcare.gov nearly impossible. The website crashed during a test with only a few hundred users. Dropdown menus were empty; the design wasn't finished when it launched and the expected use of the site was way below the 250,000 people who tried to log and crashed the site within 2 hours of the 2013 launch. In a Harvard Business School student assignment, it was reported that only 6 people successfully applied on the first day.

This was not just a technology problem; it was a fundamental design flaw that prevented this great political victory from achieving the impact it promised.[1]

Over time, a number of tech design experts and the development of the US Digital Service embraced the challenge of creating meaningful working digital services for US citizens by applying the design and development practices of start-ups and moving away from the cumbersome procedures of Big IT projects. They took a pragmatic and human-centred approach to create something that was accessible, usable and inclusive for all.[2]

In the UK, the transformation of digital services was more successful. Following a highly critical report by Last Minute Dot Com founder Martha Lane Fox into the dismal state of government digital services, the individual department websites and logs were removed and replaced with gov.uk. They used the same type face, the highly legible and marvellously simple "Motorway" font designed by Margarete Calvert for the UK road signage system, which was implemented, sometimes forcibly, by the Government Digital Service (GDS) team. This was a

---
[1] Tom Cohen, "Rough Obamacare rollout: 4 reasons why", *CNN*, 2013. (Harvard Business Review 2016 https://d3.harvard.edu/platform-rctom/submission/the-failed-launch-of-www-healthcare-gov/).
[2] https://www.theatlantic.com/technology/archive/2015/07/the-secret-startup-saved-healthcare-gov-the-worst-website-in-america/397784/

tive strategic project that raised design and usability standards across the ? of government, treated their digital outputs as services, not websites, and ;ed the way the population of the UK interfaces with government.

)ther countries have been equally effective in combining design principles with digital transformation programmes to create radically improved services. The work of Audrey Tang, Taiwan's Digital Minister, in creating a citizen-led approach to design has been feted around the world. Taiwan has also been a powerful exponent of citizen assembly's, working with groups of randomly selected groups to shape policy established during the global Covid-19 pandemic with great success and continued with on afterwards.

Some find such openness and direct collaboration on decision making with broad groups of people somehow risky. But designing without the input of those who use what we provide is the real risk.

Alongside the global examples of design success hide the horrible consequences of the failure of Big IT. The scandal over the Horizon Post Office IT system has only recently come to the public's attention despite over 20 years of reporting and aggressive legal prosecution of post office owners across the UK who we now know where innocent victims of a malfunctioning tech. The system put in to automate Post Office offices was littered with bugs. Between the IT supplier Fujitsu and the Post Office, these malfunctions, that caused the end of day cash totals to be miscalculated, led to the Post Office prosecuting the owners of the post offices in locations all over the UK for theft. They chose to not admit or in some cases, hold back evidence of faults in the system, with devastating consequences for those unfairly prosecuted.

The nature of IT projects and the way they are designed often has inhumane consequences. Like many huge IT projects, the commercial stakes are high, and delivery schedules overpromised. At this point, the idea that you iterate a design, test it with users and identify problems, falls apart. And the result is always immensely more expensive and, in the Horizon case, damaging to a huge number of people.

UK Government Advisor Mike Bracken wrote in the *Financial Times* that a database of over 100,000 US government IT projects showed that over 80% of those projects, "where big bets on technology certainty are made before user needs are really known," where written off as very expensive failures.[3]

And yet we plough on, finding every reason not to apply even the most basic design methods. In a world of Agile development, a process of parallel sprints around small specific parts of the overall design, success is measured in velocity of development. Not in whether it works, or is of a high quality, or will not cause damage, but purely as the speed taken producing outputs. Agile methods are in-

---

3 Mike Bracken, "No more 'Big IT': The failed 90s model has ruined too many lives", *FT*, 19 January 2024.

creasingly applied to management theory and culture in order to increase productivity. Agility has many advantages and benefits development, encourages collaborative working and has many excellent aspects that allow for clearer communication and transparency as to the progress of a project. But it should not be at the cost of understating the overall objective, the purpose of a project and the detailed design process that defines what you build. Projects have value to customers and the people who will use them, and need to be accessible, usable and inclusive to deliver the benefits of technology to all. But that needs a clear vision, tested and validated, to remove the risk of rapidly creating something that is not usable, that does not work and may cause damage. It is very expensive to put right what has been poorly designed. Agile needs design as the map to success that can deliver the benefits to both businesses and humans. Agile needs design to be done first.

The Rise of Services

Despite the chaos and lack of design methods in the UK Test and Trace service or Obamacare, we have become happy users of a whole series of innovative services that have transformed many aspects of our lives.

Airbnb is a great service that millions of people around the world have used and homeowners have benefitted from. The incredible choice of homes in locations from the heart of a city to the remotest yurt up a mountain are hireable for a single day, or a summer. A highly usable and easily accessible website and mobile app cleverly filters the choices presented to match our tastes so that our preferred style, location, flexibility of dates, and accommodation can be booked in seconds. All the features of good website practice, including reviews and detailed information on facilities and amenities, are presented. As a homeowner with a spare room, a second home or a company investing in property rental, Airbnb is the platform of choice and has transformed how we travel, stay and experience the world.

In essence, Airbnb uses data to deliver happiness via a transactional platform and allows property owners new business opportunities and even careers as holiday property providers. A wonderful service that we are pleased exists.

Unless you live in Barcelona. As in many of the world's top tourist destinations, the people of Barcelona, with a combination of relentless visits from vast cruise ships and low-cost flights bringing millions of tourists to enjoy the attractions and culture of a city, have responded to the changes that their city has gone through. They have seen their local districts become hollowed out as communities become transitory neighbourhoods that fail to sustain traditional communal bonds and local industries. The silence of a Sunday morning is replaced by the sound of luggage wheel on cobbles as tourists head for the airport and the station.

Uber is another example of a service that has transformed how we travel around our towns and cities. Apps that find the closest taxi, bring them to you with information and rating of the driver and where they are as they travel to find you. Step in the car and step out at your destination, the fare paid automatically at the end of the journey and an opportunity to rate your driver (and they you) for your next trip. More efficient, less polluting (less cruising around looking for a passenger to pick up and with the large use of hybrid vehicles) and less chat make Uber a fantastic, user friendly, technological marvel.

Except there is hardly a city in the world where there is not trouble around Uber. Concerns about passenger security, driver employment rights, and tribal conflicts between traditional taxi services and the new interlopers have led to conflict and the occasional banning of such services.

It's not just new technology services that go wrong. Services provide us with energy, financial management, broadband service to our homes, travel on trains and planes and are the great enablers of 21st century life in affluent and emerging economies. These services send us bills, maintenance engineers, give us service in branches and on calls to their call centres. For companies that provide these essential services, the human element is an expense that can be cut. Hide that contact number on the website so no one can find it. Provide those useless Frequently Asked Questions that solve no one's problems. Use automated systems that treat us all as criminals, mis-send huge energy bills and refuse to admit they are wrong. Services that are impossible to turn off, or use aggressive techniques to attract us and then fail to deliver benefits that are promised.

Perhaps our most likely perception of service is the human service we receive when we eat or travel, or visit a doctor or a financial advisor. The greeting from a retail assistant or a hotel reception desk, or the opposite, can leave us happy for a day or red hot with frustration of anger. Our expectation of service can make us highly unreasonable – expectations that had to be severely reset when the post pandemic "Great Resignation" of people not returning to work impacted on the quantity of staff available for the restaurants, kitchens and hospitality industry. Perhaps we learnt to appreciate those who serve us a little more as a result.

Replacing humans, however, is not the answer – though one that the advance of AI is often predicted to lead to. When, during pandemic, pupils in schools were unable to take their final exams in a safe and secure way, the UK Ministry of Education decided to use AI and algorithms based on a school's previous exam results to predict the likely results of each student. They had chosen not to ask the teachers for their predicted grades based on the student's previous work and the teacher's knowledge of their capabilities, but used a system that measured the number of students in each grade level in the historical data of exam results, and then aggregated students into each grade in the same ratios. This, of course, took no account of a student possibly performing better, or worse, than the results of the past. The result was a revolt by parents who saw the unfairness and lack of acknowledgment of the efforts students may have put into pass the exams. Parents are future voters, and the government of the day saw the error of their ways and resorted to results as predicted by teachers.

This marked an important cultural realisation that something called an algorithm could have such a huge impact on a person's future life. We may have heard about AI and algorithms, but often we fail to appreciate the impact of the invisible decision making until they impact on our lives. You might say this is political ineptitude, but it is by design: a decision that was not adequately considered and had an unintended negative impact on people. The same can be found in the AI-led justice systems judging penal sentences according to post (zip) codes, or racial bias in facial or fingerprint recognition systems.

Even more importantly than this, there are some very real global challenges that we need to address, and soon. We have failed to address climate change to prevent us now reaching the predicted increase 1.5 degrees Celsius in average global temperature for a 12-month period for the first time since the pre-industrialised era. Policy and strategy have moved – environmental legislation is making a difference around the world, but the environmental impact of plastic and waste is still at incredible levels. It is often said that 80% of the damage to the environment happens at the design stage. But this is a collective responsibility: We are all part of the design process that creates waste, not just those who are employed as designers and indeed, designers will be at the forefront of the solution, with the skills to design for circular and regenerative systems.

Our poor skills in determining courses of action are failings of design – the human act of creating and co-ordinating actions to deliver benefits, solve problems and prepare us for the future. These are not just political or economic or scientific decisions. They are design decisions and must therefore be carried out with care, a combination of imagination and governance, and that learn from our experience of forming the world to satisfy functional, emotional and social needs. We do this every day in designing the world we interact with, but there are too many scenarios where we ignore design and make assumptions and get things wrong and many suffer as a result.

As Mark Wheelhouse from the Department of Computing at Imperial College in London puts it, "the current world is beset by many urgent and serious challenges that may change the way that we all live. Action is needed now to avert catastrophic problems soon, but this action must be thoughtful and measured, not haphazard and rushed. The design mentality is exactly what decision makers (CEOs, politicians and managers everywhere) need to adopt to avoid repeating the failings of the past."

Chapter 2
The Need for Change

Change before you have to.
Jack Welch

I ran a team at the UK Design Council in the early 2000s which was tasked with developing ideas and tools to stimulate and support the use of design by small to medium-sized businesses. One of our most successful schemes was one that provided direct short-term intervention of specialist designers along with long term access to experienced mentors who could help deliver positive business impact through design. The initiative had a few names over its life but came to be known as Designing Demand. We wanted to set a high metric for success so stated that our objective was to see Ferraris in the car park of the businesses who took part in our scheme.

I'm glad to say that, for the thousands of businesses that benefited from the scheme, from kitchen drain un-blockers to cooker manufacturers, many of the companies benefitted from these interventions and went onto achieve great success. I didn't ever get to count the Ferraris, but the point is that most business went on to improve the performance of their business and deliver benefit to customers, their owners and staff. The research into the performance of these companies showed that every £1 spent on design by businesses participating in the programme delivered £5 in exports, £4 in net operating profit and £20 in turnover.[1]

In a capitalist system, organisations strive to make money. For most commercial organisations, their purpose is to make money and deliver profit for shareholders, good wages for their staff and, yes, nice cars for the owners.

Whether you make a product or a service, are a commercial organisation, a charity or a government department, the books have to balance first, and you have to marshal a complex system of elements that will allow you to create something of value or necessity. It's why businesses tend to be led by accountants and people who know how to make difficult decisions that allow the value to be delivered to customers, whether consumers, businesses or citizens.

Understanding how we do that successfully is why people go to business schools and study to get MBAs. Many will approach running an organisation through the lens of operational efficiency, recruiting and maintaining a happy talented workforce, working on what the customer wants or how to market a product. They possibly don't perceive that all of these have a lot to do with design,

---

[1] https://www.designcouncil.org.uk/our-resources/archive/reports-resources/designing-demand-review/

which is rarely taught, and students are not assessed on their understand practice of design.

The truth is that any output is a combination of important elements ensure a robust financial basis alongside an operationally capable orga and the technology required to create value. That value creation requires outputs that are desirable, and which satisfy a need for whoever you want to transact with.

If understanding the needs of our future customers, and the desires that will make them part with their money to buy your product or service, then we need to engineer, orchestrate and implement what we make so that it is desirable and of value. We need to design it.

Design does not stand separate from economics, organisations, or technology. It is the binding glue that shapes it to be of value. It is the act of balancing all the elements to make something that will successfully compete against your competitors, satisfy and provide solutions for your customers, and create a functional and an emotional relationship with a person that could last a lifetime.

A Sense of Purpose

Many people in any organisation, whether it be a business, a local authority or a charity, no matter their position, would consider it their role to improve the outcomes of what they do. They might aim for their working life to be easier, safer, more secure, or flexible. They might want it to be more profitable or optimised to cut cost. They might be threatened or excited about the impact of technology that could accelerate change or simplify complex processes. There are incentives and assumptions, data and intuition that combine in a heady cocktail of balancing factors when we have to make decisions, decisions that could make a business survive or thrive, a patient loose or gain a bed or a customer be disappointed or delighted and stay loyal for life.

Design can be seen as the orchestration and articulation of those decisions. In one sense, it is as a tool to make things usable, deliver the functions we need and attract us to purchase or use. In another, it communicates pride, beauty, purpose and creates impact. If a car is unattractive, uncomfortable or it's controls difficult to comprehend, we may be less keen to purchase it, however attractive the price is. If a service functions well enough but doesn't treat you with consideration or satisfy your emotional and functional needs, then we complain.

The decisions we make at any stage of the development of a new product or service are a balance between the capability to make something that is of value to people in a way that is financially viable to the company.

When we collectively design something, we need to ensure a balance of these three aspects – a capability to create, in a financially valuable way, something that is desirable – in order to validate our decisions and generate a vision of what that might look like. What can we make, within cost boundaries, that is attractive to the people who have a need? These elements are at the centre of any design activity – we need people who can draw those basic elements together and create a blueprint that will repeat that idea, at scale.

For much of my life as a designer, I've designed physical products. Some of the products I designed include consumer products such as telephones, car radios, fizzy drink machines, and office equipment. I wouldn't blame you if you thought this would entail lots of sketching and sculpting of form to create an attractive design that is then sent to a mechanical engineer who will shake their head and sort out how to manufacture the design for the right price.

But product design requires a deep understanding and appreciation of who you are designing for, what their needs are, and how many of the products will be made. Designing a single super yacht for one billionaire is a very different process to designing a computer that will be used by millions of people. To design a product, you have to understand the investment available for the tooling of the machines that will reproduce your design many thousands of times, and the engineering of those machines, and the processes and materials that will be used to ensure the product lasts without failing. The modern product designer needs to consider the lifetime journey of the product from materials out of the ground to recycling and regeneration. The positioning of electronic components and the shape and size of every human hand: These are crucial understandings without which a sketch is meaningless and mere fantasy.

Design is not just the result of creative imagination – though that is a vital component. Design is a reaction to a complex set of requirements that can hugely limit creativity, sometimes to the point of destroying the desirability of an object.

The designer Tom Hardy tells the story of the original IBM PC (personal computer), one of the first designed as an individual computer for "personal" use rather than one that was harnessed to a central shared mainframe computer (Figure 2.1).

Developed in 1981 at the IBM Boca Raton laboratory, the project had, by IBM standards at the time, a short development schedule of 12 months. Due to the tight timeframe, engineering management set a constraint that all parts require

minimal tooling to minimize production lead time and directed that the keyboard housing and processor unit front cover be made of sheet metal.

A sheet metal housing is constructed from a sheet that is folded to form a box, attached by pop rivets and sometimes welded at the corners and "fettled", or filed, to round the corners so they are softer. The approach avoids tooling, but the resulting image of the first IBM personal computer would have looked like a cheap, tech hobbyist kit of the period. It's a strong but crude construction, but as a product that would be used by thousands of office workers, it was clearly an ugly and uncomfortable solution. Tom objected to this approach as he felt strongly that the design would damage the IBM brand image.

Tom wanted to find an alternative solution to sheet metal for the keyboard and front panel that would still adhere to the minimal tooling constraint. He located what was then a new plastic material called 'structural foam' that only required short-term tooling. The liquid material foamed into a durable hard part with an outer skin that could be painted. The tooling lead-time met the schedule and provided a low-cost material that allowed greater opportunity to shape the product to be softer and more appealing, resulting in a higher quality product image.

However, when Tom introduced the new material approach to the engineering team, they doubted the low cost/short lead-time tooling and continued with their sheet metal concept, such was the urgency of the 12 months to launch schedule. But Tom didn't give up: He was seriously worried about the damage the sheet metal keyboard and flat metal front to the processor would do to the IBM brand image. So, he escalated the issue to IBM senior management, produced extensive data that supported his claims and won. The engineering team was directed to use the structural foam material for the keyboard and front fascia to achieve a higher quality appearance for the product.

Using sheet metal might have hit the delivery schedule, but I seriously wonder whether personal computing would have taken off if the keyboard had been housed in an angular, ugly, industrial-looking sheet metal box. I'm delighted to say that the resulting product won a design award in 1982.

Over time, Apple would create some very attractive metal cases for their computers, milled from aluminium that allowed for them to be easily recycled, which has become a consumer and legislation led issue in the intervening years. But Tom Hardy's leadership and ability to influence management probably saved the future of personal computing.[2]

Figure 2.1: IBM personal computer.

---

2 Thanks to Tom Hardy, former Design Director of IBM. Picture 28th Annual Design Review – Product Design Award *I.D,* Magazine Award – 1982 *I.D.* magazine (US).

signing for a hi-fi company with limited resources, it was my job to design using production techniques that required low investment, such as metal extrusions and folded sheet metal. It was a challenge, and I had to present the argument to the financial director that investment in the front panel of the product to be attractive was important enough to justify the high retail price they wished to charge. Design can be as much about investment and organisational politics as form and function.

For service designers, there is an added dimension, beyond the shaping of a product or designing how to interact with it. When a designer approaches the design of a service, they start with considering the role of time.

In many ways, time plays a critical role in every aspect of design. Every object has a state of unuse and then use. A vacuum cleaner might have a hook and cable winder for when in storage and not in use. Our experience of a service encompasses many different states over time, from finding and using it to not needing it anymore. A service designer's job is to work not with raw materials or industrial processes, but to orchestrate the experience across each stage of our interaction: understand our need, identify a solution, transact in some way, begin and carry on using before, perhaps, a conclusion, or a replacement, or a repeat. Services depend on systems, people and technology and we need to consider how those elements will work and support each stage of the journey when in use.

The Balancing Act

To describe this balancing act between capability, economics and attractiveness, a simple diagram was developed some 20 years ago that helps us make decisions. In the book *Change by Design*, originally published in 2009,[3] the design agency IDEO shared a framework developed some years before in business schools that explained the relationship as one of People, Technology and Business, which can also be referred to as Desirability, Feasibility and Viability. Initially developed as a method of validating prototypes of new products, the framework asks the questions: Is your concept desirable to the user? Is the business model a viable one that is repeatable and scalable? And is the concept using current technology or processes that are dependable and repeatable?

If the answer to any of these is no, then you have a problem. If it is a good business model but the concept is unattractive or fails to deliver on the expectations of a user, then it will fail. If it is attractive and exciting, but processes or technology are not ready, then it cannot be made. And if it is attractive and the

---

[3] Tim Brown, *Change by Design, Revised and Updated: How Design Thinking Transforms Organizations and Inspires Innovation*, Harper Business, 2019.

technology exciting but too expensive for the market, then the proposition will fail again.

The Venn diagram portrays the three elements together and defines the balance required to make an idea, product or service, successful.

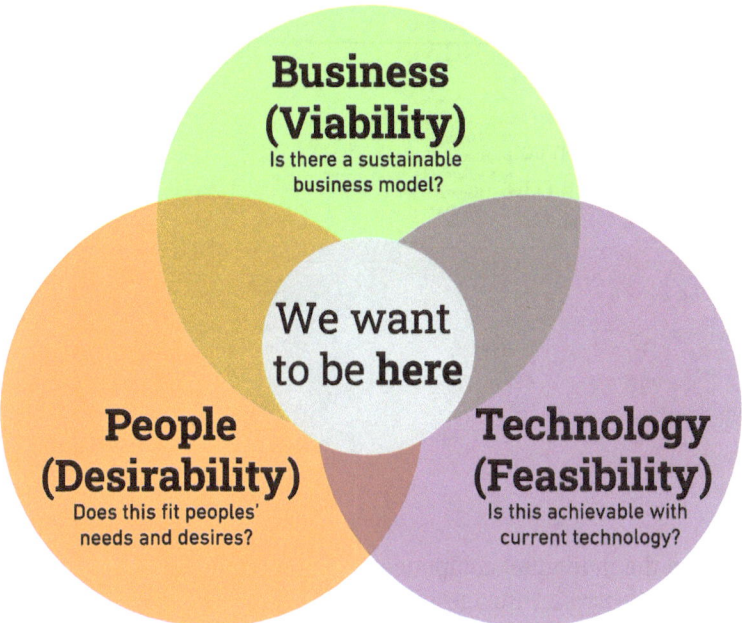

Technology feasibility describes how we make a product or service. It may not be strictly technology, it could be a process or system, or even an organisational culture that needs to be in place to make what is intended. It's the practical side of the diagram but is always related heavily to cost. Nuclear fission may be a proven possibility, but it is still wildly beyond economic means. Is the technology, or system enabler, available, proven at scale and affordable? Is the investment required for the technology or material or industrial process quantifiable in achieving a price per unit cost that is acceptable and affordable and will generate profit? This needs to be established before we can move forward.

Business viability, simply put, is the economic model able to sustain the idea. Is the benefit it provides of enough value, and affordable enough to be successful with revenue covering the organisational and production costs? Is any investment required retrievable and does it provide investors with a return?

Finally, the bit that designers are most vocal about: people and desirability. People, in this context, refers to users, the customers, consumers, or citizens who will gain benefit from the outputs, have a need or desire fulfilled in way that is attractive, fulfils their expectations and is a satisfying experience. If we unpack them further, we can see the three components as separate set of values, criteria, attitudes and historic practice that need to come together to work in harmony for a successful outcome.

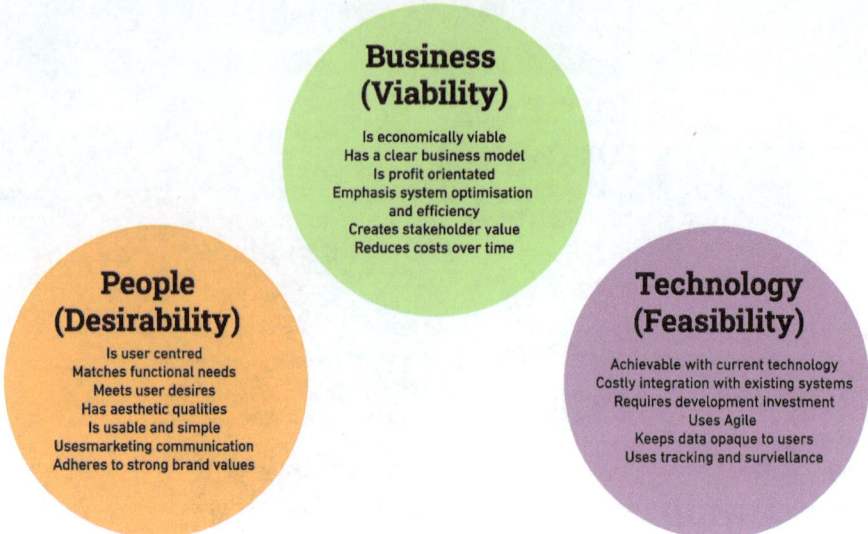

Connections between the individual components generate innovation in different forms. The connection between Business Viability and Technology Feasibility drives process innovation, optimising processes to increase profit or reduce costs.

The relationship between technology and desirability is a driver of consumer innovation, delivering benefits of new technology, from mobile devices to virtual reality headsets or the speed and reach of AI.

The connection between Desirability and Viability creates brand innovation, developing more value to customers and businesses and building better customer experiences across the journey to build greater trust and brand loyalty.

These components should not be confused with a similar Venn diagram often discussed in board rooms: People, Process and Technology. In that diagram, people are the resources of the company itself, not the customer or user. Process refers to the management steps required to develop or innovate or achieve a goal. Technology may refer to automation, or the perceived magic bullet that will cut costs and raise profits. Our belief in technology can override all logic and it is no surprise that technology on its own brings great promise but not always success. We often forget to ask ourselves why. What is the problem we are trying to solve with technology?

Articulating design process around People, Business and Technology, however, has been a useful and helpful way of describing how our decisions, and design processes, need to be balanced across these three elements to maximise the chance for a successful outcome: one that works, is attractive for people, and is financially stable. That's as important for a community coffee shop as for a global corporation.

In the design of services and experiences, whether it be for health, finance, social or business, these three components are vital. A service must answer a need to have value, a service needs an economic model to sustain it over time and be built on systems that can deliver at scale.

But Things Are Changing . . .

Patagonia is a clothing company that tells you not to buy its products. Of course we do, but we know that the clothing will work well functionally (keeping us warm in challenging outdoor environments), will last a long time and is from a company which, although, like many, there have been murmurings around the conditions for workers of their sub-contractors, is focused on saving the planet. It has a circular economic model, will repair its clothes, gives one percent of its income to preventing climate and protecting nature and is an activist organisation.

Patagonia has been going for over 50 years, but it was an early adopter of a new type of company that bought a purpose along with its desire to make profit and rewards its employees and financial backers. Contemporary brands such as Pangaia have chosen to describe their mission as a materials science company bringing problem-solving innovations, and Finisterre, who design garments in line within their overarching corporate purpose of creating sustainable fashion, are satisfying a growing consciousness and demand from consumers.

Visionary business leaders with ethical purposes are not new. Anita Roddick created the Body Shop cosmetics chain to champion the use of products free from animal testing. Steve Jobs' sense of purpose in bringing humanity back to computing has changed all our lives, and campaigners such as Lord John Bird, creator of street sheet for the homeless the *Big Issue* and John Timpson, whose high street company Timpson supports people after release from prison, show that business success and an ethos and purpose are not incompatible.

As reputation management becomes a vital aspect of corporate success, concepts such as authenticity, trust and validating the provenance of production and supply chain are increasingly questioned, made visible and desired by the purchasing public. From overdependence on plastic in packaging, the use of single-use shopping bags, to demands to punish banks who invest in fossil fuels, consumer power, though not necessarily evidenced through the cash till but certainly through social media and the press, is having an impact on how organisations function, report and sustain their businesses.

As a designer and as an academic, I have seen an increasing number of businesses, organisations and government departments lift their heads and ask: What do we need to do in this changing world?

Because change is necessary. Post Covid-19, the demands of the workforce have become more vital as people get used to a more balanced lifestyle between home and work. This is seen in the increased interest in a 4-day working week that might just be the answer to low productivity. With an ageing population in every part of the world – China is redesigning its healthcare and social models for the over 250 million people of its population who are over 65 – and an increasing number of people suffering from dementia in later years, we are having to adjust our models of healthcare. The social crises of mental health, struggling healthcare delivery and financial inequity affect us all. A lack of resilience in our data systems that struggle to defend against hackers and ransomware affect us every day. The climate crisis damaging supply chains of food is creating areas where humans can no longer survive the rising temperatures. It's also had a catastrophic impact on the supply of essential components for manufacture such as microchips.

We have to make decisions about all these things and where there are decisions, there is design. Decisions need to be strategic, but with clear understanding of consequence. Decisions need to be actionable, and not just reports. They need to have impact and so need to be measurable and human centred in order to be adopted and successful. So, they need to be designed.

In recent years the impact of the pandemic fuelled a reset and a look at new ideas that will face up to these challenges. Our views on identity, technology, race, gender, the use of data through AI, have reset our expectations of how business, society and the planet interact, and this has led to a transformation in how we view people, our economic models and our use of technology. There is a new pattern emerging and it is driving businesses and governments to behave differently, with a new sense of purpose and the need to embrace new values beyond the focus on users, profit and technology capability.

New Values

During my time as Head of Programme for Service Design at the Royal College of Art in London, I saw, as you will see in every other design school from India, China, Europe to the Americas, companies who brought their challenges and concerns for the future to the course as project briefs for the students. The Masters students with multidisciplinary and diverse backgrounds then researched and analysed their projects and bought new ideas, innovations and directions as solutions.

Why did companies trust their largest challenges to a bunch of students? Because it's often very difficult to have new ideas inside a business. Judgement is too easy, and the possibility of career damage through having an idea that is considered too adventurous or crazy, is too risky for most. Organisations are mainly operational beings, spending their time unblocking management and responding to day-to-day problems. Strategy is often not a priority and looking at the challenges ahead, scary.

I'm possibly being unfair but, in my experience, many organisations fear the future. Many of the companies who worked with the RCA students had a clear ambition and purpose. They were interested in making sustainability desirable, fun and enjoyable rather than the developing personal guilt. They may have spotted worrying (for them) trends such as the reduction in young people buying cars, or different cultural practices in communities lending funds to each other that is pointing to new models of collaborative banking, or the realisation that many customers are neurodiverse and are being poorly served by their current service experience

The students themselves have been on a journey of exploration, challenging the way technology serves and miss-serves our needs. How we can protect our identity, keep our data secure and have agency over how private data is used?

Their projects created new services to visualise the way data is used to allow greater agency and control. Ways of educating safer use of technology and enhancing the way tech start-ups themselves think proactively of the harm they may do. Through the marvellously named F*** Ethics project, (F for Face), tech start-ups found they could improve their early-stage funding by showing greater responsibility for their future outcomes and impact.

Working with students and partners on these projects showed a trend away from the one-dimensional understanding of technology as something that brings new opportunities of convenience, speed and smarter and cheaper functionality.

Technology needs guard rails, reasons not to behave badly and provide greater security and trust. It's time to consider what the next level of the maturity index for technology might be, to revisit and redefine the role of technology in our balanced system.

Ethical Technology

Feasibility, whether of technology or organisational capacity to deliver at scale, captures the readiness to proceed. Is the technology available, viably affordable to the business in a repeatable and consistent way? Does it work? These have been the essential aspects of how we measure technology capability. When we test technology, we are actually testing whether it works in a variety of normal and edge cases. We do not test for whether it is usable or understandable in the same way, which is why so much of technology is disappointingly difficult and unpleasant to use, to the point where it must be redesigned to ensure adoption is not hampered.

This level of feasibility has become easier to identify, and therefore less critical, whereas the future implications of technology are becoming a greater concern. Our redefining of Feasibility is therefore concerned with the more advanced behaviours and factors surrounding technology. Ethical tech is human centred, protects the user, is transparent and provides agency and is secure from bias. Technology has the power to remove bias, to ensure safety and strengthen secure identities and these are the capabilities needed to drive tech development and its use in our personal lives.

Ethical Technology

Responsible and human centered
User-experience design
before Agile development
Secure and ethically used data
Personalised and private use of data
User controlled
Transparency of data
No surviellence

Sustainable Business

Our models of economic modelling have been entirely concerned with increasing profit, reduction of cost and optimisation of labour and materials. But now economic viability is increasingly affected by the challenges of moving to carbon zero and becoming resilient to the impact of climate change. the subsequent danger to the sourcing of materials, climate change that inflates component costs, political threats to energy, plus the need to broadcast greater responsibility and purpose in business.

We can sense that consumer behaviour increasingly questions the impact of products and services, demanding cleaner, environmentally kinder materials and processes. There are new expectations for clarity of the provenance of materials, processes, carbon footprint and manufacturing worker conditions. Getting these considerations wrong can destroy a brand, decimate their reputation and damage the market of companies from fossil fuel to fashion.

Sustainable Business

Uses new business models
Intergrates circularity
Uses renewable and regenerative design
Considers environmental footprint
Is sustainable
Uses new materials
Services replaces ownwership
Purpose driven

Whether its regulation or corporate reputation, the need to embrace new environmentally sustainable, non-planet damaging solutions is a huge driver for innovation and cost reduction, whether economic or environmental. Business can no longer make and sell and make again. Sustainable business – from repairable smartphones to new models of sharing, renting cars or clothes, recycling and the circular economy – is forcing creativity in the business models we use.

When Adidas came to the service design course at the RCA, they wanted to know what a viable alternative to current consumerism might look like: How might a circular economy work for sportswear? What is the customer experience of returning used clothes and what is the system and business model to support such a new model? They were using designers to bring together technology and business models to create a new definition of desirability that works across ethical, environmental and human behaviour to envision a new way. A way that businesses will have to face up to and need to think about now. Inaction is a threat to survival and an increasing number of CEOs are getting that message. They need the visons that combine big thinking, technology, new systems and business models to point the way forward.

Like all innovations, it takes time to embed these new ideas and business models that replace the tradition of retail and maybe some recycling into one that builds that experience in from the start, with economic advantages to all parts of the system. These are the challenges we must solve. We need to shape new ways of providing economic growth through different models of ownership, circularity and services beyond ownership. Right now, the economic argument for the circular economy is difficult and it's too easy to ignore it. But legislation and consumer pressure will change this and the time to design for the future is now.

For many organisations, a sense of purpose is becoming as strong as their need for profit. A purpose-led business has something to say, a desired outcome that protects the planet, cares for nature or the underprivileged. A sense of purpose rallies the people who work in a company; it strengthens their resolve and loyalty and develops individual initiative to strive to create benefits for the organisation and its audience.

The final component is us. The people who use and need, desire, are compelled or instructed to use a service or product. For the last decades, the revolution in business, design and technology has been driven by "the user". This has had a positive impact and created an empathetic view of who we are designing for. We care more about what their needs are, how might we compete for their attention, be innovative and differentiate by understanding those needs and provide new solutions that are accessible, inclusive and fit for purpose. From banking apps, government digital services that replace archaic processes and technology that just works, most (though not all), have learnt to value design methods of research, insight and how to create a better method of interaction with the world that suits each individual and works in a way they can understand.

But in being so user centred, we have missed many people out. The people who deliver a service, who design and create interactions have been seen as components of delivery, rather than vital assets, to be supported, empowered and inspired. We have forgotten those who are not the individual users but may be affected and impacted by products and services around the user who are impacted by change.

The poster children of service design over the last twenty years have been the likes of Airbnb and Uber: disruptive, innovative, exciting, user-focused new business models and levels of individual service that have destroyed the legacy systems that went before them. But as we have seen, there have been unintended consequences from their success to the social fabric of communities. We have learnt to question the impact of what seemed such innovative new service models, combining technology and data to create new levels of customer experience and profitable businesses.

The next level of maturity for our balance index is to move from People and Desirability to Human and Community. We need to nurture organisations that work to ensure benefit to all, customers, employers, and those who might be impacted by their outcomes. Organisations want a diversity of employees not just to fulfil a quota but to bring new thinking to their mindsets, be inclusive of race and gender and create equitable outcomes. They want to co-create with their audiences to gain insights, consider the unintended consequences of the future on society as well as the planet and develop authentic narratives that draw people to their mission.

Human & Community

Beneficial to all
Desirable social impact
Inclusive
Co-created
Considers unintended consequences
Fair to empoyees
Sustainable supply chains
Authentic provenance

This is not some happy, "wouldn't it be wonderful?", dream. These are the hard problems that organisations of every size and objective are putting at the heart of their strategy to discover new directions that will generate tangible actions. Whether it's fear of disruption to their business ecosystem, or how to reset for sustainability and carbon zero, or through a sense of purpose and mission to differentiate and compete by providing choice to people who want to understand how to behave sustainably, organisations are looking not for examples of best practice from the past, but for future practice that will identify innovative new solutions that work in a world with new sensibilities and desires.

The New Paradigm

Design is always a combination of the functional, emotional and social context. This new paradigm, this revision of the model, a level up the maturity index of contemporary organisation design, reflects what is happening to businesses now. We need more data, more learning and more time to develop truly effective alternatives that will retain a liveable planet that is fair and equitable and hands back agency to people keen to communicate and benefit from this wave of technology we are experiencing.

Design is not on the periphery of these tectonic shifts. It is at the centre, and we all have a role in bringing together the thinkers of economics, the scientists who shape technology and the designers who facilitate the creation of desirable, people and planet-centred options for our future. We can't lop one bit off, they all interconnect and this calls for collaboration breaking through the culture of science, economics and art to find these solutions. It is not enough to be a campaigner or a tree hugger, concepts such as equity and sustainability run through the views of all aspects of this paradigm, they are not separate to it. Therefore, we need to embrace this fantastic opportunity and break through the pollical, cultural, educational and societal barriers to set a new course that will bring sustainable wealth and comfort to all.

How Do We Redesign Thinking for Change?

It's not just strongly purposeful companies such as Patagonia who are bringing purpose into their strategy. Companies such as Bosch and Logitech are enthusiastically embracing change. Whether through international legislation such as in the European Union, or intergovernmental agreements such as the Paris and Kyoto agreements, levers are creating positive force for change – it's no longer an option.

As an example, the Bosch Group, based in Stuttgart, a leading global supplier to consumers of technology and services with a broad product portfolio, from washing machines to power tools, cookers to heat pumps, and supplier to the automotive industry with components from semiconductors to solutions for the software-defined vehicle, brings user-centred design to every business unit in the company, creating a maturity index clearly outlining different levels of UX capability. They are consistently raising their ambition, defining new levels of design maturity that beside, e.g., design strategy and service design, also embrace sustainability, inclusivity and harnessing the power of AI in a meaningful way.

Bosch understands user experience and design as a tool to embrace the challenges of the future, in harness with the technological and engineering legacy and the financial goals to sustain their business. Their motto of "Invented for Life" has come to mean different things over time, and the consequences of designing for humans, the life of the product, and the sustaining of the planet are all part of their corporate mission.

Embracing the challenges of moving to carbon zero, Logitech came out loud and proud in articulating the environmental impact of their products and the efforts they have made to create more sustainable products. Evaluating the full life impact of manufacture, use and disposal of each of their products and communicating that on the packaging was a courageous and inspirational move. Working closely with design and engineering, they redesigned their product line to reduce the carbon footprint and environmental impact. As their COO Prakash Arunkundrum has said, sustainable solutions are the product of close collaboration with the design team to engineer, communicate and ensure that the functionality and desirability to customers of the product remains. The onus was on them to share the information of carbon footprint and allow the customer to make that choice.[4]

It is easy for a leader to keep the status quo. It is easier and cheaper. But the challenges ahead are very real and the risk of not preparing for the future, for not being ready to compete before the market moves or consumers behaviours swings, make leaving things as they are a risky proposition. Whether your objective is business growth, positive social impact or enhancing your relationship with your customer, you need to make decisions and having the design process and skills to visualise, prototype and validate your decisions gives you a real advantage.

And whether you are trying to streamline your operations, using design to help you identify where the value to your customer is, highlights and shows you what to keep and what to let go. Design is not a luxury, it's a vital business tool that if missing from your armoury, restricts your ability to move forward and increases your risk of acting on unproven assumptions, which are expensive to repair later.

And yet, every time businesses go through tough times, they reduce the design team, like it's a luxury they can do without. Eventually, those executives will feel the pain of such poor decision making. In the 12 months previous to writing this book, US healthcare, software and tech companies have all made drastic re-

---

[4] Prakash Arunkundrum, COO and GM, Logitech for Business, Innovation Roundtable Summit, Copenhagen, 2023.

ductions in their human-centred design teams. The damage this will do to their future success will be felt by their shareholders in the not-too-distant future.

The much-reproduced McKinsey Design Report[5] that shows that design-led companies outperform their competition by 200%, earn higher returns for the shareholders and maintain market position through all conditions, is studiously ignored by CEOs every time there is a crisis.

Yet the majority of service designers in many parts of the world have been hired not into organisations but by external management consultancy and accountancy firms. For many of these firms, their consultancy arms earn their fees from identifying and delivering change. Over time, they have correctly identified that service designers who facilitate change, based on real insight, and their creative skills to solve problems and identify better solutions that have impact, are perfect for the projects they carry out for business and governments. This is not design as they were expecting, it is design in different way that delivers real transformation and effective, measurable results.

Perhaps, in the future MBA courses will teach about the disasters caused by short-term firing of design departments. Hang on to your designers, they will lead you into a future that customers and citizens trust, act on and create value and profit, together.

How Do We Design for Change?

As a service designer, your role is not the traditional one imagined for designers. You, I'm afraid, are not the guru who sprinkles magic dust on an object and then moves onto the next challenge. You are someone who collaborates with all around you, who facilitates conversation and collaboration with customers, users, managers and employees. You will use your creativity to co-create new ideas, see patterns and build concepts, but with humility that you might be wrong and the only way to learn is to visualise, prototype and share ideas to check whether they are right or improve them.

You will understand there is no silver bullet, and that the systems of change are complex, but you have tools that provide your colleagues with moments of epiphany when they understand what the experience of people is that they make decisions about.

You will develop the language of foresight, how to understand the impact of global trends and visualise alternative scenarios that can galvanise people towards the shared authorship of better decisions and better outcomes.

---

5 "The Business Value of Design", 2018.

Getting invited to the party is a constant problem. Getting noticed, employed and impactful in any organisation is tough. You will have to be a pioneer and an evangelist and prove your value in any organisation large or small. But, as I have seen in every case, designers surprise people around them, create solutions and desirable impact that were not expected and unleash their collective creativity that makes life better and happier. Even the most cynical client gets excited about possibilities they had never imagined when they're presented by students or young service designers. In a world over-invested in fear of risk and heightened caution, we need to invest in people who have empathy, creativity and the tools to bring both the evidence and validation for the direction for change. We need to redress the management balance away from the technical and economic mindset that has failed to solve the big changes of society and the environment and reframe their mindsets to think more responsibly and bring about a balance between art, science and economics to find purpose, deliver technology we can trust and that enhances human society. This, as designer, you can, and must do.

Whether you wait to be invited to the party, wait for the brief or proactively drive for change we will explore later, but we cannot let organisations treat design as a luxury that can be hired and then fired. After all, we are all making design decisions every day, so don't lose the expertise to help us make better decisions based on a complete understanding of their impact.

Chapter 3
In Technology We Trust

*We tend to overestimate the effect of a technology in the short run
and underestimate the effect in the long run.*
Roy Amara

I love technology. I wouldn't have survived in any other time that wasn't as saturated with helpful technology as this one is. Planning each day, knowing where to go, be connected to people every moment, stay in touch with events, book trips, pay bills, listen to music, watch TV, through my phone, my tablet, my PC, my set top box. I can't remember what we did before technology did all this for us.

I also hate technology. As I mentioned in the introduction to this book, the madness of the six-monthly clock changing rituals, where every object has a maddingly complex and different way of changing the time from winter to summertime and back, remains one of the most stupid and, ironically, time-wasting human activities there could be. Giving something that my elderly mum needs to be simple and understandable to a programme engineer, who clearly thinks that simple means having a magical knowledge of the number of seconds you hold a button down before it moves to hours or minutes, except it never does behave precisely how the many pages long instruction book describes it. For all the sophistication of technology in our world, we still can't design an intuitive and consistent approach to changing time. And I haven't got time to mention the parking meter that requires you to enter your licence plate and countless other truly dreadful and anger-inducing examples of terrible technology interactions that enrage us.

Here we are, with technology in every part of our lives. We hold it, look at it, interact with it, trust it and believe it. Some of it is very visible and useful, though we're not sure how it works. Sometimes it's invisible and we don't realise it's there. Sometimes we are forced to use it when what we really want to do is talk to someone. Mostly we do love it because it brings us information, knowledge, entertainment, social connections, dopamine hits and directions for how to get somewhere and what the traffic's like. Sometimes it's difficult to use, but, I have to admit, it's mostly usable, with a little practice.

Sometimes we are fearful of technology. We worry about surveillance, or bias, or loss of privacy, though we celebrate the security it might bring to our homes and streets.

We are annoyed by passwords, registration processes, countless entering of emails into websites and apps. But technology finds better ways, by recognising our faces, fingerprints or voices to give us secure access. We mostly like it.

Technology often makes physical objects redundant. Fax and answering machines are things of the past, delivered as a service rather than a physical machine. I love that I can tune a guitar via an app on a mobile phone rather than waste all those resources on a specific tuner.

Most would agree that technology has radically changed our lives, and many would point out that this has not always been in a positive way. The move from the paper-based curated and edited from of daily information in a newspaper, for example, to open digital access to everything anyone has ever said in a click of a search engine, is amazing but has had occasionally frightening consequences.

Fear of Tech

When mobile phones became readily available in the 2000s, many feared that such close exposure to radio waves transmitted near our heads might have lasting effects and possibly cause brain cancer. It turned out that the impact of mobiles on our brains was more on our mental rather than physical health. Over the decades, the impact on our mental of mobile phone usage by new generations of users has become a huge cause for concern. There is already a backlash against social media platforms which allow untrammelled access to potentially damaging content with few restrictions, especially for young people.

As we walk our streets or sit in social spaces anywhere in the world where economic access to technology is possible, we will see people's heads directed to phones, a daemon hardwired into our thoughts, beliefs and emotions. This is a radical shift across all cultures and societies, and it's possible to see that we are becoming disconnected to the real world around us.

We are living in what is described as the 4th Industrial Revolution. This is a technological revolution, which the World Economic Forum describes as "a fusion of technologies that is blurring the lines between the physical, digital and biological spheres".[1]

---

[1] Karl Schwabb, 2015 WEO Forum Interconnection. Schwabb introduced the concept of the 4th Industrial Revolution as:
- The ability of machines, devices, sensors, and people to connect and communicate with each other via the Internet of Things (IoT), or the internet of people
- Information transparency – the transparency afforded by Industry 4.0 technology provides operators with comprehensive information to inform decisions.
- Technical assistance – the technological facility of systems to assist humans in decision making and problem solving, and the ability to help humans with difficult or unsafe tasks [24]
- Decentralised decisions – the ability of cyber physical systems to make decisions on their own and to perform their tasks as autonomously as possible.

If the 1st Industrial Revolution was the age of mechanical propulsion enabling the acceleration of our industrial capacity, the 2nd the use of electricity to power and light our lives and mass production, and the 3rd the miniaturisation and reduction in cost of electronics to entertain our lives, then the 4th is the one that has opened up our access to knowledge and communication and is increasing at such a rate that we start to feel a threat to our purpose and future lives.

The Transformation of Personal Technology

Early on in this revolution, I worked with the mobile phone company Orange in the UK. The mobile phone was transforming from being a pocketable block with a number pad and a small screen that was used primarily to make phone calls and send short text messages to a new generation of pocketable computers that became known as smartphones.

The advent of the SMS (short message service) text message was a small revolution of its own, allowing private messaging to people across a meeting room, or around the world. It was apparent from the start that the basic number pad on the traditional mobile phone was not an adequate way to form words and sentences, and we had to find a more text friendly input method.

At that time a phone was more of a business tool for professionals whose jobs required them to be away from their office, or an emergency method of communication, a secondary device perhaps placed in the front compartment of a car in case of an emergency. Being able to communicate anywhere, along with the ability to send short messages as texts, opened a more social aspect of mobile phone usage. When it became socially acceptable, and it wasn't at first, phones started to be used in restaurants and public places. In certain countries such as Italy, populations rapidly adopted the mobile as a social communication tool.

Those early phones were simple and reasonably easy to use, though ease of use, or usability as it came to be known, was seen as "nice to have" rather than an essential aspect of the software or hardware design of the phone.

Orange was interested in why the phones made by Finnish manufacturer Nokia had higher usage, and were more profitable, than those made by US manufacturer Motorola. The theory was that it was due to the way the different manufacturers marketed their phones. Nokia marketing and packaging showed pictures of relaxed, trendy young people having fun who clearly spent all their time phoning each other. Orange executives surmised that Nokia phone owners simply had more friends and called them a lot. Motorola's brand at that time was more corporate and professional, plus that the mobile situation in the US was quite different, with the person who received a call paying for it, rather than in Europe, the caller paid.

Having used the two handsets, it was obvious that the Nokia was much easier to use, and the hypothesis was made that maybe it was the greater simplicity of the Nokia that was driving greater usage.

Orange had a testing lab in Bristol in the UK, so it was decided to test the two phones together and compare how people used them. It was easy to use the Nokia handset with clear descriptions on the screen and just a click or two to make the call. The Motorola on the other hand was complicated with many notifications at each stage asking if you wanted to go to the next instruction and make the call. It was as if it had been designed by lawyers to avoid responsibility for persuading you to make a call and the receiver having to pay for it. Which it probably was.

The discovery that it was the design of the software of the phone that enabled it to be easier to use, and therefore be used more and be more profitable, was a moment of epiphany. It wasn't marketing or a more fashionable image that was driving usage. It was the ability to simply, and perhaps pleasurably, carry out the functions of the phone.

As mobile phone usage grew along with the exponential growth of the technological capability of the handset, cameras, email, and access to the internet began to revolutionise the role of the mobile phone in our lives. You might have expected that the lessons of usability would be seen as useful in ensuring everyone could use the new features easily. But this was not the case.

Orange was a revolutionary brand, with their launch adverts made by filmmaker Ridley Scott and their advertising slogan "the future's bright, the future's Orange". Their proposition was radically different from their emerging competitors Vodafone, Deutsche Telekom (they didn't mention the phone bit for a start) and across their advertising, stores, culture right down to their phone packaging, they were transformative and friendly in a way others were yet to learn about.

Almost unbelievably at the time, Orange repackaged every phone they sold in their own branded packaging, complete with a rewritten user manual to help their customers get going with the phones. This was an unheard-of effort to provide a higher level of service and customer experience.

On my first day at Orange, I was given their most advanced phone yet, developed by Orange along with Microsoft who provided the software and operating platform plus a dedicated handset manufacturer. It was an exciting development and bought to the public a host of technological marvels: email, video, access to the emerging mobile internet, and applications that could be bought for playing games or other services.

However, there was a problem. It still looked like a conventional phone with a number pad, but with a multidirectional cursor button under the screen. The screen was small and very crowded with icons directing to Microsoft and Orange services. There was a sense of competition, not cooperation, between the two companies, with mobile phone networks wary of the possibility that Microsoft would "own" the service and dominate the customer experience, meaning that the networks would remain little more than the plumbing for data and calls.

The phone was ergonomically terrible, with buttons that were difficult to view and use, a tiny, overcrowded screen and an ugly design. But it had all that technology! More than was in all the Apollo moon missions put together, Orange triumphantly announced. What could go wrong?

The phone was a disaster in its first version and mis-sold to people who didn't need all those functions and were confused by its advanced features. I was tempted to give up on Orange but realised that the answer to all these problems was design. Better design, reframing the handset for its new capability and purpose, designing the screen to be easier to comprehend and access the amazing features.

During this time, I met Steve Jobs, the CEO of Apple, wo was developing an interest in mobile phones. I was introduced to him by my once colleague (now Sir) Jony Ive. I'd met him once before, and he was interested in my role and opinions of the future direction of mobile phones. Steve had been working with Motorola on an iTunes phone and was clearly forming a very negative view of the industry. He politely asked me some questions, then told me I was completely wrong and went off to develop the iPhone.

When a designer from Nokia I knew pulled out an iPhone from his pocket, it was a magical moment. A proper interactive touch screen, a graphical representation of physical sliding unlock action, the two finger pinch to instantly zoom in and out, visual voicemail, so you could see who had left a message instead of having to call your voice mail . . .

These were just a few of the amazing innovations that were seen in the iPhone for the first time. The response from Microsoft, the company we most feared as a network provider? Some may remember Microsoft's Steve Ballmer's comments that it was overly expensive and didn't have a keyboard and his phone had all the same functionality. You can watch the video.[2] Well, history records who won.

Prior to the iPhone, it was estimated that around 10% of users accessed the internet once a month via their mobile phones. With the iPhone, 95% of users were accessing the internet every day.

Just because technology can do something does not mean people will use it. Before the iPhone, much of the technology was already available and "worked". Only the important aspect of working – the usability, desirability, ease of use, plain language, ergonomics, and the need and desire to use it – was missing and it therefore only achieved a tiny percentage of its potential.

---

[2] Micosoft CEO Stevel Bulmer laughed but then regretted his first reaction to the "$500 Phone that doesn't have a keyboard".

There's an important aspect to this history lesson in that we continually fail to learn. Technology is not enough. The finest and fastest technologies are useless without a sense of their value to people, an understanding what people will use it for and the need to design it so that it works well, not only for experts or tech enthusiasts, but normal people. You, my mum, all of us.

Steve Jobs, driven by his frustration with the status quo, of technology slowly evolving by bolting on new features to the tired old formats from a different age, realised that things needed to be completely re-invented. He looked up and away from the traditional forms of a mobile phone and radically reimagined them. A touch screen with an almost magical interface that allowed us to play, learn, be informed by the great interconnected network of the internet. A screen you could turn so it worked as a larger keyboard. A phone slim enough to sit in your pocket and a metal case strong enough to survive whatever you did with it.

Rather than looking at what was currently possible, he took, as he always did, the world's finest manufacturers on a journey with him. He inspired them, invested in them, persuaded them to take a giant leap of faith that by imagining something far better than what currently existed, they would reap the rewards of market domination. Which they did and still do.

That was leadership. With the brilliant designer Jony Ive and a team of driven creative and technological geniuses, they made it work. Have we ever seen such leadership before or since?

The benefits of this combination of technology and usability, science and beauty, are all around us. The way we pay, shop, talk, play, are entertained and are informed is almost exclusively through digital means. Organisations hold huge amounts of data. Data has become a driver of decisions and outcomes and as we rapidly move into the world of artificial intelligence (AI), a new horizon of opportunity is opening up.

We, and many businesses and governments, are keen to harness the benefits of technology. We are excited by it and want to trust that it will work benignly in our interest. The investment and growth in technology has come to define our age and, especially since the global pandemic, our interactions have gone digital.

Our trust in and optimism about technology have been at the heart of enormous changes in our lives. Working from home, paying digitally, buying online rather than a physical store, booking a holiday, taking a picture of our family, all have moved from a physical act requiring products and places, to digital, online activities with the ease and ability to navigate through enormous possibilities and choice is balanced by the lack of physical experience on which to make that choice. But the ease and efficiency of technology is seductive.

Technology Solves Problems We Don't Have

We tend to believe that all technology is good. Certainly, technology companies believe that their technology will enhance our lives, make it simpler and allow us to achieve previously cumbersome processes with greater ease and comfort, and at a lower cost for them.

But this does not always work. The desire to invent and develop new technology and thrust it upon us is a strong one. But it often, possibly always, fails. There are many examples of amazing and ingenious technology that delights with its possibilities, but crashes on the rocks of public ambivalence, lack of uptake or just lack of a reason to use it.

Heroic Failures – Segway

The arrival of the Segway was first hinted at in 2000. Our previous hero Steve Jobs hinted that it was going to be bigger than the invention of the PC. The inventor Dean Kamen had started with a design of a powered wheelchair in 1990 and by the mid-90s the US healthcare company Johnson and Johnson had invested $50 million pounds developing it. It used an innovative system of computer-controlled gyroscopes to allow for body motion to guide and steer the wheelchair over any terrain and bring the passenger up to eye level.

Dan's team saw an opportunity to extend the application of this wonderful engineering feat to all and create a new class of personal mobility vehicle.

The Segway was born in a hurricane of hype and technology optimism. An apocryphal story tells that they were given to the Post Delivery Service in Boston, a city that is very cold during the winter months. Within a couple of weeks, the postal workers had given the machines back. They complained that they got too cold riding the Segway during their rounds and preferred walking, which kept them warmer and was better for their health.

In the end only 140,000 were sold, not quite the next PC or the bigger than the internet phenomena that were foreseen at launch. You can still see them in various cities around the world with slightly embarrassed tourists following a tour guide around historical sites and universities and golf courses too. They're not easy to use as you have to lean back to activate the brake and get used to tipping left and right to steer and you need training before you ride one.[3]

What was the problem the Segway was solving for us? Originally, as a wheelchair, mobility at a level that had not existed before for people with disability.

---

[3] Mark Wilson, "Segway, the most hyped invention since the Macintosh, ends production", *Fast Company*, 23 June 2020.

But for others, it was hard to see what problem it was solving. It was slow (10 mph), expensive ($5,000), took a long time to recharge (8 hours) and replaced ... walking! It had no purpose, no value to many of us apart from a sense of wonder at its technical ingenuity.

The Segway is a great example of technology push. We can do something, so let's make it at scale and launch it on the world with our fingers crossed. And, in this case, it was a massive failure: There was no need to replace walking, it was difficult to use, and the intellectual, engineering genius and huge finance that went into it were wasted. What might that genius and money have been spent on that gave us something we wanted and was useful?

More recently, personal mobility has been reinvented in a much more useful form as the sharable scooter system that is prevalent in many cities of the world. By sharing ownership by hiring the scooter on the spot through an app, this cheap, clean form of transport is increasing popular alongside shareable e-bikes. The tech is simpler, the cost to the passenger cheaper and the access to bikes is usually conveniently close. They bring other problems, such as leaving them to clutter our pavements and walkways, but mobility designed as a service has proven much more successful than the Segway. And the only computerised gyroscopes are those in our brain that stop us falling off. Though always better to wear a helmet.

Google Glasses

Google Glasses were announced as a leap forward in sensory interfaces. A global marketing campaign was founded on a trust and a belief that what technology could do, we would want. The Google proposal that we wear spectacles which hold a miniature camera and projector that beams onto the rear surface of the glasses so we could see information, without the need to look at our mobile phones, was seen as an exciting and liberating future.

Whether they realised it or not, Google were introducing an intrusion into the intimacy of our private and social lives. If I am having a drink with a friend, or a great social evening, do I really want a camera crew of colleagues or friends to record this through their Google Glasses? Insane!

Now, I can imagine that for a police officer, a manager in a nuclear power plant or a brain surgeon, there may be situations where this marvellous technology could provide, and is beginning to, great advantages of better and safer performance. But to arm the whole population with recording devices is a massive social intrusion worth some discussion at least. As it turns out, we didn't want to pay for that intrusion, no matter what the advantages. In a more environmentally aware time, we might question the environmental cost of storing all that data, and the privacy and security of it too.

The question I ask is: Why? Why do we allow such a random, chaotic, try-it-and-see-what-happens, at immense cost, approach to changing the world. Is it not madness? What other aspects of life are created and forced on us with such blind faith and financial risk? But Google can suck up the costs and move on in the spirit of adventurous tech development. What a waste.

Speech Recognition

We can wonder what our ancestors would make of modern-day technology. The Harry Potter magic of a zoom pinch touch screen. A box that you can talk to and it can play music and deliver you a take-away dinner. What happy lives we must lead.

Speech recognition would especially amaze them. We've had access to this technology for longer than we might imagine. It's over 30 years since the capability of turning our voice into text to compose an email or be able to talk to a virtual assistant through our mobile phone has been available. Back in the 1990s Whirlpool experimented with voice operated washing machines. The design agency IDEO had been working on it and took part in the publicity launch. Unfortunately, in rehearsals the machine kept starting during the introductory speech when any phrase that accidently included an instruction to the machine was spoken. The engineers had to turn it off and add a physical "On" button. Which sort of questioned what the purpose of the speech recognition was.

Orange, always a forward-thinking organisation, fired with a desire to make technology work for us rather than the other way round, brought voice technology to their customers in 2000. The technology called Wildfire, bought for $148 million, allowed subscribers to speak commands during a call, which would be answered by a natural female voice. Perhaps the precursor to the film *Her*, where the character Theodore Twombly (played by Joaquin Phoenix), interacts with a computer that he falls in love with, the Wildfire voice was liked by users and seen as a step forward from robotic voices. The service had its business fans and many disabled users found they could access smartphone services for the first time. But the voice interface was not easy to use and not always accurate. An idea before its time perhaps, but when numbers of users dropped to around 10,000, Orange dropped the service.

Despite these setbacks, the tech industry did not give up, certain that the future was bright, the future was voice recognition. Around 2015 several banks gained favourable publicity with their plans to record customers' voices on calls and use voice mapping to provide fail-safe identity checks without going through all these questions every time a customer called. But the setup and process of recording was far from seamless, and most people didn't bother. Suddenly our smartphones had facial recognition and voice security wasn't so attractive and disappeared.

But as processing power grew and natural language listening and reading on vast cloud-based data banks connected over fast and accessible networks, the ability to replace a visual user interface with a voice-based interface became a reality. With the Amazon Alexa and the Apple Siri, an affordable and accessible consumer product was available, linking vast retail platforms and internet search to happy, hungry, purchase-ready consumers to buy with their voice.

My wife will not have a speech recognition device in our home. She is sure that it is listening to our conversations and will immediately fill up her social media with adverts for new shoes when she mentions her shoes look a little used. She does not trust it.

Trust is an important word. It's not easily handled by technology organisations. They feel uncomfortable with it. During my time working for Cisco, the US-based global supplier of all the kit that makes the internet work, the feeling of excitement in the future was tangible. The concept of the "Internet of Things", where the sensors, cameras, audio devices and huge databanks are connected over a network, was an especially exciting vison of the future. We can record data of where we are, how we travel, how we are entertained, what building we are entering, our moods and sentiment, our lives and the context of the surrounding systems of time of day, weather, time of year and all of our past behaviour. The opportunities were boundless and will change our world. They renamed it the Internet of Everything, so ubiquitous and advantageous would be its impact.

But for anyone who starts by thinking from the perspective of people, rather than technology, it was not so clear cut. What if people don't appreciate being pinged by every building they walk past. What if people don't want their data stored and didn't trust that it would be kept safe and secure by the organisations who collect it?

My elderly parents love their speech recognition device. Every day they wake up and ask it "Play Leonard Cohen". And it does – all day!

Like many couples who spent a lot of time together, they like to play fight and josh around. When my father complained loudly that his wife might kill him if she kept pushing him around like that, their speech recognition device jumped into life to ask which emergency service he needed. The rumoured service that Amazon were developing to identify domestic violence in the home was clearly working!

So, for them voice recognition provides immediate, easy and inclusive access to a service they love. It is accessible, friendly, obedient and always on.

But for others it's a security risk, an "always on" listening device ready to pounce with an order or a response. Ready to run off with your data and let it loose on any old hacker or SCAM merchant, perhaps. Trust is crucial to our relationship with technology and without it, it fails, expensively.

The Metaverse

Our next example of overconfidence, for a period, completely overtook the planet. Every organisation was preparing for a future world of virtual reality, a recreation of the physical with an enhanced multisensorial experience. Our work, play, education and relationships were being prepared to be delivered through headsets that would revolutionise our world.

Eventually, even Facebook and Meta founder Mark Zuckerberg realised that this was not the great idea he had thought it might be. Can you point to another technology leap that took so much investment and money and that achieved so little?

Facebook bought an interesting and ambitious headset manufacturer Oculus Rift and tried to convince the world that this is what we needed and would replace, or at least duplicate, the real world. It was interesting that they spent a lot of time and money with the great art and design colleges of the world in exploring what it might be used for, which does suggest they weren't sure what problems they were solving.

On the other hand, some surprising and exciting outcomes have been achieved. Apps that make you experience what it's like to be blind, or to re-live the historical experience of Afro Caribbeans travelling in the US in early 20th century, or tools to support neurodiverse children.

But this doesn't mitigate completely the waste of money and mindful arrogance of launching technology on the world with no purpose and your fingers crossed. How do they get away with it?

In one sense we do trust technology. We believe it will be the solver of problems, that it will bring new possibilities and opportunities, disrupt the old and inefficient with faster than lightspeed cleverness.

Technology doesn't have to be clever to be dangerous. Over the last ten years, a system developed in the UK to improve the accuracy and efficiency of regional post offices, a vital part of the community and source of stamps for letters, parcel deliveries and much more, turns out to have been so inaccurate and untrustworthy that it routinely miscalculated the daily takings of each micro-business that made up the national network.

The inability to believe that their system had bugs that were creating miscalculations led to the persecution and prosecution of hundreds of innocent post office owners, with occasionally tragic consequences. The terrible design of the software ended up destroying lives.

Consider the plight of retired schoolteacher Eileen McGrath. At the age of 85 she noticed that her pension had not been paid in over the Christmas period. She then received letters asking her if she had died. Calling the pension provider (never a pleasant chore and, as the service designer Lou Downe put it, the need to have to call a contact centre is a sign of system failure), she informed them she was indeed alive. A second pension had the same problem, and it turned out she had to repeatedly prove that she was alive each year to ensure her pension was paid. As Eileen mentioned to the UK paper, *The Guardian*, "This is Alice in Wonderland territory".

What madness is this? How can the systems and processes we use be so disconnected from the humans they serve? Why is the emphasis on us to monitor and correct invisible systems that we have no agency over? I suspect there are many more stories of systems behaving badly and that we have all experienced them. We are often caught in infinite loops of frustration and annoyance, sometimes anger. Being redirected to Frequently Asked Questions (FAQs) that don't match your questions, or trying to find hidden phone numbers when you just want a human to sort a problem out.

Invisible Enablers

Data and new tech solutions are allowing many of our decisions to become increasingly automated. Another recent technology bubble has been blockchain. Rooted in the mercurial advance of cryptocurrency, blockchain, otherwise known as distributed ledgers, provides a mathematically complex system of contracts that are highly secure and traceable. The complexity of creating a blockchain contract consumes enormous amounts of energy, but the uses beyond cryptocurrency include identifying authentic replacement components for aero engines and digital passports for humans as well as objects.

Generative AI has been the headline of recent times, but AI and algorithmic-based decisions have been around for a long time. Increasingly, decisions from healthcare treatments to mortgage loan approvals are eased and speeded up by rapid analysis of historic data and decision trees that open, or close options and opportunities for us.

The opportunities these invisible enablers provide are benefits around personalised experiences, built on knowledge of our behaviour and past actions, that can mean highly focused and relevant choices, whether that be the properties we are shown on an Airbnb site, to recommendations of books, to financial advice and insurance premiums. Some good, some bad.

The experience of these enablers is often invisible, decisions made in the background that may speed up and ease the decisions we make. On the other hand, we don't know the basis of these decisions and we've been aware for a while that systems can be biased and produce unfair results.

When Don Norman wrote his book *The Design of Everyday Things* on user interactions in the digital space, he looked to a concept created in the 1960s around animal anthropology called "affordance". Affordance is an invented word to describe the way animals recognise their environment and identify how it might help them make a home and protect them. In the digital world, Don Norman recognised that we needed to make things clear, that a button was a button and could access actions or information. He realised we had to design digital interactions that were still unfamiliar to us in a familiar way, that allowed or brains to identify and have confidence in achieving a goal through a digital interface.

We experience this when we see the language of icons in an app on our mobile phones. The three horizontal lines have come to be understood as the menu, and a line under a web address as a link to that website. These visual clues are necessary for us to navigate through a digital experience without fear or trepidation, confident we won't have an accident and do something we didn't wish to do. This is vital in building confidence in digital experiences, and we would not use our banking apps if we weren't sure they weren't designed to prevent us from making a potentially expensive mistake.

In the world of invisible enablers though, that transparency and good design practice are missing. We have little knowledge and no agency over the decisions that might prevent us from accessing services or information, or be directed in a certain path. When I led a team designing digital passports that would allow us to travel without friction or the need to queue at a passport desk to enter a country, the experience was so opaque that research showed us people were profoundly uncomfortable when they first experienced the journey.

We might assume that a magical, interaction-free journey is our objective, but we also know that things go wrong – we might go down the wrong lane, or find ourselves trapped in a technological nightmare we can't get out of. We need design to provide that transparency, affordance of the technological ecosystem we are in and control, to have agency to opt in and out.

There are many amazing benefits to be harvested from our increasingly invisible technology ecosystem that we plug into it at every moment, but it needs care and design, consciously and to our benefit, just like every other decision we make. And in a world where all the decisions are made by the people with the technical knowledge of the system, we need to ensure they are aware that a collaboration with designers is critical.

The march of technology has been much bumpier than people realise. On one hand, we are frightened by Amara's Law that states we are always over optimistic of the capability of technology when it is new and underestimate the (negative) impact of technology over time.

And so, we come to AI.

Data and AI

Data drives most design decisions and both CEOs and designers will use data to inform, shape and validate their decisions. You don't need to be a data analyst, though collaborating with data experts is always valuable. Driving what is measured and identifying the data that will make a difference is just as much the job of a designer as a data analyst.

Data has gone to a new level with generative AI. AI has been around much longer than people realise, but with the rise of easily-accessed large language model regenerative AI platforms such as ChatGPT that use natural language and access enormous amounts of data, the realisation of the power and the increased relevance of AI to our lives has accelerated at pace.

Ai is exciting, dangerous, oversold and as misunderstood as every new technology. It offers great enhancements to medical science, organisation efficiency, removing the drudgery of repetitive jobs. But possibly at the cost of our jobs, our identities and control over outcomes that could massively affect our lives.

AI gives as good as it gets and as we become more practised at using AI in our everyday lives, it's become obvious that it has limitations. For one, it needs a lot of explanation before it finds helpful stuff. The interface is clunky and not attractive, and you have to kiss a lot of frogs to find the prince of a good answer. Like all technology, its good at repetitive processes but not at context and the normal complexity of life. So, if we stay in control and understand its impact before damage is done, we'll be ok.

There are very real advantages of using AI for designers, and RCA graduate Aeron Sun has developed an analysis of how various AI tools strengthen the diversity of research, stimulate and aid creativity (but not replace it), and ensure compliance and good governance across the process. We shall look at this in more detail in the final chapter.

Designers are embracing AI to stimulate their creativity, create instant storyboards of scenarios they are designing, explore greater diversity, ensure compliance and check against regulations. But they are not concerned that they will lose the jobs – the opposite. Visual communication graphic designer Adrian Shaughnessy describes how the outputs of AI are impressive, but flat. He adds humanity, complexity, contradiction, emotion and empathy, that AI is not able to manifest. Will it ever do that? Maybe better than now but I will put a stake that it will not be able to replace those elements of our human behaviour.

In the visual world, AI has already a very recognisable and unique style that shouts, "AI did this". Cultural bias is very easy to see in storyboards that use particularly North American references for architecture and mannerisms. Useful, yes, and designers will find ways of using it that are superior to the creation of polite but stern emails or conversational bot interfaces. But as a friend, not a threat.

Humanising Technology

Technology is made by humans and is in the service of humans. It needs to have a purpose, a problem to solve, a reason to exist, for it to be of value to us humans. It needs us to trust it, be able to use it, be accessible to all and do no damage in the process.

Design, often understood as shaping the physical world and combing material and processes to make things we use, is just as relevant in this technological world. The craft and skill of a user experience (UX) designer is now a critical part of any software development team, or should be. It is a lesson that has been learnt the hard way, but it is fundamentally understood that our digital experiences must be designed to be simple to use, understandable to all ages and abilities. It is understood that there is a beauty in usable and inclusive user interfaces, they can bring joy through simplicity, from efficiency of process, and deliver information or services of real value.

The benign impact of technology can be underestimated. When banks first developed financial applications that allowed customers to see their accounts and move money between them, it was not expected to become the primary method for interacting with your bank. It was not requested by banking executives who showed no vision of a digital future beyond their back-end processes that run their investments and banking operations. In an age where people worry about the closing of physical branches, and there are many who depend on that physical interaction, the mobile banking app has revolutionised our agency and ability to manage not just our accounts but our lives. Can we get through the to the end of the month, the end of the week? How can I send money to a distant relative or my children in another country? How can I sort out the financial affairs of a loved one who has died?

Technology and the digital revolution have equally positively transformed as many aspects of life as it has blighted. In every case, the processes have been designed. Some well, with care, empathy, consideration of all people who will want to access the delights of digital services, in collaboration with the skill and expertise required to code and deliver these amazingly complex yet necessarily simple to use interactions.

But in too many cases, the human is not put first. We do not start with the needs we are trying to satisfy or the problems we are trying to solve. We are happy to develop what we can and launch it in the hope that some will find it useful.

Alex Barclay is a designer in the healthcare industry and describes how, post Covid, we have witnessed an acceleration of digitization that has had a very positive impact on healthcare service delivery, care providers, pharma, technical innovations, that have realised the dream to "serve more people more of the time, where they are, how they are, when they are in the way that they need". But once again, "the best technology in the world is only the best technology in the world if people can use it".

Technology has been a force for transformation in our lives, but it is not the solution to all our problems. It is an enabler, to a problem we need to identify, that we should take responsibility to design to solve real problems or open up new opportunities. Technology should be designed to support all people in all contexts, be transparent and retain their agency, and do things that are useful, on their terms, that don't drain our valuable resources and damage society, as happens too often.

How Do We Redesign Thinking for Technology?

There are a number of situations where technology influences and leads our decision making and you need to work out if that's right or not.

New technology comes along all the time and it's always an exciting vision that is painted. This will solve our security issue, create a fantastic new customer experience, solve all our service delivery problems and cost us less and make us look cool.

There are many emotions around technology: Our competitors will do it first and make us look behind the times, we can drastically cut costs; my tech lead has it as their number one objective for their road map and has a resource of 2,000 developers who must start now.

It can be tough to challenge some of these but we need to redesign thinking, press pause and ask ourselves:

1. *What is the problem the technology is trying to solve?*
As my earlier examples show, we are very good at creating technology that doesn't solve a problem. It is fundamental that you understand what the problem you are solving is, how big a problem is it and whether the investment in technology will justify and solve the problem.

From autonomous vehicles to an AI toothbrush, things have seemed a good idea, but are they really? The innovative company Arrival looked to be leading the way with their driverless logistic delivery vehicles, but after a lot of investment they have had to leave the arena. They loved the idea but how were they solving the problem and what was the problem? Autonomous taxis crashing in San Francisco – what is the benefit of this incredible technology again?

If you are a CEO or a senior leader, you need to know in your heart and say out loud what problem is being solved.

2. *You know the problem but is technology the right solution to the problem?*
A subset of our intuitive need to solutionise as soon as we hear of or see a problem is the belief that technology is the one way you can solve the problem. How many times do we hear the answer to a problem is a website, or a mobile app. Is it? What is the nature of the problem that a website is meant to solve? Is the "brief" more information, better signposting and navigation, a need to calculate or access support? A website or an app may be part of the solution, but there may be other and better ways to solve the problem.

3. *Technology can solve the problem, but it's not designed for the context of the person who has the problem.*
This is where design is tangibly important and can remove barriers and make sure your investment in technology works.

We must have all heard that the solution to our businesses problems is a new HR technology platform or a new customer management platform. But we also know that this often turns out not to work as we wished it to, or be usable by the people who need it.

4. *Choose wisely: What is the criteria for choosing a technology platform? Their brochure or your needs?*
If you are talking to a technology company, present them with the problems you want solving, and show them the people who have the problem. On no account ever let your IT department choose the vendor unless they have conducted interviews and research with the people who will be using it before they choose. IT departments are knowledgeable about the tech, how it works, all the features it has and how brilliant it will be. They probably know nothing, or are making assumptions about user-centred design and identifying the human context and criteria that must be satisfied if the IT project is going to work for the people of the company or customers.

Get a user researcher in your IT team. Make sure they have gathered the insights and been listened to and fed into the requirements for the IT provider. Make sure the choices are not just made on cost and speed of installation – it will cost you twice as much to unravel the chaos, loss of goodwill with staff and customers and sheer technical redeployment of a system that just causes more problems than it solves (see all big IT projects). Remember, if a system needs people to be trained, it's not well enough designed. Did you take training for your iPhone or PC? Then you shouldn't for your HR or any other system that is about to ruin their lives.

Incentivise your IT team to deliver happiness, not anger.

An Anecdote on Designing for Technology

My first employer was Bill Moggridge, a product designer who founded his own design company in London and went on to be a co-founder of the California-based global innovation company IDEO. Bill moved to San Francisco in the late 1970s, just at the start of the Silicon Valley phenomena and whilst there, invented the first laptop. A fellow Brit whom he was visiting on holiday in California showed him how he had combined new technologies that could manufacture keyboards and screens that were much slimmer than those used in conventional computing equipment that allowed him to create a thin and lightweight portable computer. The keyboard was positioned below the screen to create a product called the "workslate". When Bill began to work on the industrial design to make it a commercial product, he suggested that they add a hinge between the screen and the keyboard to make it easy to transport and store in a briefcase. The company launched as GRiD, and the Compass computer became an iconic product that led the way to the ubiquitous laptop: portable computers we can use anywhere. The elegantly simple rectangular design used innovative new processes for the outer case to be cast in titanium, a material which conducted the heat created by the microchips more efficiently. It was quickly added to the collection the Museum of Modern Art in New York, and it was used on the Earth-orbiting space station SkyLab.

Unfortunately for everyone, the GRiD Compass was not a commercial success. This was not just because it was expensive, or before its time, but because, as Bill quickly realised, they had not spent as much attention as they had on the outer case design on the screen design and operating system. The software was primitive and difficult to use, there was no Microsoft operating system available and the mouse had not been invented yet, so inputs where entered by software code or cursor buttons, making it clunky to use.

As a result of his epiphany, Bill changed his focus to designing software that was clear, easy to use and beautiful. For many, Bill is the inventor of "interaction design", what was then the new idea that we could design the interface between humans and machine.

Bill was designing in an age where most computers used black screens with a green font, with no graphical images, and commands requiring complex code instructions. But at this time Silicon Valley engineers and designers in research labs such at the Xerox Palo Alto Research Center were developing new ways to operate computers and created a moveable cursor device that became called a mouse (due to its being a mouse-shaped, hand-moved, device with a cable that came out of the back). Screens used familiar concepts such as paper, files and waste baskets with easier to read fonts and graphic icons and symbols. He was therefore able to design the interface of the software that could carry out useful tasks and develop the concept of usability, ensuring that previously complex instructions to use a computer could become easy, accessible to all and not require specialist skills or training. This of course was a desire shared by the young entrepreneur Steve Jobs, who, when he saw the inventions of the Xerox lab, created a completely new type of computer, the Apple Macintosh, that democratised and empowered anyone to gain access to the power of computing.

I'm telling you about Bill because he was my first boss and someone who, through their passion for design, changed the world.[4]

How Do We Design for Technology?

Design is good at technology. The design of many of our digital touchpoints is now amazing and people respond positively to well-designed websites and mobile apps.

A recent podcast asked what government had done that was positive, to which the contributor answered "getting a passport, taxing a car and many other tasks that you can now do online. They seem to have got the tech right there".[5]

They didn't get the tech right; they got the design right. Where, in the UK, Canada and the US, large IT projects have become national-level scandals and have wasted incredible amounts of money, time and human wellbeing, projects such as those created by the Government Digital Services in the UK have shown how to do it.

A single, clear, usable (visually simple to use and using easily understandable language), accessible and inclusive (for all people) consistent approach (a single look and feel), transformed the experience of accessing public services. Using a single URL for UK government websites under the title of **gov.uk** has been incredibly successful.

Like everything, we only notice it when it goes wrong or works badly, so not all have noticed the success of gov.uk. But the impact of a clear user experience design, continued across the whole process of the task a citizen wishes to undertake, has been showcased and copied all over the world.

The essence of the service design process runs through UX design. Challenging the brief by asking what the problem is, and what is the desired outcome that the user is looking to achieve. Reframing the brief, aligning everyone involved on a project and using insights from the people who will be using the service. Finding creative solutions and visualising and prototyping these to check they work before removing any barriers or faults you find when people use your prototype. A prototype that is a fraction of the cost of a platform that may have been already built before it is discovered that it doesn't work. Digital experiences that are de-

---

4 See the seminal publication, Bill Moggridge, *Designing Interactions*, The MIT Press, 1998.
5 Page 94: The Private Eye Podcast 29 May 2024.

signed to work beautifully simply and be simply beautiful. That is what designers do, with love for the people who will use the service in their hearts and the need to provide real value and create the right impact, be it business or public service, in their heads.

The digital world is mature enough now to realise that without design, you get failure, and that failure is expensive. So many great ideas down the drain because of poor design, no matter how promising the technology. We know now how to remove confusion, build trust and ensure that a teenager and a centenarian can use a banking app to spend or save their money.

But there are many more issues and challenges when we move beyond the glass of the mobile phone in order to understand the broader systems and how they work. Understanding the whole journey, beyond the digital touchpoint of a mobile phone, is an especially important task when ensuring the world will work as you intend. Downloading, registering, setting up a password, sharing your account details, transacting, first use, features, settings, completing the journey, leaving your customer satisfaction score, complaining, renewing – the real activities around using a web- or app-based service reach way beyond the screen and can cause immense frustration and confusion if they don't work.

Designing the whole experience is vital for successful technology. This can be complicated when your organisation is divided into different elements. Does your contact centre know what your marketing manager has promised?

The tools of service design work well for digital and technology delivery. Whether you are using the Stanford D-School framework or the Design Council Double Diamond, two closely-related formulas for successful design processes, the principle of understanding the problem you are trying to solve or the goal you are trying to achieve, remains vital in creating successful outcomes.

Always Start With Research

At the heart of research is the challenging of assumptions and when we are designing for technology experiences, there are often a lot of assumptions at the start of the project that need challenging.

The first of these is that you need an app, website or the technology itself. To start with a decision that an app is needed is often questionable but very difficult to challenge. Of more use is to uncover the need the app is addressing.

An app is a solution, but what is it solving? Learn to reframe the brief as the essence of the purpose of the app. An example might be:
- Find out how to do something (e.g., get a passport)
- Provide detailed information (what to do when you get to the airport)
- Provide a current status (Is your flight on time?)
- Choose from a list of options (when you book your ticket)

It's always a verb before it's a thing. Remember what it is you are trying to help a human being you don't know, do.

Research and data tell you in more detail who is the user of your app and allow you to connect and feel empathetic to their context. Empathy is at the heart of design and standing in your user's shoes will help you comprehend and have foresight of where barriers to usage might be and how to support and give comfort throughout the process.

User experience (UX) tends to start with the first screen, but a good UX designer will start before that. What is the reason for the app, the job to be done? Beyond that, how do people know your app exists and will be useful? Despite the huge numbers of apps and smartphones, and the domination of a few apps such as WeChat, TikTok and YouTube, 25% of all apps are only used once after downloading.

Using service design tools such as customer journey maps are useful when designing for digital as they force you to consider the triggers that require a solution such as an app, how users find the app and understand its use, and then whether it does what people need it do.

This sounds obvious but design makes sure you build something that is useful and often removes features and complexity that you can add in but that don't add any value. Research, and prototyping, are powerful tools to explore how much you need to make to deliver a successful minimum viable experience (not the same as minimum viable product) that people want, can use and use more than once!

In the chapter on prototyping, we will explore the purpose and nature of prototyping at different points of the process. When designing digital experiences, the flexibility and speed of design iteration is rapid which should make it easy to modify and change a design before it is solidified and built. This is much more difficult in the physical design world where change that requires modification to a manufactured item, or an expensive one-off prototype makes direct user testing less attractive.

In essence you can use research to test the idea first. Is this useful? If people see an advert for your app or tech solution, will they understand its value and consider subscribing or downloading it? If you can't answer these questions, or people don't want it, start again and have a better idea.

As a UX designer, if you find people don't want the app you've been told to design, it can be awkward. How do you tell a decision-maker manager their request is poorly thought-through, and you have evidence it's not going to work?

This is the essence of design. Designers use their abilities to visualise the possible to find out if it's desirable. This is a fantastic tool that should be taught in all business schools of the world. The problem is, it might show that your original idea was wrong, and we are not good at accepting that. We believe it is right to fight for our ideas and support them without giving in to challenges.

The designer has a difficult role in finding and creating what people want and can use as well as diplomatically facilitating an honest and open conversation that might, occasionally, mean that an idea is abandoned. And if no one wants it, surely that's a good thing and you can go on to make something people can and will use.

Writers such as Mike Monterio[6] discuss the role of designers where there is an ethical dimension to what you are asked to do. The dilemma of working within an organisation where outputs may lead to bias or unethical outcomes is a common one but is not to be avoided. The very purpose of design is to bridge the technical and economic possibilities with human need and desirability. You can argue that it has always been during the design stage that we need to consider the safety, accessibility and purpose of an object or digital experience and as we better understand the consequences of what we collectively design, ethics, environmental impact and harm to those beyond the user, are entirely relevant and our job to comprehend and bring to the table.

So right at the start we need to be prepared to say no. Or, if we say yes, use the tools of design to gain that deep insight and empathy for the humans we are designing for to make sure it works well for them. That is, surely, good business.

Testing Ideas

Before a wireframe is created, a use case defined or a line of code produced, we need to validate our idea. We need to do this in the context of the user and the problem or need they have.

To do this we need to create enough information for someone innocent of our intentions to engage and react in an honest way that we can learn from. Some ways to do this include the following.

Storyboarding

A story board is the depiction of what might happen if this digital solution is made, how it is found used and what value does it have.

A story can be words, but as you're a designer, bringing it to life with drawings or photographs brings a depth and sense that your idea is real to gain better feedback and insight. Bringing the real context and sense of where and when your solution is used will help you spot details and potential barriers as well as be sur-

---

6 Mike Monteiro, *Ruined by Design: How Designers Destroyed the World, and What We Can Do to Fix It*, 2019, self published.

prised by the good decisions you're making. Stories give the context and sense of time – when will you use this solution, how often and what will you be doing at the same time? It makes a difference how you design an app if you are in a car or a shop or at home or in a hospital.

Make the Advert

The hypotheses, or proposition of your solution will eventually be distilled down to a panel in an app store or an advert on a transport system. So what does it do? How do you describe it? Make the advert first and find out what people imagine it will do, why it will be useful and whether it is likely to work for them.

Next, Features

We still haven't done any wireframes, though that may be useful now. Once we have confidence that people want our tech solution, we can find out what they need it to do and in what way.

Features are all those bells and whistles that are easy to imagine during tech development but not easy to understand if they have value. Given that a lower feature level will be easier and faster to get to market. There are good reasons why testing which features are vital to satisfy customer expectations and even delight them with features that go beyond their wish list. However, we also need to be careful about adding unnecessary complexity and complications that aren't required or ever used.

You're probably familiar with this – it's the reason you have all those unused buttons on your TV remote control. Someone has a very good reason to put that button on, but the occasion to need it is often very rare to the point of redundancy.

In the early days of "multichannel" experiences, where online services began to be offered on mobile, there was often a culture of "cut and paste" all the functionality of the internet on to the mobile platform. But the mobile is a small screen, being used on the move, and simply doesn't need access to the full functionality of the web.

Banking apps are great examples of how the essential features are offered with the experience upgrading on the web for those more detailed jobs that require greater access to historic data, forms, or information. That seems to work for most people and keeps the mobile experience appropriate and not cluttered with unneeded features.

When designing responsively, for example (configuring the site content to be legible for different device screens), using the html screen presentation software to reorganise a screen when it is presented vertically on a mobile rather than horizontally on a PC, the designer gets a better idea of how to prioritise and organise features. Where a PC screen is broad and you can put stuff anywhere, you get a poor mobile experience so "mobile first" design is not just a desire to design for the mobile but leads to clearer hierarchy of features and navigation that makes the experience better on all devices.

Once again, design is not just an answer to a comprehensive set of requirements put together by a business analyst and hauled over the fence to the design team. It's a journey that starts with explorations that may challenge the premise of what you set out to do. Painful though that might seem, it's nothing like as painful as making the wrong thing for people who don't need it. Which sadly is still happening most of the time.

Design the Technology

Design is at the heart of how we create the user experience of the technology we use. It is impossible to launch an application or a website without embracing the skills and processes of design. UX design has become critical part of any development team and teams of designers work across the development process alongside developers who can take wireframes and detailed user interface templates and modules to construct workable, usable, and accessible digital interfaces that allow us to achieve our goals through the glass of a mobile device or personal computer. Our banking apps, search, health, exercise, mental health, travel booking and shopping sites all require UX design to ensure we can use them for whatever purpose they serve. Within each app will be specific use cases: open an account, book a room, a flight, check my steps or my financial health. UX designers map out how functions will work in diagrammatic representations of screens or wireframes and use these to test with potential users whether they understand the meaning and flow of navigation through various choices to ensure they get what they are hoping to achieve. These wireframes are then designed as graphic entities and components to provide the detailed buttons, actions, terminology and information data.

The process of UX design shares the methods and approaches of service design. Starting at discovery, UX designers embrace and question the goal of any application and the use cases that will allow users to achieve their goals. By analysing their goals, they can arrange screens to achieve their goals as simply as possible. Wireframes are essentially early prototypes that bring to life how the application or website will work. The whole experience can be created and tested with humans, before any coding is done – and this allows for the design to be improved through iteration to integrate learning from user testing to remove barriers or improve the ease of use.

At the heart of UX design is usability. Familiarity of graphical elements, or buttons that are large enough to see and activate, the size of text and the use of colour to mitigate for legibility and colour blindness (25% of men are colour blind and confused by colours that include red and green). The process of testing allows us to confirm or improve how easy something is to use. Why is this important? Because if things are overcomplicated, or unfamiliar, they won't be used. That is bad for business, government and everyone involved.

Designing for Real People

At London's Imperial College, the Department of Computing are training the next generation of digital designers and developers. Their digital coding skills are high and their inventive mindset impressive but in teaching the rigours and rituals of Agile development, student feedback led them to take a different approach to the core tenant of Agile methodology which is that "our highest priority is to satisfy the customer through early and continuous delivery of valuable software". With the emphasis on the rituals and processes of Agile, the course heads Robert Chatley and Mark Wheelhouse decided to take the emphasis away from "completing the process" to turning back to the original spirit of agility and responsiveness to problem solving.

Working with Nick de Leon, Carolyn Runcie, myself and the team at the RCA service design course, we developed a course called Design for Real People. A paper written by the Imperial team described the objective of the course to combine service design techniques "with agile development and delivery of web applications to enable students to create digital software that addresses challenges faced by real people in a particular context".[7]

Through techniques from design such as developing personas of users and using journey maps to understand their needs, computing techniques such as "vertical slicing" where slim parts of the solution are developed in detail, rather than dividing the activities into technical layers. In their example, it's better to understand the overall shape of the application rather than spending time of sorting a database that may not be needed, and is therefore a waste of time.

Their learnings have been that it's not good enough to do things "by the book". It's vital to take a user-centred view, listen to insights and iterate your design in response to user feedback. A simple and essential truth that is vitally important in the education of those who will engineer our future interactions with technology.

---

7 R. Chatley, T. Field, M. Wheelhouse, C. Runcie, C. Grinyer and N. de Leon, "Designing for Real People: Teaching Agility through User-Centric Service Design," 2023 IEEE/ACM 45th International Conference on Software Engineering: Software Engineering Education and Training (ICSE-SEET), Melbourne, Australia, 2023, pp. 11–22, doi: 10.1109/ICSE-SEET58685.2023.00007

Chapter 4
How to Make a Poor Decision

> *Any man can make mistakes, but only an idiot persists in his error.*
> Cicero

Our concept of leadership tends to emphasise the importance of single decision makers. A good leader is one who is decisive, who weighs a situation and makes a call. A CEO who has an idea and runs with it, pushing away the barriers and naysayers until they touchdown and look up for the acclaim.

Their intuition tells them they are right, their conversations with friends and associates form their worldview, their shared, common sense. They hear the advice of one or two trusted advisors or critical friends and feel they know they are right.

It must have seemed a great idea to automate bank branches. By putting in self-serve ATM (teller) machines, your visit to the branch becomes more efficient, allows people to serve themselves, avoid the queues and provide faster service. In the UK and many other countries, banks invested heavily in machines that would read cheques, dispense or deposit cash, transfer money and all the things people go to bank branches for if they don't want to do it on their mobile or online. Once the shiny robot machines were turned on, the branches would be able to dispense with staff as they wouldn't need so many.

Sadly, things didn't turn out as predicted. Difficult-to-use machines that were frequently out of order meant people needed to speak to the attendant. That was probably why they'd gone to the branch in the first place, as that is the great advantage of a local branch: that you can speak to someone about something you don't understand or perhaps just need help with or, as many customers have told researchers who asked them, they believe that real humans deliver a higher level of service that they expect and feel they deserve.

Unfortunately, the strong belief of many financial service CEOs that technology would solve problems, reduce costs, and staff numbers and still maintain a good level of service, did not work out. It led to long queues of people along unused and often out-of-order machines. It led to complaints and bad feelings. Even the staff agreed with them and complained about the extra work for the fewer staff.

Doing the Right Thing

Believe Housing is a fantastic social housing organisation, which builds and maintains rental properties for over 30,000 people. They care about their residents, want them to be happy and feel well served and have a strong conscious and ethos to do the right thing.

That's why they decided to replace the gas boilers of all their properties with electric heat pumps to ensure that they were able to reduce their carbon footprint in line with the historic Paris agreement to attempt to limit the global impact of climate change to an increase of within 1.5 degrees Celsius.

This was a massive investment and a major inconvenience for the residents. Their houses and apartments had to have their traditional gas boilers removed and replaced with new heat pumps that act as reverse refrigerators, taking the cooler outside air and converting it into heat. It took time, considerable inconvenience and a change in behaviour as the residents got used to the different way of heating their homes.

The classic gas boiler, used in 90% of houses in the UK and across many other areas of Europe, provides hot water that is passed in pipes around the rooms of a house to heat radiators mounted on walls. In other countries, especially Scandinavia pipes provide underfloor heating. In the UK, central heating, as it is called, provides controllable warmth through a thermostat that can be turned up or down to vary the temperature in a room. For the residents of Believe Housing, the opportunity to say, "I'll just turn the heating up before Doris next door pops in" is an example of the control residents have become used to having over their environment to create a cosy warm environment in their home.

Heat pumps behave differently.

Heat pumps use electricity to generate what is sometimes called background heat. The use of electricity is the reason heat pumps are being rapidly adopted across even the coldest parts of Europe. Electricity is much cleaner than gas with a fraction of the carbon footprint of piped natural gas, which emits carbon when burnt by the boiler and is much less efficient. Heat pumps are mounted outside a building and look like oversized air conditioning units, of which they are the reverse. They can create heat from outside air temperatures as low as −16 degrees Celcius. However, they typically deliver an ambient temperature inside of around 16 degrees Celcius, with additional electric heating units used to increase warmth in specific areas of your home.

So as well requiring extensive refit work, they are very different in use and require a different approach to heating, without the ability to run it up in with the speed and convenience of a gas boiler.

When the landlords fitted the new heating systems to their properties, there was a period of adjustment. But there was another impact they hadn't foreseen that turned out to have a major impact on residents and the success of the initiative.

Electricity at the time of the changeover, although more efficient, was considerably more expensive than gas. That meant that in heating their homes to a lower temperature than they were used to, and having to get secondary heaters to make it cosy, their monthly heating bills went up by two and a half times. These are social homes for residents who are less able to afford their own homes.

It was quickly apparent that the residents were having to make some difficult choices between their energy bills and food. People began to eat less in order to pay their heating or turn down their heating and endure discomfort during cold weather in order to eat. This was a serious problem, and it was rapidly realised that they had no alternative than to remove the heat pumps they had fitted and replace them with gas boilers.

Not an easy decision. A great and worthy idea with the best of intentions that didn't anticipate the consequences and impact in advance and so led to a heavy cost financially and damaged the trust and relationships they had with their residents.

When the Disruptive Innovators Network of housing associations in the UK asked its members to bid for support from service design students at the Royal College of Art, Believe Housing applied and was chosen. The work the students and Believe team did over a period of months and now years shows how different routes can be taken for different types of people within the resident communities, The team's onsite research uncovered the difficult decisions residents were having to take to respond to the increase in their electricity bills and the hardships they were enduring. It was powerful evidence for the management teams. They also uncovered the different attitudes across the residents and created four different archetypes that represented the data patterns and insights from interviews of their respective attitudes to change and energy consumption.

It was a masterpiece of collaborative service design using the tools of qualitative and quantitative research, interviews with residents, spotting the patterns and using archetypes to build empathy and understanding so that the management team could best navigate change towards cleaner energy. Their process concluded with a series of pilot schemes tailored to each of the different types of residents. Metrics were set up to measure progress and eventual success across initiatives that are in practice today with positive results and outcomes.

This is what good looks like. The impressive and decisive leadership of the housing company, despite their laudable and best intentions, created a problem they had not foreseen that cost them and their residents.

It happens all the time and every day. Strong leadership, unaware of the assumptions they are basing their decisions on, creating traumatic outcomes that cost considerable amounts to correct. The wonderful thing was that Believe reset and responded and ensured that others heard about their story and how to avoid these unfortunate outcomes. If only there were more like Believe.

Good Design, Bad Decision

A personal case study. When I joined Barclays, I was given an exciting role to lead a team of brilliant designers, product managers, subject matter experts and behavioural economists to create a new investment platform that would provide a safe and accessible platform for people to save and invest their money.

Building resilient financial savings is the goal of good financial management: for those unforeseen and unavoidable costs that suddenly appear, a rainy-day fund for a future holiday, a stable retirement and looking after children and grandchildren.

Historic changes in the financial conduct law, intended to protect people from hidden costs when using financial advisors, had led to an unforeseen consequence. The practice of financial advisors having their fees included in the cost of a savings or pension product, rather than paid directly in a way that would be clearer to customers, was made illegal. This meant that the true cost of financial advice was now very clear, but also beyond the means of most people when paid as a single sum. As a result, they stopped receiving financial advice.

Another case of well-intentioned transformation resulting in unforeseen consequences that had detrimental impact on enormous customers. Sensing a pattern here?

The good news was that new self-serve investment and saving services were developed allowing people to buy and sell shares, save and invest in various funds and financial products via the internet. These quickly became hugely popular.

Of course, investing and even saving is not straightforward for everyone. The creation of easy-to-use investment products that encouraged people to save in a tax efficient way opened up investing to a large swathe of the population which had previously entrusted this to a financial advisor, stockbroker or perhaps a friendly neighbour who dabbled in investing.

Barclays had a successful service that bought and sold investments and stocks and shares via a telephone service, with virtually no digital presence. Meanwhile, competitors had successfully launched online platforms where people could choose investment funds and trade stocks and shares, with the appropriate risk warnings, as they wished. Barclays wanted to cut the cost to serve and compete with the online investment platforms that had been signed up to by many of their own customers.

Creating the resulting platform was the story of a successful and happy project that combined subject matter experts (SMEs) in investments with developers, marketing teams, behaviour economic experts (who understand the nudges and the way to design safe investment behaviour within a complex regulated industry), and of course a brilliant design team (including copy writers) who could create usable and accessible web and mobile screens that customers could use with confidence and without risk.

A visionary and innovative platform was designed, with the emphasis on user testing at each stage throughout the "agile" development schedule. Terrific user feedback drove excitement and expectation. Working with a brilliant technology partner, the coding and development began.

Two years later, a "minimum viable product" (MVP) was launched. With the functionality that could be built in time, but with none of the features we knew consumers wanted, the project was a massive failure. It was a salutary lesson in building an MVP that no one wants just to get it to market. I've seen it happen so often, even launching products that don't work, just to say they have been launched. If you are a decision maker, consider the insanity of these stories and redesign your thinking.

We've looked at many examples of technology push and assumptions that people will embrace a new idea without ensuring the barriers to usage are sufficiently ironed out or simplicity designed in. In too many cases, we continue to prize rapid delivery without ensuring things work, put faith in technology without ensuring it is appropriate and relevant and not loaded with superfluous functions and features.

Why do we make so many poor decisions, why do so many start-ups fail, innovative ideas fail to become adopted, hunches prove to be wrong and business investment get wasted? In the US 10% of start-ups fail in the first year and over time, 90% fail.[1] The main reason? They make a product nobody wants.

Nobody means to make a product nobody wants. Nobody means to make a decision that is wrong. Yet the traditional model of decision making only rarely leads to success and most likely, to failure.

We saw in the last chapter how technology push fails. Despite the brilliance of technology and engineering, if you don't know the problem you are solving, then you will have an expensive failure on your CV.

How do we find out what people want? Why don't we ask them in focus groups and they will tell us? We've already looked at how that can give false answers if you don't accurately represent the context of the decision making when you ask the question.

---

1 Kyril Kotashe, "Startup Failure Rate: How Many Startups Fail and Why in 2024?", *Failory.com*, 9 January 2024.

Data Will Tell Us What We Need to Know!

The universe of data we now swim in is increasingly providing the answers and predicting what we want before we know it ourselves. Data allows organisation to recognise our behaviour and serve highly personalised services, information and experiences.

You would think. Every few months my mobile phone provider sends me a discount offer to go and see the musical *Frozen*. At this point I relax and realise that the invasion of data and AI to understand and predict what I like is still a very long way off. I will never go and see *Frozen* and if the customer management system of my mobile provider thinks I will, I have nothing to fear.

A head of data for a large international bank told me that he knew when people would start looking for a mortgage a year before they did. Impressive stuff! Data is such a powerful tool and when collected, analysed, understood, and categorised in the right way, can be a tremendously powerful tool to help us make decisions about what people do, and will in the future, value and desire.

The collection of data as large fields of captured historic activity is known as quantitative data. The volume of data collected in every second of our lives has given us a powerful new force for decision making. We trust data, it can't be wrong and is therefore a powerful tool on which we can make decisions confident that they will be correct as data never lies.

Trust

Data can be a contestable asset. At some organisations I have been in, there are many sources of data and it's not uncommon for the different data sets to disagree with each other. There are good reasons for this, and data experts will talk about cleansing data, ensuring it is up to date, categorised correctly and without bias.

With so many ways of capturing data through the devices we walk around with, the websites we visit, the geographical locations we travel through and the choices we make when we buy or consume anything, it is possible to capture a vast amount of information that can be used to predict and help us in our lives. Linking our data to our identity, via our mobile phones or PCs, allows us to receive highly personalised information, choices and advice.

For the most part, we are happy to receive information that is tailored to our needs, through sometimes this may be scary or, as in the case my mobile operator, ludicrously wrong and inaccurate.

On other occasions we might be surprised, or not even be aware of how data is curating our view of the world. What different information organisations know about us may well limit our choices and be making decisions about every aspect of our lives from our ability to get a loan, what choices of property we see when booking a holiday location or what healthcare treatment we might receive.

The Price, and Value, of Data

The ability to capture data and communicate that data over connected networks has fired the imagination with many possibilities for new experiences and new services. As data is not just collected by our own phones, PCs and smartwatches, but by the things we pass by, and objects that communicate between themselves, the phrase Internet of Things, or IoT, described by some overexcited tech companies as the Internet of Everything, the position of the human, and the planet within these scenarios, has been questioned. What are our rights, and what is the impact on the planet on storing the enormous amounts of data captured every second?

The impact of digital photography is just one example. The average smartphone owner in China or the US takes 20 photos a day resulting in a total of 5.3 billion each day and a total of 14.3 trillion images in the world. This creates the need for trillions of gigabytes of data storage, immediately accessible on demand, hosted in vast data farms that require millions of gallons of water per minute to cool, even when they are situated close to the Arctic.

I used to think my days of damaging the earth as a designer of products was over since I became a service designer working with digital platforms, but it turns out I had just hidden the impact of physical waste under the carpet of digital waste and the enormous energy requirements required to keep it hidden.

From a human perspective, we gain hugely from the ability to be geolocated, so we can plan a route and know the weather at our destination, by having an immediate view of every purchase we make, and (arguably) of not carrying cash and buying a snack bar from a vending machine that can sense when it needs to be restocked. Our streets might be perceived as safer by the use of cameras recording every second of every day, in the corner shop we visit that recognises the criminal who attempts to rob an item from the shop.

Our data is shared, of course. It's the business model of giant global companies such as Google. There's a reason you get Gmail for free, if you hadn't realised. For the most part, we are all happy with that. When Spotify tells what our annual top 20 tracks we have listening to over the year, they are just lending you back the data they use with the music publishing industry. It's a mutually beneficial thing.

Giving back data is one of the great quiet revolutions of the last few decades. Using data that is collected for the benefit for a company can be hugely beneficial to the customer too.

As a design student at Central St. Martins, I entered one of the RSA (Royal Society of Arts) Student Design Awards. (These were started back in 1923 by the way, they have been giving prizes to design students for that long!). The brief was to explore products for the street and create an electronic bus timetable.

As part of my research, I visited London Transport, the authority that oversaw the running of public transport in London, including the Tube and bus journeys. It was an amazing experience to see how they ran such a complex system and a revelation to find out that they knew exactly where their buses were and could predict when they would arrive at each bus stop. This was incredibly useful information to them and allowed them to regulate the frequency of buses and take account of changing traffic conditions and possible delays. I innocently asked if the passengers could access that data, but this was before smartphones and mobile networks that could transmit that data. You need a perfect storm of relevant data, a network and a way of visualising the data for things to get interesting.

What London Transport, now called Transport for London, or TfL, did do several years later, (I'm sure it wasn't, but I like to think it had something to do with our conversation) was install displays in bus stops which were able to display when the next bus would arrive. What a great, user-friendly, useful service that is!

It's interesting how organisations prioritise collecting, analysing and making decisions with data to drive sales or optimise their operational efficiency. And how slow they are to grasp how data can be of benefit to their customer.

A less attractive feature of data is the ability of organisations to lose it or have it stolen or misappropriated. From airlines to banks to governments, it seems all too easy to have the personal information, bank card details and even identities of huge numbers of people, stolen and used for terrorism, money laundering and straightforward crime.

Every time I open my browser, I am told another password is unsafe and I should change it immediately. It doesn't fill our technology experiences with confidence and breeds suspicion and distrust in what and how services that access our information use and take care of that data.

In developing scenarios for connected services, it's easy to imagine exciting and useful benefits and uses for services. Working on a project for digital passports, for example, the benefits of being recognised wherever you went, to walk off an aircraft and out of an airport without passport control, to have every shop you pass recognise you and send you personalised discounts to lure you in. For every hotel to welcome you without the need for a check-in and for every hospital in the world to have access to your health records whenever you have need to visit. What a utopian vision this is!

Or is it?

Many of the possible experiences I have shared here require sensors and networks and blockchain-validated identities fed by instant facial recognition to ensure that is you and only you that receives this marvellous level of attention and personal service. But when does that stop? When can you turn off this intensity of attention? And what happens if you find out that people with darker skin may not benefit from these advantages.

I began to explore these areas working on projects around digital identity. Digital identity, built on the concept of "self-sovereignty" and using blockchain-validated data through agencies such as a passport office, can provide an almost uncrackable level of personal security with the fantastic benefit of not having to share your identity data with any third party such as a business, airline, retail store, etc., who will probably lose it at some point. A business or country customs point receives only the validation that you are who you say you are and nothing more. It's possible to imagine that you'll never have to fill out a form again once your identity is validated in an instant.

RCA graduate Octavia Coutts began to research various scenarios for a digital identity whilst a student. She interviewed a mother who told her of her daughter who was keen on football. Her daughter, who was tall for her age, found that her age was constantly disputed by the opposing team's parents. Her mother resorted to bringing her daughter's birth certificate with her to prove to everyone from bus drivers who refused her a child fare and to parents that she was indeed under 13 and could play for the team. Even then they didn't believe her and accused her of faking the birth certificate.

So, there are lots of reasons why a digital identity that was easily accessible on a mobile phone that recognised your visual appearance, updated in real time as you age, would have a benefit.

In developing the technology for these systems, we could see that we were entering a new world where the human would be merely a traveller through connected, data-fed channels that were invisible and intangible to the traveller. Walking through customs gates, into a new country, how might you know where you were? What would happen if anything went wrong or there was a fault in the system? Unfortunately, we can't take the word of a technologist who tells you there can't be a mistake. As we have seen on many occasions, from flying an aircraft to running a post office, technology can be a dangerous game if trusted without conscious awareness of what might happen when technology fails.

Creating scenarios by mapping the passenger journey through an airport with a digital passport showed us that the human experience might not be so comfortable and magical as the technology vision suggested. It was clear that there were moments when we needed to have agency over the experience and be able to control it if need be.

Developing scenarios for use of data and enabling systems such as blockchain, AI and data-fed decision mechanisms allowed the design team to develop a set of principles to consider when designing any data enabled service. These principles included transparency, feedback, alerts, permissions and clear signposting in the physical and digital space. In applying these principles as we designed the experience of travelling with a digital passport, we realised the importance of recreating familiar and understandable points of recognition along the journey.

Affordance

When Don Norman connected the concept of affordance to graphical user interfaces to ensure we understood that something was a button or a folder, he was building a natural order of recognition. But in the invisible world of AI algorithm-supported experiences, we have no recognition. What is happening? Why, and is it working or stopped working. We don't know.

When we create fundamentally new experiences through the use of technology automation, the transparency, personalisation and seamless experience that can be created seem highly desirable. But when we develop these new invisible interactions, we need to stop and consider the place of the human in the system. These systems are, or should be, in service of us, not the other way round. From algorithms for our children's exam results to sentencing offenders or delivering healthcare, design is as important as it is to a physical product or environment. Too often we forget that we are still designing, just unconsciously, whilst running away with the incredible capabilities of new technologies.

The Value of Data

To use data to make a better decision, we need to understand and manage the three discreet states of data.

We start with gathering of data. In many ways this is the easy bit, but recording and categorising data correctly will ensure data is useful. Deciding what to capture can be critical, especially when there are so many data points available. We are looking for data that will help as have insight into what people are doing and assist in creating a better output for them or you. Deciding what data is captured is not just a job for a data specialist, it needs to be managed by product managers and service designers who know what they need to know.

The next step is to analyse and visualise data to be meaningful and useful in our decision-making process. Spreadsheets are not the best place to understand data, and visualising which patterns, comparisons and conclusions you can draw from data is much easier with data visualisation. From Red Amber Green dashboards to complex emotional and sentiment scores, we need to see the patterns on which we will make decisions.

The value of data is not in the mere holding of it: It's only realised when we act. What does data help us to do better? Targeting a customer with a marketing campaign, or warning them of a greater health risk, or encouraging them to save for their future are actions that can be massively enhanced by accurate and appropriate collecting of data, visualising the patterns and truth hidden in that data and then designing the actions that will achieve value to you and the people you are serving.

Surprising Data

Transport for London (TfL) are the integrated transport authority for London. They are responsible for the day-to-day operation that includes the Tube, or London Underground (London's metro or subway underground train system), buses, the overground train network, all roads, cycling and walking. It's a tremendous responsibility, with the Underground moving up to 5 million people around London every day with an average 24.7 million individual trips per day.

Since the development of touch-card technology, recording the start and end points of journeys, the TfL system has come to generate a huge amount of data. In a typical day there are 19 million smartcard ticketing transactions. Over 97% of the stations also have free Wi-Fi. In 2016 TfL undertook a four-week pilot to gather information, using a combination of the gate-to-gate journeys and tracking each device via the Wi-Fi systems as people travelled. The purpose was to understand not just where but how people travelled across the network and improve the operating performance of the network.[2]

Using depersonalised data, they analysed the different routes used by travellers on a particular journey, from Waterloo to King's Cross. What they found surprised them.

The typographic map of the London Underground is a famous design icon itself. Designed by electrical draughtsman Harry Beck in 1933, it ignores the geographical distances between stations to organise the lines and stations as a diagram that simplifies and eases the navigation around the system. Different lines use different colours, and their stations and intersections are shown in a beautiful and simple system that has become copied by transport systems around the world.

There are many ways to take any journey on the Underground system. The data from the trial is displayed in Figure 4.1 according to Beck's design method to show the percentage of journeys taken on each of the available routes from Waterloo to King's Cross.

Figure 4.1 shows the record of 18 different routes that were taken. The fastest, taken by 26.7% of people, is via the Jubilee (silver) line to Green Park and then

---

[2] 2016 pilot of Wi-Fi data collection – Review of the TfL Wi-Fi pilot – our findings https://tfl.gov.uk/corporate/publications-and-reports/wifi-data-collection

Chapter 4 How to Make a Poor Decision

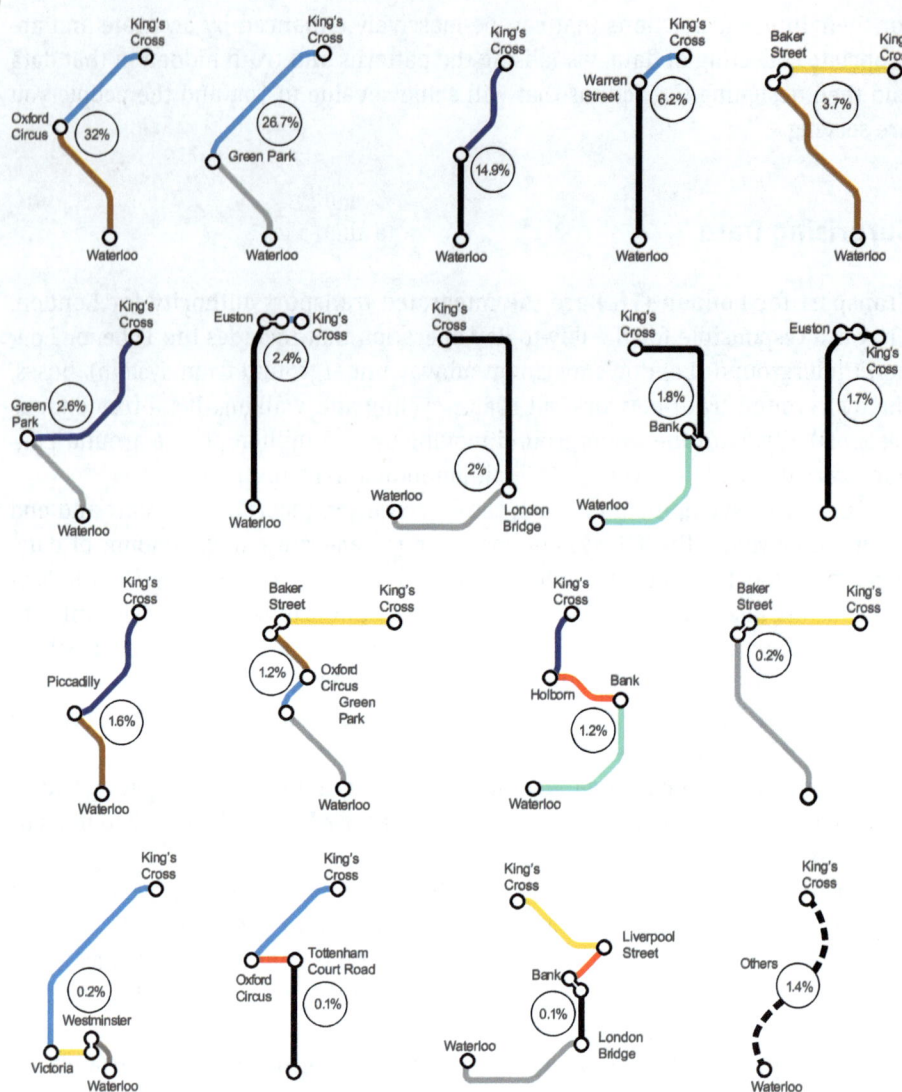

Figure 4.1: Data research of alternative routes taken by passengers from Waterloo Station to Kings Cross.

the Victoria Line (light blue) to King's Cross. But that was not the most popular route. Thirty-two percent took the Bakerloo (brown) line to Oxford Circus before completing the final leg via the Victoria line. Some travellers took incredibly complex routes via up to three intermediate stations. Why? Possibly familiarity with a certain route? Or better access to different platforms: It's impossible to know without asking them.

Hanna Kops is the Head of Experience at Transport for London, and a visiting lecturer at the Royal College of Art. It's thanks to data such as this that she and her team were able to put together the award-winning TfL Go app that beautifully brings the heritage of the Beck map into the digital age and is in the process of being extended across the whole system through signage and digital screens in stations. The data from the trial helps TfL Go guide people to the fastest, most accessible and step-free routes with real-time information and updates with information on walking and cycling too. We will sadly never know why 0.1% of travellers go via London Bridge, then Bank and then Liverpool Street before arriving at King's Cross.

Balancing Data

We can see from the TfL example the surprising insights we can get from data. Unfortunately, data can be meaningless unless we can find a way to make it coherent. We need to cut data in the right way to make sense of it. When we do this well, we get insights and clarity that inform us of the difference between what people say and what they do. This "cold" data is fact, we can believe it and use it in a variety of ways. The value of data as a design tool is in combining data fields in interesting ways that provide insights into behaviour or actions.

For example: We can record the frequency of actions and identify a type of customer, perhaps by age group or location. The entertainment industry, for example, may want to understand what the characteristics of people are who might like one genre of film against another to accurately market new similar films to people who will want to see them.

The health service may use data to understand if there are particular segments of society who are slower to recognise health issues and make appointments with their GP and therefore are at risk of delaying treatment.

A financial service can use data to categorise all the reasons people contact them and prioritise how to assist them more rapidly.

These examples give some idea of how data can count, categorise and be modelled in a way that the information is helpful in delivering a service, or marketing more accurately, or prioritising resource and effort in a meaningful and customer-relevant way.

But data doesn't tell the whole the whole story. It tells us that a certain group of people don't access the health service early enough, but not why. It tells us that a certain profile of people like a certain genre of film but not the elements that the film needs to contain. The financial service may have a clearer picture of the topics people are contacting them for, but not what their issues are or why these issues are important to them, what is the problem they are trying to solve?

Data sets are items of information presented as fields, or units of information. Age, location, frequency of visits to cinemas or health centres, all these can be captured and sorted to see patterns that are useful in understanding behaviour and events that we cannot see from our single standpoint. The scale of data helps us see where similarities, patterns exist and allow us to focus our attention. That is vital when we look to enhance, improve, design and redesign a service or create something new.

But it's only part of the story. In a much used, and sometimes misused, example, a set of data fields display identical entries. The data sets of two different people display that they were both born in 1950, have been divorced and remarried, have two children, like dogs rather than cats and have wealth over $10 million. If we were to use this data, we might send them similar marketing material for a new financial service, suggest the same hotel when they are travelling, imagine they would share a preference for how they are treated when they book a restaurant or travel.

When we reveal the identity of these two people and learn that one is King Charles III of Great Britain and the other is Ozzy Osbourne, the lead singer of Black Sabbath, the pioneering heavy metal rock band from the 1970s and star of real-life docusoaps for those who are too young to know, we can laugh at how two such different people can share the same detail.

We can argue that King Charles and Ozzy Osbourne may indeed share some needs and preferences for how they navigate through life but if I am marketing, designing, and delivering a service to these two gentlemen, I would like to understand which I am designing for at a level deeper than the data would tell me.

The data examples I am using here are quantitative – they measure quantity, in the present and past tense, at a level of precision and often at a massive scale. It's a vital and powerful tool for helping us shape a world that responds to reality rather than assumption and is fit for purpose and relevant to those who live in the world.

Data can reveal previously unseen truths, find interesting outliers or new information previously hidden that should not be ignored, and support the delivery of new products, services and experiences. But it's only half the story.

Listening with Our Eyes

Looking at data can be so revealing, we can imagine we can hear people's pleasure, concerns, pain and problems. The importance of visualising data in a relevant way is vital to understanding it – we need to be creative to simplify the patterns, understand the data before we can react to it. Wonderful books on how we visualise data are not just examples of how beautiful data can be, but the impact data can have in challenging our assumptions, in understanding scale, the shock of comparisons across nations or different parts of society. It gives perspective and, more than that, triggers our desire to act and identify where that action needs to be. Equally importantly, it sets our ambition for change: What is the scale of the issue we need to address, and how can we measure whether our responding actions are having impact and are successful?

But its' still not enough.

I have seen many wonderful data maps that visualise important areas of customer behaviour, say complaints received into an organisation. Categorising these complaints provides useful insight to understand where the biggest issues are to allow action to be taken, a project formed, the problem addressed with the objective to reduce and remove the issue.

That project team can dig down into each issue and examine the data. Perhaps there is more information there, but what is the root cause of the complaint? Can you discover that from data?

If we want to understand what the data is telling us, we need to move to a new level of data, one that will allow us to hear the voices, the descriptions, the real context of the issue. And that is not possible with qualitative data, we need the other branch of research to unlock the human experience, find the insights and comprehend the perceived and actual barriers that impede our complaining customer from happiness. We need to speak to them.

As we've talked about earlier, the tools of research: ethnography, interviewing, experiential, co-creation and workshops – the tools of direct interaction with real people, their context and objectives – are what make design valuable and different to management, accountancy, marketing and all the other tools in the service of our decision-making processes.

Why do we make bad decisions? Because we don't speak to people. We don't look deep enough into their reality; we don't ask them why things are difficult to understand, what they desire or need, or would be useful to them. We then insist on trusting our own intuition and assumptions about their needs and context and what the likely solutions might be. We do not put enough investment in listening with our eyes and ears and moving beyond the shallow atmosphere of data fields and patterns to find reality.

But when we do, there are great treasures to be found. A snippet from observation might trigger a competitor-beating innovation just as effectively as a technical research and development lab developing new ideas without a problem to solve or an idea of the people who might benefit.

We've seen how going into the airport toilets revealed a completely disconnected opportunity for designing a better experience for travellers. We've seen how assumptions of what a problem is and what the solution should be can end in disaster.

Design is a risk reduction process: It prevents you from making a costly mistake and heightens the chances of developing the right thing to solve the real problem. We really should be teaching this in MBA schools, I can't imagine why we don't.

When an organisation sees the data showing that they have an issue in a particular area of the business offer to customers and data shows they are not using, or are complaining about that feature, we can flag it up and measure the impact on our business or objective. But only when we speak to some of those people do we hear emotion. We share the pain they have gone through as a consequence of what is recorded simply as a data point. Here are some real examples for research with customers who had complained about their service:

> "No one was accountable, we're just a number!"
> "They didn't do what they promised!"
> "I tried to get help, but I hit a brick wall instantly"
> "He completely missed the point. I was pulling my hair out!"
> "I was angry! It kept me awake! Why are they doing this to me?!"

Not easy listening for the product manager trying to cover up their poor service. But all vital evidence required to change to rectify this issue.

You don't hear the heat of emotion from quantitative data. You don't get the detail about the messaging and inability of the company to understand their problem and point of view. Data isn't showing you that people are anxious and losing sleep over the issue that you have caused them. Data flags that there is a problem but if you want to solve it, you need to get up from your cosy office desk and go and talk to people.

The magic and power of qualitative research is in the detail it exposes. The solutions are apparent immediately. In those examples, we can see a cultural problem, perhaps caused by an overtly process-driven culture and lack of empowerment for the staff member to take the customer's point of view rather than the company's. We can use the power of the emotions heard in the interviews to draw attention and ensure action is taken rapidly before more harm is done. We can take that learning into the development of a new way of working, one that supports the staff to support the customer and change the culture of the entire company.

Research Wisely and Carefully

We cannot talk about research without discussing ethics. The attitude that people are there to be researched can be, in many contexts, insulting and condescending. Whereas I am arguing that we need to talk to people who will use a service, or who we are trying to solve a problem for, this needs to be a conversation rather than a questionnaire. Judah Armani, in his book *Society Driven Design*, explains how design is a dialogue, a conversation with, where we understand what "preferred" looks like and work together with people to arrive at new solutions.

To find the truths with which we can make decisions and design preferred futures, we need to both measure and to listen. Qualitative data that will inspire us and provide insights and knowledge we could never have second-guessed and the quantitative data that maps what people have done and are doing to validate and instruct us. It's impossible to make a good decision without both, the black and white and the colour of real experience and collaboration on creating solutions and opportunities that fit the people who will benefit.

Chapter 5
The Design Approach

A short exercise before we start this chapter.

On your mobile phone, write the word designer and then look at the emoji that appears, It will be a male or female wearing a beret and holding an artist's paintbrush and palate. An artist, in other words, in a cliched French way.

Then Google "famous designers" into a search engine such as Google. You will find around 50, maybe more, fashion designers. So, between our messaging apps and search engines, we have a perception that design is about art and fashion.

This is a list of projects carried out by service design students at various colleges in the last few years:
- Imagining the future of on street electric vehicle charging
- Make sustainability pleasurable
- Develop services around DNA testing to proactively promote healthy lives
- Help support those who are homeless
- Redesign the expensively failing prison probation service
- Design digital banking for the neurodiverse
- Work with NGOs across continents to improve water security and quality
- Develop services for carers of disabled or elderly partners
- Increase volunteering in young people
- Reduce the number of people who, after leaving prison, return there

The reality of design is that it is a problem-solving activity that zooms between strategic intent and the detail of what we experience. It is poorly represented by our messaging emoji and search engine results and as result poorly understood by society. And that means we are underutilising valuable and effective tools that have the power to make new solutions that solve our future challenges.

The premise of this book is that design is a process that helps us make better decisions. We are sharing methods often developed intuitively, but backed up by academic research, by designers to help them design the objects, interfaces and services that we use daily. In this chapter we will unpack these methods and processes to share why they can be useful to everyone in situations and contexts where you may think design has no place or relevance.

In the early 2000s, Damien Newman, a designer at a research centre in Cambridge, UK created a sketch (Figure 5.1) of what he saw as the process of designing something new, in an effort to move his colleague's perceptions that design was simply the act of making something beautiful, usually at the end of the process, after most decisions had already been made.

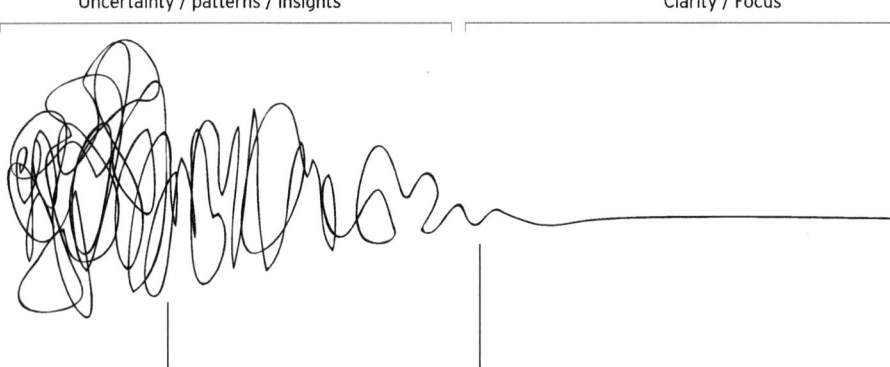

Figure 5.1: The Squiggle, Damien Newman.

Damien's diagram, known as "The Squiggle" (Figure 5.1), became a much-shared depiction of the more complex but incredibly useful processes used in design. There's even a t-shirt of it available.

The squiggle shows the uncertainty of the process, how it goes up and down, forwards and backwards but eventually becomes a straight line as you move towards a single concept that can be delivered.

Damien went on to superimpose on his squiggle how initial noise and uncertainty are replaced by patterns and insights that lead to clarity and focus. Over these he also placed the actions that drove the process: research and synthesis, concept creation and prototypes to the end stage where the design was complete.

The squiggle is a compelling, honest, revelatory, and amusing image that helps us realise that although the design process seems messy and uncertain, there is an underlying order that allows you to progress to a successful outcome. That process is better than the accidental and risky outcomes that come from an excess of solutionising in a vacuum of information and insight.

A few years after the invention of the squiggle, the UK Design Council were thinking about how to explain design to non-designers too. During my time as Director of Design and Innovation, we had built a team of design thinkers who were researching and exploring and building tools that would help the target market for the Design Council, small businesses, to optimise their value and find growth opportunities in export markets through better design.

Set up after the Second World War to promote design to businesses as they retooled and came to terms with a new, competitive economic world, the Design Council was well respected; a retail store in the centre of London sold items which were deemed to be well designed with an accompanying tag to confirm their design quality. The shop, and the magazine *Design* had a real impact on the swinging 60s and public culture as retailers such as Terence Conran's Habitat stores bought Scandinavian products and contemporary styling to fusty Edwardian British homes.

But by the 90s and 2000s British companies were losing out to foreign competition. Better engineered and beautifully styled German cars sold for higher prices and in greater numbers. The traditional British way of engineering to reduce costs had led to cars that were poorly built, broke down and despite a heritage of innovation in cars such as the Mini, and prestige of manufacturers such as Jaguar, the wheels, sometimes literally, came off the UK auto industry.

The same was happening in the US. Japanese manufacturers such as Toyota brought well-made, reliable, feature-full and lower cost cars into markets that had been dominated by Detroit's gas guzzlers. New processes and manufacturing practices, collaborative efficient workforces and smaller cars that used less fuel in a time of fuel supply crisis, changed the US market forever.

Conventional manufacturing-based economies were faced with the need to transform in the face of new competition that was truly global. It was not good enough for a US or UK company to put on the national flag and hope that would bring in customers and business. Companies had to appeal, innovate, provide new and improved products and services, ensuring longer guarantee periods and service levels not previously considered important.

By the end of the 20th century, the UK Design Council moved away from developing a sense of design for the broader public. The public got it, and were buying products from Japan, Korea and then China that were well designed. Effort had to focus on the home industry. Manufacturers needed to understand and integrate design to compete and grow.

Again, perceptions were against design. Economics, more efficient manufacturing, cutting costs, using marketing to sell products, rather than design them well. Design was seen as a less important priority compared to the hard stuff of engineering and cost control. The Design Council had to develop new tools that were practical, captured the company manager's imagination and helped them see the value and importance of creating better designed and more innovative products that would help them compete in a global marketplace.

Richard Eisermann, my successor at the Design Council, asked the question "what is design?" If there wasn't a clear and easy-to-communicate definition, that businesses could immediately understand and act on, then all the support and evangelism for design would be ineffective.

As a result, the Design Council investigated how people were answering the problems they faced, how they developed their new products and services and what problems did they encounter. By understanding how they were "designing", without being so conscious about it, the value of design could be articulated, and the positive impact shown.

In talking with a huge number of people who had set about solving the problems of their business or developing better products, they heard many times how they had identified a problem and immediately seen a solution that would solve it. By rapidly making progress to modify or redesign a new product to solve the problem, they reported that in most cases, their new solution was unsuitable for the people who had the problem and that the problem they had solved was not the real problem.

Many of the people researched said that they felt that if they had only taken time to understand the people, the context and the underlying reason for the problem, they wouldn't have wasted time developing a solution that didn't fit the problem and was unsuccessful in achieving what they set out to do.

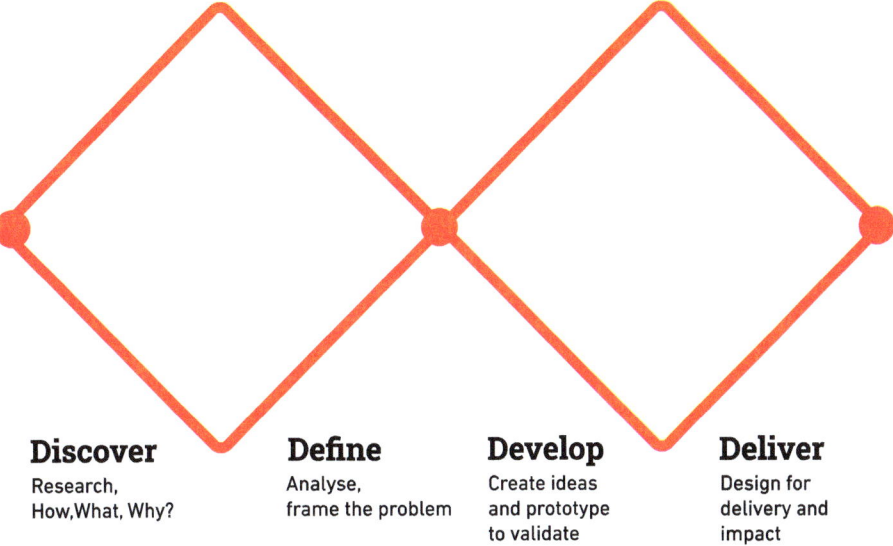

Discover
Research,
How, What, Why?

Define
Analyse,
frame the problem

Develop
Create ideas
and prototype
to validate

Deliver
Design for
delivery and
impact

Figure 5.2: The Design Council Double Diamond, revised.

The Double Diamond

The Design Council team including Chris Vanstone and Andrea Siodmok, began to explore how they could capture a diagram (Figure 5.2) of the design process that would help people see that doing initial research and analysis of a problem would create valuable insights and a reframing of the problem that would focus creative efforts to generate good solutions more successfully. What they would then develop, with all the effort that takes, would be more likely to be successful. If you combined that analysis with creativity and then the practice of designers to visualise, model and prototype a design BEFORE it is built to check it, test it and validate that it was likely to be successful, you had a set of actions that could ensure success and reduce the risk of the consequences of jumping to conclusions, creating solutions from assumptions rather than facts and reduce the risk of having to modify a product after you've delivered it, which is extremely expensive and time wasting.

In a separate piece of research, the Design Council found that £1 spent on design repaid itself with £24 profit to your business. This is an extraordinary return on investment and, as other research tells us, validates the importance of design in any organisation's strategy.

In creating the diagram, they brought in other factors that hold back better design decisions. The attitude and mindset at different stages of the process require us to think differently. At the information gathering part of the process where we explore what the root cause of a problem might be, the types of people and their context who have a problem that needs solving and how the organisation is causing the problem through its operation, or technology or some other part of it's "system", we need to consider many things. We need our thinking to be broad, to include many things, to look under every stone and consider many aspects.

At other times we need to do the opposite and focus, analyse what we have found and focus on a single brief that all can be engaged in solving.

And when we create possible solutions, it's advantageous to have many ideas, and to defer judgment, let them fly to understand which has value, which will lead to an effective and possibly innovative solution that will bring competitive advantage. It's necessary to prevent a mindset that tries to kill ideas too early, that is a barrier to building on ideas and imagining new solutions and concepts.

The Design Council wanted to sum all this up in a simple diagram that could capture the process and mindset from the findings of their research and visualise design in a compelling and easily remembered way.

The resulting diagram has become known as the Double Diamond. The diagram that Chris Vanstone drew on a napkin, links two diamonds together. The diamonds represent the diverging thought required to think broadly with the convergent thought required to focus, reframe, and agree on the problem to be solved. The second diamond captures the divergent thought of creating many possible solutions, not because it is desirable to build many solutions but to ensure that all angles have been considered, all possible solutions understood and evaluated according to their impact on achieving the objective of the project.

To support the ease of understanding of the Double Diamond diagram, four stages of the process were laid underneath, one for each half of the diamond. These were Discover, Define, Develop and Deliver. The precise definitions and actions required for each of these has changed over time but the general application of the Double Diamond provides a framework for a simple, risk reducing process that allows anyone to solve the right problem in the right way.

Discover

If there is one aspect of the design process that all versions and methods share, it is to consider and research what you are designing before you start designing or making decisions that will have impact. As Herbert Simon put it, changing existing situations into preferred ones.

To discover is to find the new. Things we didn't not know beforehand. Things that surprise us and make us see a situation differently, with more empathy perhaps or more clarity so that the decisions we go on to make are founded on evidence.

The Discovery phase is our opportunity to find and understand that evidence and to do so we need to think broadly. The first half of the first diamond represents a diverging way of thinking where we open up and look at every aspect of the problem we are trying to solve.

In understanding a context there are several layers we can use to start to understand why things are happening the way they are. The first is people: who are we making decisions for?

Who Are We Designing For?

I was talking once to a manager about some interviews with customers who had complained about the problems they had experienced with the company. "Oh yes, I met a customer once, 20 years ago" he told me.

That someone could have worked in a company for that long and only met a customer once was shocking to me, though I suspect not uncommon. In that particular company, the people who worked there described themselves as customer centric and felt they were doing their best for customers. However, what was clear from the large number of complaints was that they were not looking after their customers very well. It's possible that what they thought was good for their customer did not match what their customers expected and wanted. If they had only met one once in 20 years, that's not so surprising.

In another conversation the head of marketing told me that they knew all about their customers, because they were in marketing and knew how to sell to them. It's a common misconception that the marketing department are the owners of the data and insights of their customers because they "talk" to them. It's true that many marketing departments hold the funds for market research. But how many connect that with product managers, people who are developing and innovating around their products and services or trying to improve customer satisfaction, reduce complaints and wonder why sales are static? "Let's just have another marketing campaign", they often say.

But this disconnection and apparent ownership of the customer is false and dangerous. Every person in an organisation needs to understand their purpose and their role, and creating silos around something as important as knowledge of the customer is a big mistake.

In the process of design, we cut across these silos and share our understanding of the customer across the organisation. We can use that shared knowledge to fuel our collective creativity and ability to care about the people we are serving. This is a fundamental shift in how organisations work and when we shift our thinking, it creates innovation, business success, behaviour change and positive impact, both inside and outside of the organisation.

If we are trying to redesign thinking, then our first step is to reverse our traditional approach and start with people. We tend to end with people and construct our organisations, policy and strategy around our capability; what suits us and our organisations, what product or technology can we make and then try and persuade people that it will work for them. It's not surprising then that policy fails or products need enormous marketing budgets to persuade people to buy them or exciting innovations fail. The essence of redesigning thinking and the design methods we use is to start with people.

People are old and young. They represent every demographic and behavioural type. They are neurodivergent, abled and differently abled, proud and ambitious, scared and cautious. This diversity and inconsistency make it difficult to start with people rather than the steady things we know and can control.

But we are designing for other people. We expect people to desire, choose, purchase, use and be satisfied with what is offered to them. To ensure we create real value, we have to understand people and listen to them.

It is difficult for many to put themselves into other people's shoes. We have our own experience; our own worldview and we often believe our intuition and that we know what is right. But the first part of thinking differently is to put that to one side and learn how to learn about people.

During my time at Cisco, I worked with the local authority in the town of Almere in the Netherlands on a project about ageing. We were exploring how technology could support the wellbeing of people as they age – would it be helpful?

Almere, 20 minutes east of Amsterdam, is a great place to go to think about how we age. This small city with a wonderful Art Gallery designed by Kazuyo Sejima and Ryue Nishizawa, was built on a polder: land reclaimed from the inland Lake Ijsselmeer in a process that took 9 years from 1959 with the first house built in 1974. By 1984 it was a municipality and has become the Netherland's newest city.

Those pioneers who first moved to the new city stayed and over time grew older. The modern infrastructure of fibre optic connectivity was in place but for the city authority, the question was how to use that infrastructure to support the senior population of Almere.

At the start of the project everyone was full of ideas and things we could do. But crucially, we stepped back and asked ourselves, who are the people of Almere?

Our first thought was to search online to see what we could find out about the people who lived there. What we saw was surprising in its diversity. A dude in a hat still young inside. An 80-year-old man in a tuxedo on a dating app. People taking part in demonstrations to protect the natural environment around them. People forming communities and using gaming technology to play against each other and people with mobility problems carrying heavy shopping to and from their homes.

This was a start, but we wanted to get to know these people better in order to understand what their needs are, and how they might access the services they needed. Interviews and visits were set up across the community in care homes, private homes and in community centres to understand who the people were and what their needs were.

From those interviews we constructed a set of people who captured the diversity and range of needs across the community. Some were physically less able and needed support, others were ageing well and could help those less so. Some were lonely and this seemed to lead to rapidly deteriorating health.

This project shaped how Almere began to think and connect with the people who it made decisions for. Their leaders referred to the people they felt they now knew; having listened to them, they understood their needs better. When they made decisions about traffic flow in the city centre, they would look to the pictures of the people they had heard from and consider what they might say.

The project was about how technology could help the population thrive in old age and once we had understood who they were, we could start to generate ideas that had value to them and could have a positive impact. Several technology solutions were tried out: supporting keeping fit across the community and in individual homes over video and another to share their community choirs over video with other choirs around the world. The impact was positive and immediate, with people coming out of their homes to take part in the weekly event producing a measurable impact on their health and wellbeing.

Understanding who we were designing for and on behalf of who we were making decisions for was essential and drove greater creativity and better ideas that worked and had positive impact. How could anyone be so arrogant as to make decisions without listening to those who they were designing for? Well, it turns out that's exactly how most decisions are made, with no attempt to listen and observe, to learn and create solutions that people need and want.

Why Don't We Just Ask People What They Want?

The focus group has been as a driver of consumer goods, packaging and government policy for decades. Sit down with some people and show them your product and listen to what they say. Understand what is important to them so you can design your policy to fit them. Shape the car to reflect their daily lives. This is all good and legitimate research, but there can be problems.

In the 1980s a new form of audio device was developed by Philips. It combined large speakers with a radio and cassette tape player and could be used outside, in the park, at a picnic or just walking down the street. The boombox was born.

It was a new type of product and Philips didn't know whether it should be treated as a youth-orientated fashion icon or a traditional audio device in the usual black or silver of that genre. So, they set up a focus group to find out what people wanted.

They prepared versions of the boombox in various colours ranging from the conservative black to bright primary colours that captured the feeling of youth and summer days in the park. Everyone agreed: The colourful ones were what they wanted. Philips were happy and got their answer.

As a thank you for taking apart in the focus group, people were invited to take away one of the boomboxes. So, they did. Only they all took the black ones, leaving the favoured colourful versions behind . . .

What happened there? Why did they say they preferred the colourful options but took the boring ones?

We can only guess, but I believe that what Philips had done was accidently recreate the real experience of purchasing the product. When confronted with the choice of taking it home, they began to think of what their partner might say, or where it would sit in their home and how would that fit into the décor? Suddenly the decision is very different from just ticking a box in a survey, this time the decision was real. And they did the opposite of what they said they would do.

This is a huge problem with the techniques of focus groups and market research. There is a huge amount of money spent and trust afforded to the results research. Yet in many cases, it can be inaccurate and unhelpful in predicting human behaviour. It's usually done too late, with products or services that are already designed, meaning bad news is difficult to respond to without great expense.

It's very easy to ask someone in a survey or focus group how much they would pay for something. But unless the context of the question feels like it's real, we are just guessing and the results are unlikely to represent the decisions that will influence people to buy, or not, a product.

"If You Want to Experience Something, You Have to Experience it"

So said the great Bill Moggridge about how we need to learn to see what is really happening. If we want to gain insight and find the real problems people have, we need an array of techniques to ensure that the context in which the question is asked is authentic enough for the answer to have some value.

Given that research if such a vital part of a successful approach to solving a problem, it was common for many design students to immediately do a survey, send it out to anyone they know or can find and wait for the results. Sadly, surveys may make you feel like you're doing research, but the quality of the returns is usually disappointing and unhelpful. This is because surveys are good at validating an idea and seeing who confirms and agrees with question like "do you think your politicians are good or bad?" But they are less good at providing insight into why you think your leaders are heroes, or terrible.

As Bill said, to find the sort of observations and insights that fuel innovation and creativity, we have to roll up our sleeves and talk to people.

Research for Design

During the 1980s, Bill Moggridge's design company IDEO had the realisation that better solutions and creative problem solving came from understanding and watching people. Pioneers such as Jane Fulton Suri and Matt Marsh in San Francisco began to work closely with designers on conducting new forms of research and observation that could expose behaviour, what customers did or tried to do, to discover their real needs and frustrations with current solutions.

Their techniques included ethnography, the extreme deep dive form of research where you follow and record everything people do to understand their fundamental needs and desires. From this came the ability to solve, improve, adapt, or reinvent solutions that would generate innovation and competitive advantage.

In a famous example Jane saw a roll of industrial tape on a van driver's dashboard which served as a holder for the morning coffee that he drank in the car on the way to work. These little observations became vital to the design and innovation process and allowed IDEO to design innovative products and services in healthcare, office equipment, financial services and more. It became part of their ethos, their differentiator that ensured that their creativity was rooted in evidence and discovery that couldn't be gleaned by sending people surveys. That ethos is now at the heart of the design process that we can all use to create preferred situations.

What's Really Going On?

London's main airport at Heathrow is the entry and exit point for millions of people every year. As a hub to many other destinations, it's one of the busiest in the world. Cobbled together by various terminals, it's an unloved but necessary point of transit.

When the decision was made, after a lot of political turmoil, to expand Heathrow and build a 5th terminal, a huge infrastructure project for the next 40–50 years it required some foresight to ensure it was future proofed and took account of trends in our climate, how people might travel and developments in technology.

The Terminal 5 building has, therefore, large gutters and water storage capacity to cope with predictions of periods of draught followed by intense downpours. The impact of increases in the numbers of travellers from Asia, who may prefer to travel in groups rather than individually, were considered. Predictions of an ageing population, healthier and wealthier with a propensity to travel into old age were considered and to explore how these and other environmental or demographic changes would impact on the design of the terminal, a research project was set up to explore and research how these different types of travellers were currently experiencing.

A team from the Helen Hamlyn Foundation, who were set up to educate designers in how to design for an ageing population and for those with disabilities, initiated a ethnographic survey where they would follow people around the airport and report back on what they did, and what requirements should be added to the design specification of the new airport terminal.

They quickly found that many older people were visiting the toilets and bathrooms in the current airport, so they noted that more toilets would be needed if the average age of travellers increased.

Strangely, perhaps, one of the researchers decided to explore more fully and followed the travellers into the public toilets. Once there, they saw that many people were standing around inside the toilet area. When the researcher asked them what they were doing, they replied that they were listening to the announcements as they couldn't hear them in the noisy retail environment outside.

They were listening to the announcements, not using the toilet! Once this was understood, it was easy to set out clear seating in the centre of the terminal with lots of digital signage and, of course, great audio quality so that passengers of all ages could sit in comfort, hear their flight information without stress and not miss their flight.

We all need to get in the toilets of life because it is when we are curious and willing to go deeper and find out what we might be missing, that we see the solution and the opportunity waiting to be grasped. Innovation is a lot easier when you've metaphorically visited the toilets to find out what is going on.

This deep, ethnographic, or deep dive, experiential research delivers incredibly rich insight, but it's expensive, takes time and might only cover a few people. But the richness and exposure to the reality of how people are living their lives and interacting with products and services is incredibly valuable to our decision-making process and how we might design, or redesign, our solutions. This depth of research is what inspires our creativity, gives it a foundation on which to conceive better ways and allows creativity to flourish.

Like many things in the design process, there are counterintuitive aspects that take some people a while to accept. For instance, it is a widely accepted rule that the insights gleamed form as few as 6–8 people, when studied and interviewed honestly and openly, will discover 80% of the problems and opportunities present in a current service or product experience.

On the other hand, if you want to validate the insights you have unearthed, then our friend the survey is an excellent tool to reach a much larger number of people and see if they validate your findings. Do they have the same problems, do they recognise the issues and desire the same or similar things to the smaller sample of people? The trick is to know which research technique is appropriate and when to use it.

But whether following people around to observe what they do, or studying them with an ethnographic approach, the great gift of research is to talk to the people you are working on behalf of, your customers, users, citizens who will transact with your product and service and gain benefit in some way.

Interviews

When we listen to people and hear of their needs, concerns problems and wishes, we shift our perception of purpose and see the light. Sometimes this happens to a CEO when someone they know mentions a problem, or gives them some advice or tells them about a competitor's new idea. Because it's the CEO and they are in charge, the currency of this information and the actions the CEO takes is out of all proportion with the veracity and diversity of insight they should be working with. This "divine intervention" acting on a single data point can throw a company seriously off course.

Listening to your customer is good, but you need to listen to a representative range of them.

Experience the Experience

Sometimes organisations carry out what is termed mystery shopping. They may pay someone to visit their competitive stores or use their services to find out how they compare with their own.

During a senior management team away day, we invited the directors and managers to do a spot of mystery shopping on their own company. Dividing them into three groups, one group was asked to visit the physical store nearby, the other to ring the call centre and the final group to buy their product online.

The first thing we noticed was the group buying online had all typed their own company name into the search engine and as a result, their solution was top of the list. STOP! we cried; no normal person would do that, we explained. They would put in the service they were looking for, or the problem they had and not any company name.

That gave a rather different result. Their company was a long way down the list, which did not please them but did allow them, possibly for the first time, to discover what it's like to be a customer of their own business.

What we were doing to those senior managers was to share an invaluable and vital tool used in the design of service called the Service Safari. It's a ridiculously simple tool and provides fantastic insight into how to improve a service, but hardly ever has a manager in a company done it.

Here's an exercise: Think about visiting the supermarket (and I mean visit, though you could do this same exercise for the online experience too). What do you do? Consider what the triggers for the visit are: weekly routine, emergency purchase of milk, etc.? How do you make your list or remember what you need? How do you get there? How do you find stuff, how do you choose, what is the checkout experience like?

A Service Discovery is the detailed observation and recording of every step, every micro-event, touchpoint, moment of a journey and it immediately exposes the good and bad of that journey. If you have a pulse, you will probably immediately get creative and start solutionising. Great, but hold that thought for later.

Now go and do a Service Discovery on your own organisation. Imagine you are a customer and be honest with yourself, try and forget your own knowledge of how the organisation works. Be as ignorant and unaware as a normal customer would be. Observe and capture every moment.

I wish every person in an organisation would do this; the insight and understanding they would gain, the empathy and understanding of what needs to be put right is unavoidable and completely tangible. You may have seen a PowerPoint about what your customer's experience is meant to be, but I can guarantee the PowerPoint slide does not represent the real experience they have.

For the service designer, this is the point at which you can identify with customers and start to become intimate with the real experience they have. This technique is about putting you into the customer's shoes but, even better, do it with them! Then you see what happens in the toilets, the detail you can't imagine unless you've experienced the experience.

I wish every fast-moving consumer goods company executive had the experience of opening the packaging of their own product. I wish every policy maker understood the experience of the citizens on whose behalf they make decisions. Experiencing the world as others – of all capabilities and contexts – do is the beginning of better understanding which leads to better impact but is also the beginning of love, for people you service, sell to and who work for you. Design is the emotional balance of finance and technology, and love and happiness are the output when we get it right.

Within the title of design research are a catalogue of tools that allow people to express themselves in a deeper and more truthful way than asking them to fill in a survey.

Co-creation, Co-design

Including the people you are designing for in the process of design is an extremely powerful way of gaining insight, deeper understanding, building empathy, learning what people really desire or need and removing your own bias and assumptions (which is another important benefit of doing research).

Whether you are a decision maker or a designer (and as I repeatedly point out, if you are making decisions, you are part of the design process, just without realising it), then working alongside the people who will experience the fruits of your decisions is a radical step, but one which takes the pressure off an individual to make a decision that is wrong and possibly damaging.

The art of co-design is in the preparation. Co-design requires bringing representative people into a space, and along with researchers and designers, providing the information, prompts, stimulus, and paper and pens to reflect on the current and comprehend the possible.

It's a coming together and sharing of power and the pencil to shape new possibilities, together. This is done at an early stage; in many ways co-design is a research tool as much as it's a design tool. Involving people who can share their experience and motivations with the opportunity to visualise and express that experience is a powerful act of discovery that can further fuel creativity.

For many designers, co-design is a better way to design that removes the bias and assumptions of the designer but stimulates and shares their skills of visualisation, listening, being inspired, and forming new and better ideas and solutions.

We are used now to checking the time from our smartphones, which, even in their closed state, display the time. But it wasn't always such a prominent feature of your phone. This came from co-creation sessions with users who were asked to draw what they would like on the first, or home, screens. There were many creative ideas flying around at the time, including the owner's name so that they didn't pick up someone else's identical phone.

People did draw many versions with different information or images on the screens but the one aspect they all had (though in several different forms) was the time. Perhaps it was a clockface, or in numbers, but it was always the biggest thing on the screen.

From co-creation sessions came the realisation that people needed to be able to personalise their home screens and, of course, upload a photo there – and it turned out that putting a picture of your favourite family member or pet was a better way of identifying which phone was yours than displaying your name.

In designing with others, we need to respect and ensure an inclusive approach. As with all shared and collaborative decisions and design practices, we need to be aware that they can favour the loud and confident and hide the quieter and less extroverted people. But innovation and creativity thrive on diversity of every sort (pluralism is my favoured word, where plurality is at the heart, not tokenism).

Some of the best co-creation sessions are very visual, with images and objects that stimulate discussion and show how our decisions may be impacted by different issues and contexts. When the UK Policy Lab wanted to co-create strategy and policy on our urban high streets with consumers, they showed them realistic images of the kinds of business that might exist in ten to twenty years on high street, including new services and repair shops for our household robots. The images shifted the participants' positions and brought out new responses, hopes and fears about the future of their local high streets.

Handing Over the Pen

Sometimes interesting innovations fail because of a poorly thought-through detail. To improve the process of acting on a complaint, a service was set up to notify a complaining customer at all times of the status of their complaint, what was happening and how long it would take to resolve. The concept of transparency and information works well on our public transport systems when they are delayed, so it seemed a good idea here.

Sadly, the constant stream of notifications and poorly worded explanations that were being sent did not rebuild the broken relationship as had been hoped. Indeed, it made it worse.

To try and ameliorate the method of communication, we asked some complainants to attend a workshop where we gave them smartphone-sized bits of paper and a Sharpie pen and asked them to write the notifications. We identified when a small, or even no information was helpful and when a longer, more detailed update was helpful.

Sometimes it's great just to had the pen over and see what comes out. There is evidence that people are not so good at taking a leap into the future and tend to measure their experiences based on what is current, but when you need to understand what they don't want, it can be extremely effective.

Card Sorting

Other simple tools for uncovering unarticulated wishes are to use cards that can be sorted by people into their order of preference. It's a simple way of understanding what is important to people, or what concerns them most and is close to the kind of multiple choice "rate these in order of importance" surveys we might take online.

In designing for a luxury brand, a product team had decided that what was important for their customer was a feeling of being special, having inspirational experiences and a sense of uniqueness. In testing these assumptions, it was important to not just list the words they have thought about but find some others that hadn't been considered important. There is little value in simply validating your ideas by not including any others.

Luckily there was a good research person who was able to spread several other values and words that might connect with the potential customers, which was just as well as they chose completely different words as their most important. To everyone's surprise, these were quite mundane topics such as be attentive, care about the little things and be thoughtful. No one picked the bespoke, desirable, and exclusive cards. It was a shock to the team but a terrific moment of insight where we were able to set about designing a service that gave them what they really wanted, rather than what we thought they wanted.

Epiphanies

All these tools allow you to uncover information about how people think and what they might do in the future. The purpose is to discover what you don't know and validate whether assumptions you have are correct or not.

If you talk and conduct research and you have only validated your assumptions, you need to ask yourself if you have been curious enough and whether your research was deep enough. My rule of thumb is that you can expect to have around half of your assumptions proved to be correct. But for the other half, you should have found out things that surprise you. You should have had epiphanies that completely change your perception of what people do and need. You should see your task in a new light, informed by something you did not previously know or expect. If you do not have at least 50% surprises and epiphanies, then you haven't looked hard enough. Go back and be more curious.

Mapping Journeys

The journey map is at the heart of service design. It is a tool that allows you to bring together all the research techniques listed here with the data and insight to connect the person you are making decisions for with their current experience over time.

Capturing, recording, analysing every step of the journey that we have through a service is a powerful tool. Following the people we are designing for through the minutiae of their experience, the journey through time of how they interact with the world uncovers the barriers, challenges, confusions, expectations and frustrations that are present in the most basic scenario.

We tend to think of journeys through time as processes that occur like stepping stones across a stream. We see processes as tangible outputs that deliver us what we need. Order, collect, pay, consume. Okay for a pizza delivery perhaps, but even that simplest of transactions is full of choice, doubt, time and fulfilment or disappointment.

Because we are in control of processes, and can invent them and monitor them to determine if they achieve their purpose, we are more comfortable at process design, rather than as experience designers. We do not address the mental friction of choosing from a large and complex menu with many complicated alternatives. We lie about delivery times so people don't complain or demand redress. A bank will be comfortable that their compliance and regulation is protecting their customers when it fact it is driving them mad with frustration and treating them all as potential criminals.

The act of mapping is discovering what is really happening, moment by moment. Watching recordings, asking the people who interact with your organisation what they really do, what are they thinking and what is their emotional context at each point, reveals all the truth you will need to know. Then you can redesign your organisation to have greater value, be more successful and solve the challenges that occur when people interact with you.

Working with organisations as diverse as financial institutions to a local fire and rescue service, it is common to witness the epiphany when people discover how difficult or unpleasant working with or for them is. In one recent example, a Head of Comms who was walking through their own internal communication platform, was forced to realise how impossible the platform was to use and find out even the most basic information.

But this pain is healthy and useful. Identifying the pain points and opportunities along the way give you the chance to put them right, prioritise those points that are barriers to profit or happiness, identify the opportunities for innovation and competitive advantage or that move the dial on achieving your goal.

Good Journey Mapping

Journey maps need to be thorough and based on the person you are designing for, not yourself. You therefore need data: quant and qual, that reflects the reality of their experiences.

They also need to be extremely rigorous in the detail. It is not enough to say "visit website" as a part of the journey. We need to know whether they searched for it on a search engine or used a QR code on a bus stop poster. We need to know everything through every moment of time to find out where the friction, problem, barrier, misunderstanding and confusion, disappointment, confusion, impatience and every other emotion may occur.

A good journey map uses a template which can be modified according to the context that reflects the key stages in the journey. The start of the journey is not when they walk into your store or download your app or search for a product: It starts before then with the need, the trigger that starts the journey.

The traditional journey map starts with the issue that needs solving, the job that needs fixing, the emotional desire that needs fulfilling. Going back to the root need or desire is what is at the heart of the "Jobs to Done" theory that analyses what people are "hiring" your organisation for. It's a question we often forget to ask.

From then we have to navigate to information that will help us find what we need. Of course, a need, or especially a desire, for something we didn't realise we might want, may come from an advert or new technology that does something we didn't even think of before. This still requires an array of micro-events to be in place for us to find, compare and choose the right solution for us.

We then transact. We may purchase in a store or online, we may be influenced by packaging, or availability or features, or the amount of trust we have in the brand and of course the price we have to pay. Every element of the journey is complex and affected by a multitude of decisions in response to presentations of information, promise and intuitive emotional connection. It's important you are aware and designing all of these, the person on the journey sees only their choices and experience along the way, innocent of which department is responsible for creating each moment.

Only now do we get to use, the bit that most designers are concerned with. How easy is it to use "out of the box"? Is it a satisfying or disappointing experience? Do I send it back?

94 — Chapter 5 The Design Approach

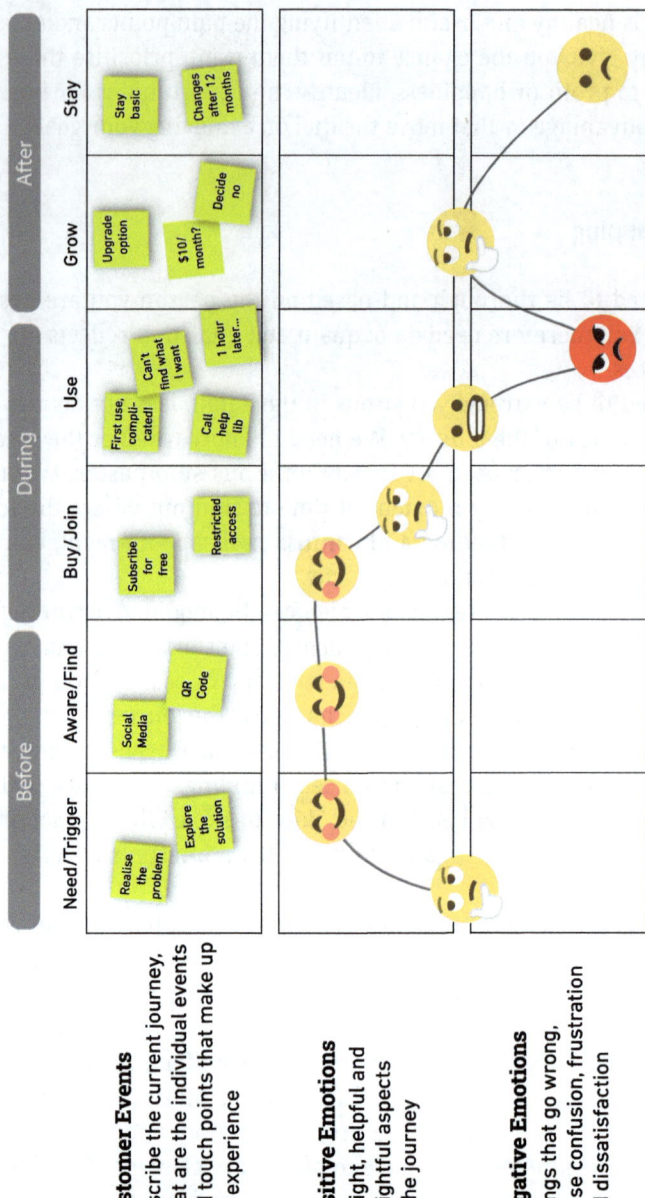

Figure 5.3: Journey mapping.

Over time the journey goes on, perhaps as a service is sporadically used or maybe used daily, until such time as I don't need it, or I see a newer shinier and more advanced version that fulfils my needs better.

This abstract definition of the journey states becomes very tangible when you use it to record every moment of the current journey. You can name them what you like but they must represent the true journey through time, before you have got involved and, in a sustainably concerned world, what happens during and after use.

The journey template (Figure 5.3) can be enormous and go round the walls of a large meeting room. That's because, if it's accurate and useful, it will detail every single step of the real journey experience. The journey map can be extended by identifying and adding beneath it the touchpoints, systems, processes, and people who are involved and responsible for each part of the journey. It takes curiosity and courage to do this, but it gives you an x-ray of what is really going on and what and how your organisation is operating at each stage.

It's a powerful tool and visualisation of what is rarely visualised – reality. That is why it's powerful and so effective and allows us to pick out the bits that work and more importantly, the bits that don't. Prioritising the broken, removing discomfort and barriers and identifying opportunities for innovation all spring from journey maps, allowing us to completely understand and take action to renew, improve and redesign.

Other Design Methods

The Stanford Design Thinking method (Figure 5.4) is perhaps more directive than the Double Diamond but has a similar order of defining the problem before creating or ideating.

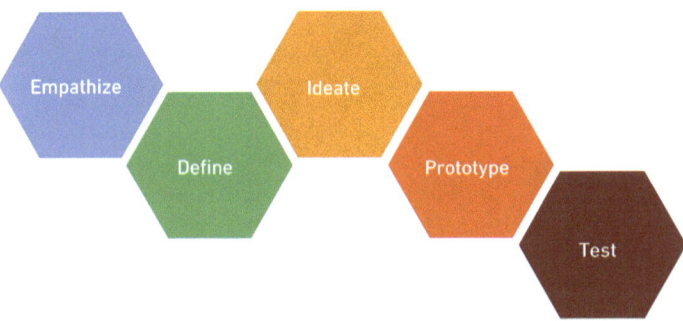

Figure 5.4: The Stanford D-School 5D Design Method.

This process starts with empathy: understanding user needs through observation and recognition of what drives behaviour. From this insight comes problem definition that is captured as a problem statement. From this we can ideate and image the solutions that will solve the problem statement. Then we prototype and finally test the idea to get feedback from the people who will use and benefit from the idea.

We can see the similarities between the two methods and both have been effective in helping leaders and managers understand that there is logic and value in design methods that decrease risk whilst increasing desirability.

Design is a method, not a luxury. It's a method we can apply to many things, all use and learn from and it prevents accidents that are based on assumptions.

Chapter 6
What Is the Problem?

> *Memo: Piers for use on beaches.*
> *They must float up and down with the tide. The anchor problem must be mastered.*
> *Let us have the best solution worked out. Don't argue the matter. The difficulties will argue themselves.*
> Winston Churchill, 30 May 1942

Projects tend to start with briefs. "We need to develop a button, an app, a website, an advisory service, a product, a forum, a campaign, create some regulations . . ."

A brief is a brilliant thing. It sets out what people will work on to create workable, impactful solutions that will win business. Raise revenue, solve a problem, exploit technology, capture an opportunity. In Winston Churchill's case, create an innovative floating harbour to allow millions of troops to land on the Northern coast of France (without saying how, just framing the problem as economically as possible).

A brief is a valuable document that will need to be returned to and referred to during the life of a project, to ensure that everyone is working to the same target and not drifting off with some other agenda. Whether making a government policy or a new product, governance is a valuable thing that can monitor progress and deviation from the brief and keep everyone focused.

Unfortunately, all the examples at the head of this chapter (apart from Churchill's) are terrible briefs. Why? Because they ask for a thing, rather than express the problem that needs solving. Or who has the problem and in what context.

The Value of Challenging the Brief

Harriet Birt is a user-centred designer who has won awards for the simplicity, transparency, and usability of her design of digital apps. She wanted to work with people where she could genuinely make a difference, adding value through creative problem solving from unique angles that led to innovative solutions.

Harriet combined her design consultancy with a role in a UK-based fire and rescue service and was excited to be working with an organisation dedicated to saving lives. Her role was to work on a project to redesign an app for firefighters to deliver home fire safety visits, to assess and advise on safety in people's homes.

The initial app was intended to help firefighters carry out these assessments more efficiently, meet operational targets and reduce overall costs. However, 18 months after the app's launch, home fire safety visits were still taking too long, and the fire stations weren't completing enough of them.

The project had decided that what was needed was to improve the app and it was assumed that the user experience and user interface design was at fault. Harriet decided to take a design approach to explore the brief and ask what do people need to access to ensure the safety of their homes and also what was the fundamental problem that was being solved?

It rapidly became apparent to her that the language used in the app was not suited to the intended audience – which was proven when she did ethnographic research with homeowners and firefighters. In addition, she found a variety of actions and pieces of information that could support home safety more effectively than the current app.

When Harriet talked to firefighters, she found that 63% of them had not received training to use the app. It became clear that the app's design issues were only part of the problem. The lack of training, combined with cumbersome devices, inefficient systems, inconsistent delivery, and firefighters feeling undervalued, meant that the app wasn't working as intended, to the point where only 5% of the 80 firefighters she talked to were still using the app 18 months after its launch. Many stated that the app took them too long to complete, so they stopped using it in order to meet their targets.

The need to redesign the app was based on an assumption rooted in someone's opinion as to why firefighters weren't using it. By applying the "Five Whys" technique, Harriet began to uncover the deeper issues underlying this assumption, which allowed her to propose changes.

She proposed a new approach from delivering visits to all residents, which often led to inefficiencies, to a targeted approach that prioritised those who truly needed the service, and who the service identified as those groups of people in a vulnerable category.[1] This strategy had the potential to save the service thousands of pounds.

Amongst the recommendations was that firefighters receive adequate training to deliver visits more efficiently and effectively. To address the needs of residents who were concerned about fire safety but didn't qualify as vulnerable, Harriet contributed to designing an online self-assessment tool and proposed developing a separate app specifically for the public. This app would manage tasks such as notifying

---

[1] Fire and rescue services identify someone as vulnerable if there is an increased risk of fire, such as those who:
- are aged 65 years or over
- have sight and/or hearing loss
- have mobility concerns
- have mental health concerns
- have memory concerns
- are unable to escape unaided if there is a fire
- are a family with children under the age of 5 years

incidents in their area, reducing the need for printed materials, sending notifications when faulty white goods were recalled, and alerting residents to bad weather, heatwaves and other safety advice.

All of this had shifted the focus from simply designing a better-looking app to addressing the root causes of the problem and solving those. Harriet's story shows how curiosity to locate the real problem, the courage to challenge the original assumption and a collaborative spirit to help firefighters and vulnerable citizens be safe, saved money and was more impactful.

The cost of developing and maintaining an app is huge. Eager designers, developers and coders are all trained to build apps and can't wait to be asked, especially if that's their business model that earns their revenue and livelihood. An app is a tangible thing that a product manager can put on their annual achievement appraisal: "I ran a successful app development program".

But this costly resource can, in many circumstances, be a waste of effort, time and money if the app is not the solution to the problem. Harriet's story shows how curiosity to locate the real problem; the courage to challenge the original assumption; and a collaborative spirit to help firefighters and vulnerable citizens be safe, saved money and was more impactful.

Describe the Problem, Not the Solution

If a brief asks for an app, or a website, rip it up and ask what problem an app would solve. It a simple and critical rule: A brief should not describe the solution. It should describe the problem to be solved or objective of a project and the people who will benefit.

This is another counterintuitive design rule that feels wrong to many. "What we need is an app" is a much-heard clarion call. But rarely is there an equal effort made to first understand the problem and decide what the solution should be.

So, having gained insight and knowledge from the data you have and the interviews you have heard with the people you are designing for, it is critical that we use that to generate our brief, which is the description of what we want to achieve.

Understanding what the real problem is, is not easy. We need to frame the problem, or reframe the problem so that the root cause is clearly articulated and the real underlying problem identified. If we take a moment to do that, our creativity, development and intellectual resources can be harnessed in solving the problem in the right way and reducing the risk of meaningless development that will not achieve your objective.

As we've seen, understanding the existing customer journey is one of the most useful tools for framing the problem. Looking at each step of a journey from the customer's or user's point of view allows us to feel the pain, see the opportunity and link it to the systemic elements that might be causing problems.

Once you have a detailed journey map, you can stand back and isolate the pain points, the events that don't go well, and then isolate the causes. A service may fail through lack of information, or too much information and not enough guidance. It could fail for many reasons and standing back an analysing these causes brings us the rocket fuel for creating meaningful solutions that have impact.

How Might We?

Service designers use this moment to create a statement that is framed as "How Might We?" This statement is another critical moment in the design process and one that is the pivot point that can make or break all your decisions and subsequent development.

Crafting a "How Might We?" statement is difficult and may take many iterations. A good "How Might We?" takes account of the patterns in your data and insight, the real root causes and captures the essence of what you need to achieve.

To identify the root causes, take time to look at how different pain points might be connected. Some typical themes are:

Not enough information – many people get lost in a physical or digital space. Is there a sign, is the navigation clear, how do you find what you need (for which the Frequently Asked Questions page is NEVER the answer)? When I ask people to spot opportunities, they very often say "a website". That is not the answer. The problem a website is trying to solve is usually lack of information. The opportunity is to navigate the user to the correct information, which MAY BE a website, but other solutions may apply. If we understand what the problem is, then we can decide whether a website is the best way of providing that information. And see if other solutions may be better in the context of the user who needs more information.

Why, Why, Why, Why, Why

When we see a problem, we start to solve it. We rarely ask ourselves the questions "Why is this happening?" or "What is the cause of that problem?"

Looking at any problem you want to solve, ask yourself why? And then ask that question again. And again. In service design we play the game "5 Whys", where we insist that every answer is greeted with another question: Why is that?

Playing 5 Whys can be very revealing. In a customer experience workshop in Dubai with one of that region's most eminent retail chains, a team brought a real business challenge. A particular web page, a critical part of the process of onboarding new employees into the company, was causing problems for the new recruits. This seems a great problem to bring to a design workshop, a nice clear brief that designers can solve.

Going the through the whole journey that a recruit experiences before and after the problem page, the team isolated the problem and asked themselves why, why and why again. As they went through the process, a new understanding dawned on them. They problem was not the design of the page, that problem was a symptom of not recruiting the right people for the role they'd intended. The issue was their marketing, advertising, role description and recruitment strategy. Not the design of the web page.

What Does a Good "How Might We?" Look Like?

We use the statement how MIGHT we rather how CAN we to ensure that we are focusing on the issue we want solving. Using CAN asks a different question: How can we use our available resources and capabilities to solve the issue? How Might We is divorced from the detail of how and is preferable in that it describes the ambition, the positive alternative to the problem we face and what the impact and outcome should be. It should not describe the output.

At the risk of repeating myself, the key concept here is that a How Might We should not contain the solution within it.

To give an example: The people using your service are unhappy and show it in a low customer satisfaction score. You have a workshop to look at the reasons and craft some How Might We statements:
1. "How might we encourage our staff to be more polite?" Not a bad idea, but a solution rather than statement of the brief. Polite staff may be nice to customers, but the statement says nothing about being knowledgeable or helpful. Politeness may be one aspect of an excellent customer service experience, but not the whole solution.
2. "How might we create and train a completely new workforce?" This essentially means firing everyone and starting again. This is an extreme act and probably the last resort when you have admitted defeat. Not a great How Might We.
3. "How might we ensure that every staff member who encounters a person understands and can deliver our brand values?" This is a much stronger How Might We as there a lots of ways it could be developed, is likely to be more sustainable and flexible, as long as your brand values are sensible ones that enhance the service experience.

In forming the How Might We statement, we use a template that divides the sentence into three elements.
1. How Might We ... plus an action. This might be: provide a ..., or improve, ensure, create a new ..., whatever describes in adequate detail what you intend to do.
2. So that ... the users, the people we are designing for, who will be described here in the sense of the problem or desire they have. For example, people who live in the country and do not have access to public transport, or people with health issues that prevent them from working, or people who are looking for sustainable garden equipment – whatever it is you are aiming to solve is placed here.
3. So that ... the positive, desirable outcome is expressed here. This is not the same as the output, the thing you will do. This last part of the sentence allows you to articulate the impact of the brief, what will be the better outcome and result of you solving this brief. For example: so that people can access their local community centres, or people live longer and healthier, or that people have a clear choice and can reduce the environmental impact of garden equipment and influence manufacturers to be more thoughtful.

Let's have a look at some more examples from workshops with a diverse range of challenges.

For refugees with children arriving in a new country:
How might we reduce the communication friction for refugee parents so that they can make the best choices for their children's education that enables them to be successful?

For the employers of social workers who are losing staff at a high rate:
How might we prevent social workers from feeling overwhelmed, because of being overworked and mentally drained, so that fewer resign from the profession and more have quality time with their family?

And a beautifully simple example:
How might we give value for the unseen work for paediatric nurses so that workload evaluation is accurate and patients can receive a high quality of service?

A good How Might We captures enough detail to bring the brief alive, makes the problem and context clear and frames the "so that" as an outcome, not an output, that can be measured.

It's usual to draft a few statements like this before you arrive at the final one, Your statement should capture the broadest scope that allows for creativity to solve it.

What Does Success Look Like?

It's at this point that you can and should establish how you will measure whether you are successful or not. By defining the "so that" conclusion, you are defining the outcome and impact and therefore it should be possible to identify how you will know whether you have reached your objective and had a measurable impact.

Taking the three examples above, how would we measure their success.

For the children of refugee parents, it might take years or even decades before we can see the impact of a good education choice and their reaching a position of thriving in their new society. But perhaps there are weaker signals that would allow us to conclude that things are going in the right direction. Regular school attendance, good reports and marks, for example. Making progress through secondary education and perhaps attending further education. Finally, employment and salary scales might be the ultimate measure, along with a strong social role in the local community. It's not for me to decide, there are experts who will know how to measure success but this is the point we want to hear from them so they can help us define how we will measure both progress and final impact.

For social services employing social workers, outcomes may be quite rapid as the number of resignations against a long-term average should be measurable within years or even months. For the paediatric nurses, change could lead rapidly to positive results, and the additional requirement for a better patient experience may be felt reasonably quickly, again with weak signifiers such as reduced complaints or better recovery rates.

This point is the centre of the process, where the broad discovery of exploration around a problem or a new possibility is followed by analysis, establishing root causes and patterns that expose an underlying issue.

Amongst the many advantages of redesigning our thinking to use design processes and methods, the reframing of a problem is perhaps one of the most essential. It takes data and facts and uses our human ability to appraise and make decisions to set our direction. It can be a simple, factual sentence that does it, but the power of our understanding and insight comes to the fore in setting the direction of our creativity and resources to make change real. This is the tipping point, the point of embarkation, where we can make change happen and know that it is the right direction. The next challenge is to create the solutions that will achieve our ambition and be the measure of our success.

How Do You Redesign Thinking to Define a Problem?

Challenge all your assumptions, ask 5 whys and frame the problem, not the solution.

How to Redesign Design to Define a Problem

Challenge every brief, understand the problem it's trying to solve and help people to frame or reframe the problem or opportunity. It's your battle cry, this is what we will do and solve.

Chapter 7
Time for Creativity

> *The creative process is about surrender, not control.*
> Bruce Lee

Creativity is a mystery to most of us. It is perceived, perhaps, as a luxury, something done by others, who can wear the label of being creative or are "a creative". We often don't believe in our own capability to be creative, imagining that it is something to do with art or literature. Creativity is low on the agenda of skills that are perceived as useful to everyday life, such as rudimentary maths or the ability to analyse information or turning up on time and sending a polite but firm email.

In a world of social strife and inequity, climate crisis, wars caused by insurmountable differences and historical legacy, and economic headwinds and political challenges, you'd think we might occasionally contemplate that we need some new ideas to start to solve some of the issues. Perhaps we need to create some new visions, some new directions, that we can aim at and achieve? Practical, not fantastical, but new all the same, or at least an improvement on what has gone before, but which is no longer working. Perhaps we need some creativity to think differently and find some better directions? But then again, I have 150 emails in my inbox, so I'll leave it for someone else to fix the difficult problems.

Despite our reluctance to consider creativity as a key requirement of human endeavour, creativity is increasingly recognised as the most useful skill we will need in order to answer the challenges of the 21st century. Up to the age of around 7 or 8, we are encouraged to embrace creativity and develop our skills in drawing, painting, and making. Creativity is of course more than that and as we mature towards adults, it becomes about thinking differently, "out of the box" and developing problem solving skills.

And then it stops. In curriculums that focus on the hard topics of maths and engineering and STEM (science, technology, engineering and maths), there is no time for creativity. The focus on the skills many governments prioritise has the effect of unbalancing the combination of scientific knowledge and creative thinking required to resolve the multitude of challenges we face.

Science cannot resolve everything without comprehension of human behaviour. Technology is part of the solution but needs the stewardship and accessibility at the design stage to make what we should make, not can make and ensure it is relevant, accessible, desirable and trustworthy. We need highly expert and creative engineers to make the things that are beautiful and work for all.

Yet we separate it out, remove it from our priorities, place art, music and design in the "soft" bucket of skills that are nice to have, but not essential.

Not only is that a huge and costly mistake but we are throwing away the heritage of humanity in combining technical excellence with innovative and creative ambition. From the Eiffel Tower to a Zaha Hadid building, from the UK telephone box to the iPhone, it is the combination of scientific exploration and invention with human-scale beauty at the point of touch and form that makes humanity amazing and liveable. Yet we continually devalue our creative skills and emphasise the technical.

As a result, we spend very little time, if any, examining problems and applying our creativity to solving them. Our workplaces are designed for intensive managerial correspondence through our screens and keyboards and meetings, held in intransient rooms with big tables and no writing on the walls allowed.

Creativity is scary to most people. They will tell you they are not creative. Creativity is a department somewhere else in the building, perhaps marketing. Creative people are seen as flamboyant, emotional, different, and creative work a risky career for our children to take.

And yet, in the time of rapid developments in AI, creativity is likely to be the strongest differentiation we will have from the march of autonomous job replacement. Of all the roles that could be replaced by AI, creative roles are the feeders into the data and the most likely to keep value and relevance in our future society. Although AI is moving rapidly into areas such as video and content creation, the ability to invent and create new scenarios will be easier for us humans, depending as it does on what we have done in the past to predict what we might do in the future. As John Maeda pointed out, the algorithms didn't predict the success of the 2019 Marvel film *Black Panther* because there had been no films about black superheroes before then.[1]

Creativity is a skill that people desire. Educated in technocratic methods, creativity is increasingly desirable to the upcoming generation of future leaders who realise creativity and a human focus on problem solving are essential in developing human value and innovation in harmony with science and technology. It's not a luxury or an add-on or something to be feared, it's an essential part of our education and a tool to solve the very real problems and challenges that face us every day.

What I enjoy about the design of services, through service design, is the holistic nature of the discipline. In looking across a problem rather than focusing on one part such as the digital or the physical product, you are forced to embrace the systems, the interactions, the emotions and the functions of a service, all at the same time. With the bias for action that someone who is a designer is bound to have, and an optimism that they can make everything better, there is a drive to turn insights and data into action and use creativity to find new solutions. This

---

1 John Maeda, Design in Tech Report, 2019.

is important for all of us; we should understand creativity, and not fear it, and harness our own, along with the creativity of all around us, without fear and self-repression.

A previous Vice Chancellor of the Royal College of Art once suggested that creativity was not for everyone, and he did not think a creative post room would be a good idea. He was reflecting on the essential job of a post room and that creativity might be risky and endanger the core function: Change for change's sake is not desirable.

I reflected on this concern of inappropriate creativity when I read an article on a development by the French post office, France Poste.[2] Staff in their post offices had noticed that their customers were picking up packages of clothing bought online and then rapidly returning with those that didn't fit to send them back to the retailer. The observant post office staff decided that it would be helpful to install a changing room inside the post office with a mirror so that their customers could quickly try the clothes on, reject the ones that didn't fit (the trend to order three garments, small, medium and large and then return the two that don't fit has become an established practice for online fashion purchasing), without the trouble of going home and returning to the post office at another time.

I can understand that careless and frivolous creativity could be seen as dangerous, but the France Poste example is one of great observation, empathy for their customers, piloted and tested before rolled out, that delivers a competitive advantage that will sustain customer loyalty. Brilliant design and good for business!

Creativity is not a threat or a risk when it is properly embedded into our decision-making design process. When we consider the problems and challenges we have in our businesses and lives, they tend not to be solved by emails and meetings but are more likely to be successfully solved by thinking creatively, holistically and pragmatically around a problem to find an outcome that will have a successful, positive impact.

Despite the enormity of the problems around us, we spend so little time thinking collectively about how to solve them. We hide behind our screens and go to yet another meeting or trust that someone somewhere will have a moment of divine inspiration and the tenacity to push their idea through and solve our problems.

If we are to face up to the challenges of our customers, our citizens, the safeguarding of our technology and the crisis of our climate, we need to invest a lot more time in thinking creatively and stop seeing it as a luxury, or something

---

2 "French post office opens changing room for online shoppers", *The Guardian* (UK), 10 January 2024, Agence France-Presse.

done by people who are "creative". We all have a role in this, and all have a contribution to make.

So put that laptop away and start being creative.

Creativity is Scary

Whether through our education, or perception that creativity is only for the arts, many have a problem with the concept of creativity. Creativity is often seen as the result of a moment of almost magical or mystical inspiration, often in a place of isolation such as on a misty mountain top or in the shower. An idea can suddenly form in our minds which we identify as new, better, an innovative way of solving a problem or finding a new way of tackling an unmet need that we recognise.

It can be the result of frustration, perhaps within your job where you see a better way of doing something and can result in entrepreneurship and new businesses. It might be an insight from observation where you see that another way would be better. It might be a vision of a new technology or invention that could save the world.

It's important that we identify creativity with moments of lucidity and clarity, as the conditions of creativity are helped when we are not repressed by our everyday thoughts. When we have perspective of our problems because we are contemplating nature, or relaxed and with clear minds, such as when we are in the shower, that is the moment when we feel we are more likely to have creative thoughts.

But we can be creative at other times too. It is possible to drive your creativity and consciously force ideas out into the open.

For designers, creativity is a solo activity that comes to life when shared. It's internal and collaborative at the same time. Ideas need concentration, silence, deep thinking. Creativity also needs permission, the removal of self-repression and concern about how others might judge you, or you judge yourself. It needs time – not that much – but focused time and usually space, different and away from the office noise of "business as usual" or BAU. BAU is the enemy of creativity and innovation.

Everyone is creative. Whatever role you play in an institution or society, you have the right to use your insights, experience, and observation to trigger thoughts about how you might improve them. We need to wake up and acknowledge the agency we have in the world around us. We can worry about whether our ideas and creativity will be heard or be the right ideas to solve the problems we are concerned with, but none of that can happen if we don't have any ideas and are not prepared to think creatively in the first instance.

Again, people think that certain people are qualified to be creative, that you need to be expert in a field and to have deep knowledge of a subject to be able to consider a new idea. In the kind of creative session I will describe, it is not uncommon to hear an expert refusing to take part in a collaborative idea generating process. They are often appalled, and possibly threatened, that less qualified people than them, with perhaps only slight experience of a problem, can be listened to with the same respect as themselves.

Don't they have a point? Why would creative ideas, without experience and specialist knowledge, be valuable? Let's deconstruct the elements of creativity to challenge and explain why it is a good idea.

When we think of a new idea, we automatically measure that idea against the reality of the current world we live in. It is almost impossible for people to have an idea without immediately self-judging that idea and considering the possibility that it could work, what barriers there might be, and whether their colleagues would consider the idea stupid. Often-heard comments such as "we tried that before and it didn't work" or "there's no way we could afford that" or "that's ridiculous, it will never work". These thoughts kill our confidence and the ideas we've just had, dead. It therefore takes very confident people who don't care what others think to drive forward their ideas. Think of Space X and how Elon Musk decided to land a rocket back to earth upright on its base. Absolutely crazy, but he did it.

So, to allow the flow of ideas to emerge and survive our own repression and the fear of others, we need to construct some conditions.

Permission to Have Ideas

I am constantly amazed at how, when given permission, in a safe space and without fear of judgement, people have brilliant ideas. They don't realise they will have ideas and are usually not comfortable about being expected to have ideas. And yet, when the moment arrives, they do. Lots of them.

We need to give ourselves permission to have ideas. We need to reject the suggestion that you must be an **expert** to have an idea (in my experience, the more expert you are, the more repressed your creativity is). We are all customers, citizens and access services and experiences and know what good and bad looks like and can bring that experience to think of how to improve things. But only if we have permission and are free from aggressive judgement and negative comments.

But isn't it important to make sure we don't have stupid ideas, ones that are impractical or too expensive to produce or the technology doesn't exist yet? What do we do with all these ideas, we can't make all of them?

This is where the shape or format of the various design process diagrams become especially useful and very important.

The Double Diamond makes this very explicit. The Creative part is the first half of the second diamond. It is a divergent activity with the freedom to imagine, create, soar into new territories without fear of consequence or judgement. It is followed by a convergent process that measures effectiveness, analyses cost, risk and practicality. But without soaring creativity you have very little to analyse, no opportunity for the new idea, no innovation, and no competitive differentiation.

It's okay to have a hundred ideas because one of these will be successful. Even if none of them are any good, they will start the chain reaction that will unveil ideas that will solve, practically and effectively, your problems or define the route to success.

CEOs and politicians traditionally have a single idea and, surprised and delighted at the combination of their creativity and power, can enforce their idea and run down the pitch of development, carrying resources and finance with them till they triumphantly deliver their objective at the far end of the pitch without fear of challenge or distraction. No one dare challenge or threaten to detract them from their grand projects.

From banks to governments, healthcare policies to technology push projects, the world is littered with appalling ideas that remained free from challenge or testing, devoid of insight from people who would use them or empathy for their context.

Design a risk reduction process. It is a way of making the right decision in the knowledge of what a wrong one is, with the humility to realise you can be wrong before you become right.

Have a lot of ideas. Tease them out, share them and imagine what they look like. None of these ideas is real, yet, but we can imagine, and model and produce a simple prototype and see if people like it or can suggest improvements, without spending anything at all. Isn't that an attractive proposition?

The design methods give you permission to have lots of ideas because we need a lot of ideas, and we can separate the act of having ideas from the act of analysing them. This might seem wasteful, but not as wasteful as having a single wrong idea that is developed at speed and great cost and then found to fail, which is how most things are developed in the world now.

What About My Hunch?

We like a hunch. I just feel it is right, my instinct and experience combine to make me strongly believe that my hunch is right.

The Double Diamond appears to say that you must do research and base your ideas on your deeper knowledge of insight of what the problem is. That seems to leave little room for hunches. But the Double Diamond does leave a lot of room for lots of creative ideas, which in a way can all be described as hunches.

At the 20th anniversary of the Double Diamond held in the design company IDEO's London office, one audience member was clearly unhappy with all this talk of design process. Perhaps he felt that creativity is a free thing, and one should have the right and freedom to follow one's intuition. Gill Wildman, part of the Design Council team who created the original diagram from their research, answered that the space inside the diamond is where the hunches live. The difference that the diagram brings is that all hunches are treated as equal, and the process will allow all ideas to be validated against the objective of the project. Prototyping and testing will ensure those ideas that best solve the problem or opportunity are the ones that are taken forward.

Having a hunch is not a divine right to build your idea. It's a divine right to allow the idea to be examined, visualised and prototyped and tested and then, if successful, merit design and development resource being used to make it real. Ideas have the duty to accept they might fail, and not be taken forward and not waste valuable resources that could be used in ideas that are more promising and impactful.

To be creative, we must remove the ego and power politics of whoever thought of the idea or their power within the organisation. Design methods challenge all ideas, assume you have a 50/50 chance of being right or wrong, celebrate as much when we are wrong as when are right.

In the Innovation Centre of France Telecom, designers were working with technologists, research development scientists, marketing and business leaders to create "moon-shot" innovations to capture new markets and opportunities in the exiting emerging world of triple play mobile, broadband and content. Projects were accepted into the centre for a period of three months, and, at the end of that period, a decision was made as to whether they would continue for a second three months of development. My French colleagues explained to me that, based on customer feedback, a project could continue, be accelerated, or closed down. Whatever the result, the team drank champagne. The killing of a project to free resources for another candidate was as successful as finding a project that was working or working so well that it should be accelerated.

This is the attitude we should take into our creative mindset. Failure is success and reason to drink champagne, and at such an early stage a painless and reasonably low cost one. Failure can be learnt from, and someone who has failed is more likely to succeed next time.

The Philosophy of Failure

Judah Armani, author of *Society Driven Design* and founder of InHouse Records and an award-winning social innovator and educationalist, is a fan of failure. For him, "failure needs to become our best friend" and is an essential part of learning. In failing, we drive iteration and if we can overcome organisational or our own unwillingness to admit failure and can instead learn from it, to drive our ambition to create better solutions.

Going further than just admitting failure, Armani uses the Socratic dialogues – Plato's examination of theoretical positions through the eyes of Socrates – where the starting point is our innocence and lack of knowledge. In this way we "learn" about our own assumptions and perspectives and use dialogue to learn and understand people and systems before creating new interventions.

So, creativity demands that we overcome our perceptions and prejudices against our own ability to be creative, it removes the fear of judgement and embraces an ethos of learning through failing, not protecting or defending ideas or using our political power to discriminate between one idea and another based on our personal preference. There is a sense of science here that creativity has rules that both liberate us and remove the bias of our power to ensure that once we understand the problem or opportunity, we can then create the solution or innovative new direction to be followed.

How to Be Creative

We have challenges and they need to be solved. We can make things work better, for people, our organisation, business or the planet. There is no other way to rise to these challenges than through creativity. It might be creative accounting, new technology, cultural change or system transformation, but the only way we are going to make progress is by being creative.

There are rules for creativity. Creativity requires that we put things down and move away from the everyday activities of our labour that are the enemy of creativity. There is always another email to write, meeting to attend but at a certain point we need to set up the correct platform, set the stage and prepare the ground for creativity. Here are my rules:

1. Stop Business as Usual. This can be difficult, but it is vital that the three essential ingredients of creativity – people, time and place – are satisfied.
People and time go together. You need people first, and they can be a surprisingly broad group of people from around the topic area you are exploring for new creative solutions. People with empathy for people who use the service, whether they are inside or outside the organisation. People who understand and have

some experience of the issues, perhaps feel the pain of a customer or someone who is accessing their service. People who are keen to create improvement, make things better. They can be managers, people-facing, curious and without an agenda for their one and only idea (see previous). They may have a range of perspectives from legal to accounting to delivery to marketing to design. The wider the input the better, especially when creativity becomes collaborative when it needs to be delivered.

I usually recommend that the one person you should not have in a creative session is the boss. It is not that surprising that people try and impress their boss and usually do not want to challenge or disagree with them. Therefore, a senior manager in a creative session can create a creativity distortion field where everyone agrees with their ideas, and all agree that theirs is the best. However, in some circumstances, I have seen bosses and senior managers really enjoy the flat hierarchy of a truly open creative process and marvel at the joint creativity of their teams. But usually, their role is to be presented to, and make the tough decisions about which ideas go forward, based on the objectives of the project. If in doubt, leave them out.

You don't need that much time to be creative, just focus, which makes it even more strange how little time we use in creatively solving the issues we face every day. But time is required, a time where people can come together to invest their shared efforts in creating new possibilities. Carve out the time and combine it with a different space, one that provides a place where everyone is on neutral territory, so the quiet can coexist with the loud, there are no distractions and people can be relieved of their "business as usual" pressures and other distractions.

Most offices do not have the spaces that are conducive to creativity, and space can be a liberating factor in creativity. Creative spaces are simple and have surfaces that you can pin ideas up on to and share tables that you can commune around rather than meet at. Spaces can be digital and virtual white boards and virtual meetings can be very successfully used for creativity.

Sometimes you need a different space, one that gets people out of their everyday mindset. It does not have to have beanbags and loud colours, The Disneyfication of creativity is seen in advertising agencies, consultancies and corporations and usually heralds the death of creative thought. In my experience, a successful creative space is neutral and messy which does not have the Post-its torn down by the overly efficient office managers at the end of the day.

2. Be in the Room. To be creative requires focus. You need to concentrate and not be distracted. Laptops should not just be shut but not on the table. Phones on silent and away. This is an investment that needs to be respected if it is to be successful, so attention is vital.

This is the time to bring all your knowledge of the data and insight of the behaviour of your users, customers and citizens, your business culture, organisation behaviour, systems, and things good and bad to focus on making them better. It's the time for ambition to do not just the right thing for them and your organisation now but to dream of what brilliant and beautiful could look like. It's time to sort out the things that don't work and dream of how things could be. It's time to be creative, so get into the zone.

Creativity in design is a collaborative venture, where ideas come from individuals and are shared and built on. For this reason, it's important to understand and respect the people you are collaborating with, to build both your and their confidence and confidence in the joint endeavour.

One technique for this is to establish who your co-creatives are and what their skills and attributes are. One method is to ask everyone in the room to describe and draw their superhero skill. In a world of comic book superheroes, it's fun and revealing to express what your superhero skill might be to each other.

For example, you might feel you are experienced and understand the organisation and the people in it and who use it. You might express that as a wise Owl and let's add a cape to the drawing to emphasise that this is your superhero skill.

You might believe you are a detail person, and you might draw that as a magnifying glass or a microscope. With a superperson cape of course. These exercises also broach the difficult subject of drawing and one of the tools of creative sessions is drawing. So, getting people used to drawing and overcoming everyone's belief that they can't draw is a helpful start to being collectively creative.

Creativity needs a level playing field too. Innovation and creativity are fuelled by diversity of people and points of view. We cannot afford to ignore the voices of those we don't normally see or hear. If we design without a cross-section of diversity and neurodiversity, our ideas will be less able to succeed in the world we are designing for. A quiet person can have the best ideas and if they are drowned out by the noisy, we will lose that value, that possibility of a better solution that fits all.

Inclusivity

Creating an inclusive environment is a vital part of workshops. Whether colleagues, students or customers, we have different capabilities, cultures, languages, and a range of different approaches. Inclusivity is the principle that all participants have the same, equitable inclusive experiences. For creativity, it is particularly important to ensure everyone can contribute and not feel left out.

1. An inclusive space. Any space should take account of physical access needs to buildings and the space. If working with a number of teams, you need to allow space between teams to reduce interruptions and ensure each can communicate. You may need extra spaces for participants who have different

hearing capabilities or collaboration styles. Ensure you do this well in advance of your creative session.
2. Think about neurodiversity. We all have levels of diversity of approach, thinking and working collaboratively with others. Informing all to respect and embrace all types of thinking will contribute to successful outcomes and greater understanding.
3. Respect culture. You want to ensure that there is diversity of heritage and cultural traditions across your team. Applications of methods and concepts can be very different in different contexts – make sure everyone understands the value of exploring these differences.[3]

Everyone Has a Good Idea

The ability to have a good idea should not be associated with having a level of expertise, intelligence or creative reputation. Everyone can have a good idea and has the right for it to be respected and considered without fear of shame.

I have sometimes come across people with great expertise who are unable to come to terms with a room full of different people who are perhaps less expert than them. This kind of arrogance is, thankfully, rare and sometimes there is no other answer than to ask them to leave. Hopefully they will stay. It is very important to create an environment that is safe and fair and removes the threat of judgement, either by yourself or your co-creators. We need to have everyone's ideas, to remove all barriers and mine the creativity of everyone.

With many teams who are about to collaborate together, especially before an idea-generating session, I use a simple online tool that helps people identify what type of creative person they are. One example that works well is "My Creative Type", (www.mycreativetype.com). After completing a simple online questionnaire, you are sorted into one of eight different creative characteristics: Adventurer, Dreamer, Visionary, Artist, Innovator, Producer, Thinker or Maker. It's a sort of Myers-Briggs for creativity, is fun, a great icebreaker and reveals a lot about yourself that helps you understand why your teammates think differently and don't always agree with you. I'm an Adventurer by the way.

We need to get used to the idea that everyone has an idea, and that creative people are not the only people to have them. In fact, the role of the creatives is more usefully to visualise and bring an idea to life, but not always to be the one who has the idea. It's a team effort, which will light up your imagination, give

---

[3] SDN (Service Design Network) – Service Design Day Workshop: Starting with Inclusive Design You Tube video providing detailed analysis of running equitable inclusive workshops. https://www.youtube.com/watch?v=1FFrQXs7gOw

you ambition and positive outlook and improve your life and. Hopefully the lives of others too if you're successful.

Everyone Can Draw

This one always gets a sharp intake of breath.

People tend to believe that drawing is an ability that only few have. We are discouraged from drawing at an early point in our education, leaving those identified as "artistic" to be the ones who retain the ability to draw.

Another way of seeing drawing is as a valuable communication tool that is as useful and simple as writing, only much quicker and better at visualising context than having to write a description. To be effective, a drawing does not have to look beautiful; it just has to communicate an idea and its context.

But people are very afraid when in a creative session they are asked to draw their ideas. There is as much self-repression in drawing as there is in being creative.

But in service design especially, the concept of capturing an idea rapidly and simply is an essential part of the process. There's a reason service designers love pastel-shaded Post-it notes. They are small and when using a broad-nibbed pen such as a Sharpie pen, also beloved of service designers, it is difficult to write a long treatise or explanation of an idea. It is much quicker to try and capture your idea as a drawing.

An example I often give is to draw a stick person. A circle for the head, a vertical line for the body and four lines representing arms and legs. Done. Then I add a small rectangle to one of the arms. This is the simplest representation of a mobile phone I can do. I then draw, to one side, a rectangle with another one alongside it to represent an open door and a door frame. I have communicated the idea that a door will open when I approach with my mobile phone. It takes me a lot less time to draw that then it has taken me to write out this paragraph.

This lack of confidence and lost method of communication is a shame and perpetuates the idea that everything we are talking about in this book is the unique attribute of a certain sort of creative person when it is a vital and incredibly useful tool for us all. Don't be afraid: Everyone can draw.

Rules of Collaborative Creativity

The innovation and design company IDEO were pioneers of collaborative creation sessions where teams of people gather round for timed periods to generate ideas. Brainstorming, ideation, co-creation or collaborative creative discussions, call them what you like but they have value in rapidly forming large numbers of ideas that can be critically analysed and formed into new solutions.

There are many examples of new and innovative products, services and solutions to big challenges being generated in this way. The advantages of collaborative creativity is the diversity of thought, the speed and breadth of ideas generated and the ability to quickly communicate them and work them into tangible concepts that can be tested and developed.

They have the advantage of greater democracy and dissipation of the power structures around idea creation (if it is the boss's or a senior manager's idea for example). But it's also true that these techniques are criticised for giving advantages to some personality types and not providing access to diverse opinions and communication styles.

Using a great facilitator is one solution to this – possibly the most important skill for a service designer is one of facilitation: the ability to bring the right people together and create the right conditions where all voices and style of voice can be heard equitably.

For a successful creative workshop, there are several important aspects that a facilitator must master:
- A safe and equitable platform for creativity that allows all to take part in a respectful and encouraging way. Set the tone to remind participants of their responsibilities to ensure a fair and equitable discussion that includes all.
- Clear objectives for what you are trying to achieve in the workshop, so nobody wanders off in a meaningless direction.[4]

Defer Judgement

A workshop is a positive space to collectively explore a concept. It is not a place to criticise individual thoughts or comments, so it is vital to ensure everyone understands that this is not a place to criticise individual thoughts.

This is a difficult one for many people. It is our intuitive behaviour, and one that we think makes us look smart, that we should offer judgement at the first instance. But if we want to develop a kite that flies, we shouldn't shoot it down too soon. Once it has flown and we can appraise it, there may be a time to improve or put aside, but we can only do that once the kite has flown and has not been shot down at the first instance. Design processes emphasise the necessity of letting ideas come into being in our minds before we start to analyse, so this rule is a vital one that needs to be strictly enforced. Defer judgement and let the ideas fly.

---

4 IDEO.org Human-Centred Design Toolkit: The Facilitator's Guide – a guide, templates and planning tools to run a workshop on human-centred design. https://www.ideo.org/tools

Encourage Wild Ideas

It's okay to think beyond the now. It's okay to dream and think further out, even if ridiculous. Go to your extreme "what if?" And "what if?" beyond that?

Wild ideas are free and cannot damage anything. They can move the goalposts, trigger bigger thoughts, reframe our horizons and reset our ambition. Could we do that? Dare we think of an idea that big?

If we don't have crazy ideas now, when will we? Sometimes it's the crazy ideas that show us the route forward. It was, again, a wild idea to land a rocket back on Earth on its base, but they did it. It was a wild idea to go look for India the other way round the globe. It was a wild idea to go to the moon, and then bring the astronauts back safely.

Our greatest enemy once again is our own self repression. You have permission (and a good facilitator needs to give that permission very clearly) to think big and embrace the unthinkable. If Steve Jobs hadn't imagined a phone without a keypad and a screen image that could grow and shrink under your fingers, we wouldn't have the iPhone. So don't be afraid, push yourself to think beyond the present, beyond the possible, it just might lead to the idea that will solve your challenge or break through the horizon of opportunity.

Stay Focused on the Topic

Having said go crazy, don't go off track on your objective. If you're trying to get to the moon, don't wander off to Saturn.

The value in creativity is that it is in the context of the framing of your brief. More than that, it's in the service of achieving what you have already defined as success. This makes creativity focused, targeted and easier – you can understand what you are trying to achieve, and all your ideas are small, medium or wild crazy versions of solutions that will get you there.

One Conversation at a Time

Conversation and dialogue are a vital part of creativity. In a traditional brainstorming, we need to respect each voice and allow it to express an idea (whilst drawing it as the same time, of course). A poorly led or facilitated session will dissolve into chaos and when everyone is pumped up and has ideas, it's difficult to listen and wait your turn.

Creativity methods such as Crazy 8s have the advantage of being silent and solo during the idea-generating stage and then allow for full sharing of all the ideas by each individual before they begin to be analysed, grouped and rated according to their ability to solve the challenge of the brief. This makes for a more equitable and fairer platform for idea sharing, but we should still remain wary of power politics and stronger personality types driving the agenda.

Be Visual

Capture your ideas in a visual way. Use even the most basic drawings and diagrams to capture the essence of your idea – you can add some bullet points if you need, but drawing is such an efficient and understandable way of communicating a concept, it can really help others to understand and appreciate each idea.

Go for Quantity

This is your chance to think of everything you can that will satisfy your objective. You can have other creative sessions where you will build and develop ideas in different directions, but this is the chance to capture as many as you can. There is no advantage in having less ideas at this stage. Having 100 ideas means you have a much greater chance of having the one that will be successful. Harvest, capture, express, consider and create as many ideas as you can – you will have plenty of time to evaluate and analyse to sort the wheat from the chaff later.

Creativity Methods

Creativity can be structured, organised and prepared for and there are several methods you can follow to generate ideas.

1. Crazy 8s
Crazy 8s were invented by development teams at Google as a way of busting difficult problems. Rather than cogitating in the corner with a technical conundrum, they believed organised impromptu sessions where they invited other engineers and colleagues and asked them to have an idea in one minute and then repeat with other ideas 8 times, hence the name. The method is described in the book *Sprint*, which captures a whole raft of methods for developing innovative, or just problem-fixing ideas in a focused way. Much of what has become to be known as Agile has come from this approach.[5]

---

[5] Braden Kowitz, Jake Knapp, and John Zeratsky, *Sprint: How to Solve Big Problems and Test New Ideas in Just Five Days*, Simon & Schuster, 2016.

Crazy 8s are frightening to most people. The idea that it is possible to have 8 ideas, and to do it in 8 minutes, seems impossible, However, in my executive education classes at the Royal Collage of Art and with individual clients, I have taken around a thousand people through this and, in all but one case, people came out of the experience amazed at their ability to have ideas having successfully got to 8, or at least 7 ideas in the process.

How to set up a Crazy 8:
The Crazy 8 method has a nice amount of ritual to distract participants and get them ready for idea generation.

1. Prepare your paper.
It is preferable to use a piece of A3, or US tabloid sized paper, which is often found in a photocopier tray, but equally A4 or US letter size paper, or a page of your foolscap notebook is fine.

In the ritual you take your piece of paper and hold in landscape, or horizontal format, with the long edge at the top and bottom of the paper. Then fold it in half, so that the two short sides come together, and the long edge is halved. Turn the paper through 90 degrees and make a sharp crease.

Do this two more time, folding along the long edge each time. When you open the paper up, you will find that you have eight segments defined by the creases in the paper and you will use each one of these for your different idea.

Alternatively, you can draw a line vertically down the centre of your notebook, then a horizontal line halfway across at the middle of the page. Finaly, draw two more horizontal lines one above and one below at to quarter the halves and you then have 8 segments, one for each idea.

2. Set the timer.
Ideally, you have a facilitator who is running the meeting. It is the facilitator's job to ensure everyone is following the method correctly and set a timer on their phone or clock for one minute

3. Get Ready.
Ensure everyone has a pen (preferably a Sharpie-type thick felt pen, but anything will do). Ensure that no one is jumping the gun.
Prepare to create that ideas that:
- Respond to the brief and problem or opportunity that has been framed, usually as a "How Might We" statement, and be aimed at the agreed definition of success.
- Build on the insight and data already collected and shared.
- Take one whole minute, do not jump onto the next idea.

- Divide the minute into sections, a guideline would be: thinking of the idea, (30 seconds), thinking how you can draw it (10 seconds), and then drawing it (20 seconds). A minute is a surprisingly long time.
- Do not rush through and have 8 ideas in one minute! Respect the time and the idea.
- Don't panic, you will get through it.

4. Start.

There are different approaches to the 8 minutes. The concentration and intensity of everybody working silently in creating ideas can be distracting, so you may try some ambient music, though some see that is distracting.

The facilitator can encourage. I liken the experience to going to the gym and learning new exercises to build your creative muscles. It aches a bit the first time but you get used to it. Encourage people at the halfway point, encourage wild ideas or building ideas towards the end.

5. Finish.

At the end of the 8 minutes congratulate and point out the amazing achievement of the team or group. In a workshop of 30 people in 6 teams, each team has just had 40 ideas. The whole room has generated 240 ideas in 8 minutes. When did that ever happen in anyone's lives before! I usually show a GIF of a firework display to celebrate the conclusion of the last minute.

This is the power of the Crazy 8. It's not the total answer and it's just a start but it is inspiring and exciting to see how creative we can be. And then we do some more . . .

6. Thematic idea creation.

It may seem cruel, but I always follow up with a second exercise with ideas stimulated by certain themes.

Ask people to have a second piece of paper (ignore the groans). This time we will fold it just twice so that there are 4 sections defined by the creases.

We then provide a theme for each of the next 4 ideas. These tend to be slightly easier for people, so I generally give 40 seconds rather than a minute.

Idea 1: "How would Apple solve your problem?"

I use Apple or an equivalent logo of a global brand that everyone recognises. Apple represent design excellence, human-centred user interface, radical ideas around retail and other touchpoints, and the strong innovative mindset and leadership of Steve Jobs. It doesn't matter that this may have no relevance to your problem, thinking like Apple allows the participants to step into a different framework of possibilities.

Idea 2: "How would Disney solve your problem?"
Disney deal in fantasy and imagination. They can do anything, fly on a magic carpet, create a fantasy world where the laws of physics don't exist or make a film that delights and inspires our imagination. Like the Magic Wand question in research, we are liberated from reality and can say what we would really want, if only the world had magic in it.

Idea 3: "How would your competitor solve your problem?"
Many people find this particularly liberating as it is in a related field yet with different rules or a more innovative mindset. I am always amazed at how creative people become when they imagine they are working for a competitor.

Idea 4: "How would a great Disruptor solve your problem?"
Examples I have used in the past include disruptors such as Donald Trump or Elon Musk or more positive disrupters who resound with participants in different parts of the world.

This can be especially liberating and being given permission to behave badly or cut through all rules and barriers can unleash a lot of creativity and is always fun.

These structured idea-generation sessions can be enlarged to cover many potential themes, all with the objective of removing or repression and creating a framework where we think freely and differently, outside of consideration of the barriers and problems that might retrain our creativity. There is plenty of time for that but in this instance, let go, think the unimaginable and drive your ideas out into the open.

Sharing Ideas

To conclude this creative session, ideas are shared within the teams or the other participants. This needs to be done in a timely way so a few rules:
- Describe each of your ideas succinctly using the drawings to communicate the idea.
- Do not explain how it works or why you thought of it, just share the ideas. Take a maximum of 30 seconds per idea.
- Nod in agreement and enjoy the ideas you are hearing but don't question at this moment, remember that judgement is deferred.
- Remember the ideas you like, make a note of those you think work best, you will be asked to rate them once everyone has presented.

Brainstorming

The traditional method pioneered by the likes of IDEO use many of the same techniques but are more fluid and open-ended. People, time and place are still all important, but equity and inclusivity are even more important as brainstorming is a constant multi-person collaborative conversation where ideas are shared, built on, developed and allowed to flourish in a group conversation.

The rules of engagement are as before: Defer judgement, one conversation at a time, encourage wild ideas but stay on track. Several techniques have been developed over the years to facilitate single conversation and an environment of listening and respecting different behaviours. A favourite of many service design facilitators is to use an artefact such as a rubber chicken which is held by the speaker and handed to next contributor.

A brainstorming should last around 20 minutes, as ideas run out and exhaustion sets in. The emphasis should again be on drawing and time is needed to clarify and organise the outputs. Voting is a method for capturing and agreeing on the best ideas.

Co-Creativity

We've touched on co-creation as a research tool, but this can be an effective way of creating ideas with the people who will be using the service or product outputs. Co-creation can sometimes refer to collaboration across different people inside an organisation, but the real power comes from including and collaborating with people who will access the gain benefit from what you are designing.

Working with people who might use your service requires a different approach to working with a team of designers or managers, but the value in understanding and sharing the pen is enormous and creates a new relationship between those responsible for defining and designing a new interaction that is intended to benefit people.

Many people are not used to imagining what doesn't yet exist. It is usual for people to express ideas that are based on the world around them or that they have seen in the world around them. This is not meant to be condescending, it's just that we spend very little time imagining what could be and therefore the situation and context of co-creation is important to get value and insight form the participants.

Designers are used to filling blank pieces of paper where many find that intimidating and uncomfortable, so we need to prepare the way and stimulate co-creators to build their horizons and creativity and give them the agency to start to for the products and interactions they need and desire.

Co-creation is not the same as having your customer design your product or service; for all the reasons given above, co-creation can be an excellent tool for research and not a tool for design at all. But the benefits of creating together, understanding the implications, what might work and what might not, the potential barriers to adoption, unforeseen consequences of a decision in the context of people's lives, make this a powerful and highly effective tool for designing better outcomes.

There are many good examples of co-creation techniques: The UK Policy Lab have produced a set of tools and guidelines to explore different ways of collaborating and co creating[6] and agencies such as IDEO provide excellent method cards to inspire and guide on how to co-create and generate ideas you would never have imagined.

Voting on Ideas

One way to start to sort the ideas once they are presented is to ask everyone to vote on those that seem to offer the best solutions to the original objective.

Before doing this, look at the ideas and where there are similar ideas, cluster them together as one idea so that votes aren't wasted on repeated concepts.

Traditionally, participants are given three votes and using coloured stick dots or virtual dots if on a virtual whiteboard, choose their favourite 3 ideas. It's not easy, but encourage people to not be influenced by the dynamics of the group and if you think an idea has value but no one else has put a dot against, don't be put off, be true to yourself.

Once the ideas have been voted on, the discussion about how they can be formed into a new solution begins.

Capturing Ideas

At this point, ideas and concepts that are agreed on can be captured and traditionally this is done on an idea canvas. An idea canvas forces us to consider a number of essential aspects of the idea that will validate whether it is impactful, feasible and likely to be successful.

The standard template for an idea canvas can be used across all relevant ideas and is an excellent way of preparing for presentations and sharing of ideas

---

6 Sanjan Sabherwal and Neha Sharma, Launching our experimental policy design methods, UK Policy Lab, May 2022, Openpolicy.blog.gov.uk

with colleagues and for prototyping and forming into tangible, deliverable product or service.

Another useful canvas is the theory of change (Figure 7.1). How does an idea achieve its objective? An idea transforms, restarts, fixes and opens up new possibilities. Do you know how your idea will do this? Then use the theory of change canvas to kick your own tyres and make sure you know why your idea is going to get you to your objective.

What Next?

The real output of these ideas comes when they are placed into the vision that can capture not just the idea but the context, experience, delivery feasibility and action plan that we call the blueprint. The idea is just the start, not the end. It is just one ingredient in creating a full-service experience, one that is accessible, desirable, fulfils its objectives and is economically, technically, organisationally and sustainably deliverable.

How Do You Redesign Thinking to Be Creative?

Creativity is a team game that will generate ideas that will fix your problems, open up new opportunities and set your North Star.

Don't be afraid of creativity. Don't have just one idea. Allow time and space for creativity, emails don't solve business problems or global challenges. Having lots of ideas is good – it doesn't mean you will build them all, but you will increase your chances of having a really good idea.

And defer judgement – this is the time to celebrate creativity; you can choose, kill and prioritise ideas once you have had them and let them fly.

How Do You Design with Creativity?

It sounds strange but some designers are frightened of creativity, The certainty and solid ground of research is the foundation for the next stage – creativity. But even designers can find it difficult to step off land and imagine the new.

But creativity is the supper skill we all have and forget to use. It leads to ideas, and those can be tested, evaluated and chosen according to their effectiveness. So don't worry, imagine, visualise, create the new scenarios that can be prototyped. Then you'll know.

126 —— Chapter 7 Time for Creativity

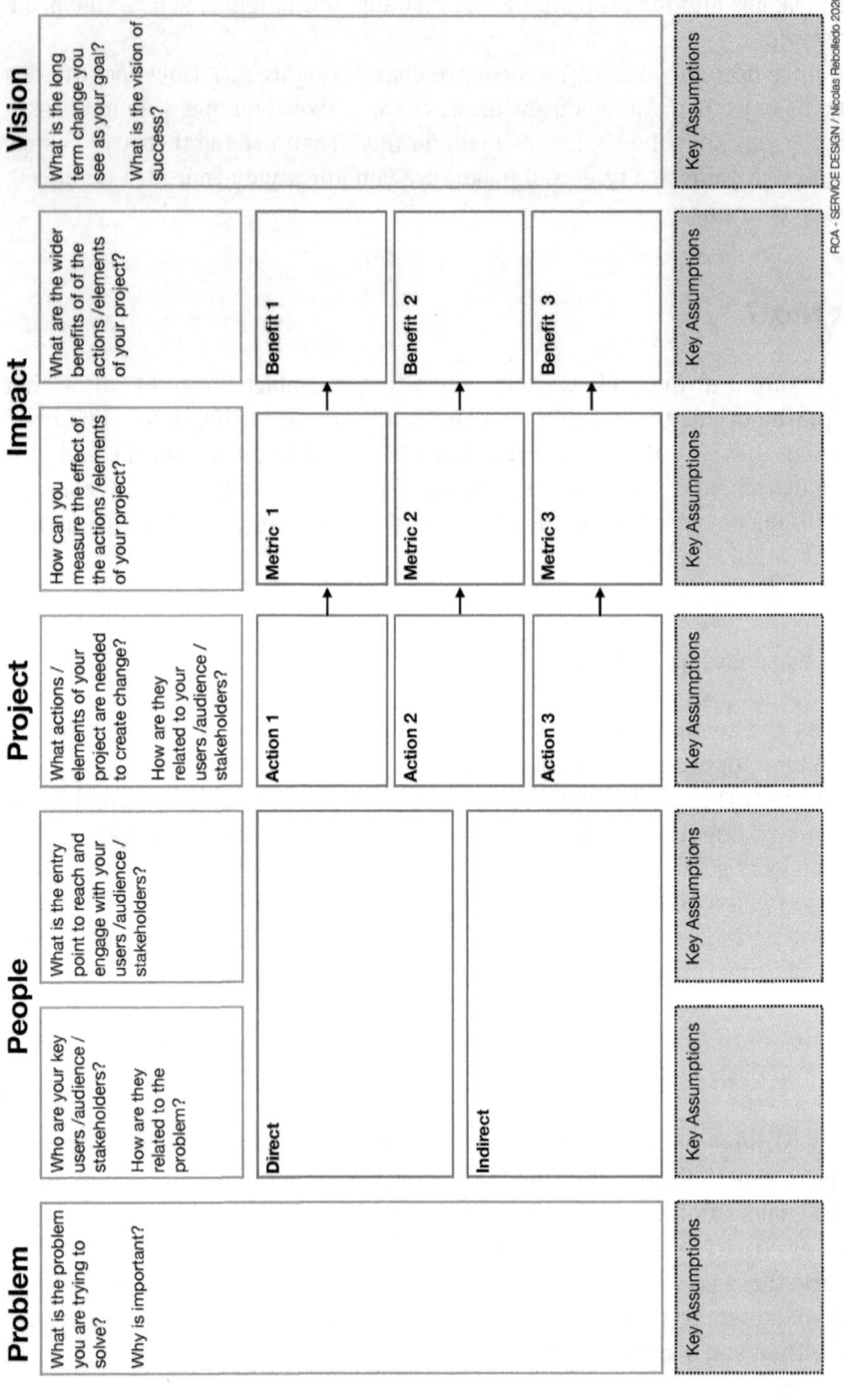

Figure 7.1: Theory of Change Canvas, Nicolas Rebolledo 2016, based on Nesta DIY 2014.

Chapter 8
The Power of the Prototype

Developing a prototype early is the number one goal for our designers, or anyone else who has an idea, for that matter. We don't trust it until we can see it and feel it.
Win Ng

If you want to find out if something might work or not, or if your idea is attractive to the people who will use it, or if you want to understand where problems you hadn't foreseen might lie, what do you do? Build it and see what happens when you launch?

Sadly, for most companies and organisations the answer to this question is yes.

Yes, to spending lots of money developing the idea, with teams of agile developers or workstreams of resources working to deliver your idea. Yes, to launching it with marketing pushing it hard to make sure it has the impact you wish.

Yes, to finding out that it's not what people want, or that it is a neat piece of innovation but it doesn't work in the way people want it to. Or yes to launching a really cool product or service that actually doesn't work. Can you imagine doing that?

Now imagine that at business school, at a module of your MBA or economics degree, they teach you a magic process where you can test all these things BEFORE you spend the money and development resources and marketing budget. It's called a risk assessment and validation process whereby you can massively increase the confidence in the success of your idea, modify the design to remove barriers that people will have and massively decrease the risk associated with innovation or developing a new product. Along with the promise that you could reduce the chances of after-launch modifications that will cost you 100 times more than they cost you when you use this process.

This process is prototyping. It a process of simulating the important elements of your idea and experiencing how something works before you have actually make it.

Prototyping is one of the most important and valuable tools in this armoury of redesigned thinking. Before we start to understand how it works and why it's so valuable, let's break some perceptions about prototyping.

For many, a prototype is a near final version of a new idea. Perhaps not beautiful, but engineered and built in a cruder way than the final product: one that will show everyone that it is possible, that it will work, and it will do what you wish it to do. It may not use the finished manufactured parts but will prove the concept, show that it is possible and works.

Another example of a prototype is a piece of paper stuck on a mobile phone that has some buttons drawn on that say, "Start Training Here". No technology, no engineering: just the essence of what you want to check people understand and want to use. It costs nothing, but tells you everything.

This is what we mean by prototyping. A prototype can be the simplest, cheapest thing in the world, but it tells you something you need to know. Do people understand what this is? Do they want it in the first place? And can they use it if they do? Possibly the three most important questions that never get asked.

Imagine creating an innovative idea, perhaps through an excellent brainstorming or Crazy 8. You have a choice: send it the development team and get them to start engineering it. Or make a fake advert for the idea.

We tend to make adverts right at the end of the process when conventional marketing is given a brief for something that has already been developed and asked to sell. But what if we redesigned this way of thinking? What if we made a really glossy advert of the idea that doesn't exist yet, but will shortly swallow up huge resources and money? What if we showed that advert to the customers or the people who will use it? They would see a new idea and they could tell you if they wanted it, if they understood it and ask you about how it might work or tell you how they don't want it to work.

When you heard back from them and they said they didn't want it, what would you do? Go back to the drawing board? Listen to their reasons and redesign your idea to overcome their concerns? Keep trying until you got a great reaction and they really liked the idea and how it worked and were asking you when would it be available?

This is what prototyping is about. It allows you to find out where the risks are, right at the start. All that development work, engineering, system changing, and organisation transformation might be completely wasted, and have to be redone later, if you were so stupid as to make something without capturing the essence of the idea and checking people want it. Make the advert first. Listen to what they say.

When you're a designer, prototyping is the difference between being a designer and being a fantasist. In their sublime short treatise on prototyping, designers Nick Durant and Gill Wildman state that "without prototyping, there is no design". You can do all the research you like, imagine as many solutions as you can but that is all just a potential idea until the moment when you create a representation of what that looks like and bring it too life.[1]

Bringing it to life is what happens when you prototype something. You do not need to bring the technology, engineering or system to life. You need to bring the essence of the experience, what will people see and do, to life so that we can react. React, interact, love, hate, suggest, be perplexed – this is what happens

---

[1] Gill Wildman and Nick Durrant, *The Politics of Prototyping*, 26 June 2010, self published, ISBN-10 1446131424.

when we have the emotional interaction that is triggered when we see something that represents the value and potential of an idea. And that can be done with a fake advert, or a Post-it on a mobile phone, a cardboard box that represents a bank, or a health clinic reception or a seat tipped on its back to send you to outer space. No technology, no rocket fuel, no reality required, except the essence of what people will see and do.

Our traditional thinking says we have to have built something to believe it. But by the time we have built something, based on assumptions, usually incorrect, about what people want or how they will use it, we have already massively increased our risk of failure. But to turn our thinking around and make the advert first is very counterintuitive and hard to do. But that is what we need to do to save us the enormous cost of correcting something that we find out is wrong after it has been delivered.

Solving an Argument

Designers are good at prototyping because they make stuff. They can visualise an idea, mock up the advert, create a fake digital image, or use a simple app to simulate how something works, without having to do all the stuff that would make it work in real life.

When they visualise a possible product or mock up an advert for something that doesn't exist, or visualise a choice on a Post-it or mock up a driverless car from a cardboard box, we immediately react. We engage, we ask questions, we think about what we might do, what our fears are and what might go wrong. This is such a magic aspect of design and it's one we can use at every moment, if we wish.

I often see design students, managers and top civil servants stroking their chins trying to decide what to do. What they need to do is:

Stop Trying to Get it Right in One Go

Have an idea and imagine the simplest way you could test your hypothesis. Do the simplest thing you can to test your idea, with your colleagues, with their colleagues, with the people who will actually use it and listen to what they say.

If you want to solve an argument about the best solution to a problem, prototype it and ask people. Or as I sometimes say, fake it until you find out if you should make it.

The humility to understand that you don't necessarily know the right solution is a powerful part of thinking as a designer. As we've heard, Plato, in his Socratic stories, casts Socrates as an innocent who asks questions and forms his opinion of the world from the answers he receives. We have forgotten this, and our concepts of leadership rarely allow us to admit we are wrong. But a leadership style that is empathetic, considerate and listens, will embrace this approach and as a result create better outcomes.

Prototypes, in the form of simple modelling of available choices in a way we can engage with and pass opinion on, have several valuable outcomes.

1. They resolve arguments. By visualising two alternative choices, even in a diagram, or a more experiential way, we allow ourselves to see the impact of each idea, and this enhances our ability to decide which is best. It takes away the personal belief and replaces it with evidence.
2. Prototypes reduce risk. The engagement and understanding that comes with interaction with even a crude prototype cannot fail to teach us of the potential impact of the concept and also where there may be barriers or issues that we haven't foreseen. Showing an idea in way that implies it will be real in the future is a powerful trigger for opinion and comment, positive and negative. How can we know what people might feel about our ideas if we haven't asked them? Understanding the unforeseen consequences, or fears, or unrealistic hopes (think most technology projects) is a gold mine of insight that can be considered in the design and ensure there are no barriers to adoption, no worries in people that might lead to baseless rumours at launch.

    Prototypes reduce risk because they give you advanced knowledge early enough to do something about it.
3. They break down opinion. I ended point 1 with the statement that prototypes produce evidence. They do, evidence of what things look like, how we might react to them and where unforeseen problems may lie. This evidence means that the boss's hunch can be proven right, or wrong. It may take a little confidence to share bad news to a senior manager but if they don't want the truth, then they're in trouble. You can make them smart by showing them the real insights and learnings from a prototype. But whereas opinion becomes political power in leadership, being open to learning and iteration of ideas is a stronger and more effective aspect of leadership and will help everyone be more successful.

Understand Different Types of Prototyping

I have emphasised simple prototyping in this introduction and for many decisions, a simple drawing or paper mock-up will make the issue tangible and provide insight into the right direction. But prototypes can be highly sophisticated and realistic and use all the tools of behavioural science, detailed interaction design, look and feel and context to discover how successful they may be and whether they need to be modified before they are built.

This the big point of prototyping – you don't need technology or engineering. That is a different test, a proof that something is feasible and works correctly, but not whether it is desirable. It is therefore very common to see technology and engineered proof of concepts called prototypes that prove something can be made but not whether anyone wants it or can use it. It's a balance and if you don't balance these two distinct attributes, along with the need to make it at the right cost, then you have failure.

Paper Prototypes

These are literally protypes on paper and represent a fast and effective way of visualising an idea or feature to understand whether it is desirable or works better than another idea or feature.

My favourite paper prototype is a Post-it stuck to a smartphone with a series of hand-drawn buttons giving several options. When you "click" the paper button, the tester rips of the Post-its and replaces it with another hand-drawn set or buttons. In a short time, we can learn whether people want the app, understand what it does and use it. We can ask them questions as we go, ask them what they expect to happen next, before we change the Post-it and evaluate a huge amount of insight from this simple insight.

Other forms of paper prototype include handing the pen over in a co-design workshop and asking people to draw their own software or product. The simplest form is the storyboard, where a scenario is described that allows a potential user of a service or product to imagine themselves in that scenario and ask questions and provide insight into how they feel, what question do they have, and what do they expect to happen, every step of the way.

Wow, what a great idea! Why don't they teach this at MBA 101?! It would save us billions!

3D Prototypes

From paper we graduate to cardboard and the representation of space and how we might interact with it. I have seen banks, hospitals, cars, prisons and hotels recreated in cardboard.

IDEO ran a project during lockdown on the future of transportation by creating cardboard cut-outs of vehicles and role-playing new scenarios around car sharing and other features of public transport and autonomous mobility.

Why does it work? Constructing obstacles and barriers, pathways and spaces allows us to experience a higher level of interaction and feedback our feelings and expectations. Putting healthcare managers in wheelchairs and placing them in a mocked up hospital ward made of cardboard can provide them with a whole new level of understanding and, hopefully, empathy for the patients they manage.

Advanced Digital Prototypes

For those familiar with the UX world, digital tools allow rapid and realistic simulations of every aspect of a digital experience to be tested or increasingly changed in real time. Software packages such as Figma and others that can deliver code directly from a prototype have driven an element of conformity in UX design. But the power and speed of prototype creation aligned with testing of users to refine and iterate the design is extremely powerful and proof that prototyping reduces risk by anticipating barriers, correcting misunderstandings, achieving expectations and increasing accessibility.

When to Prototype

There is a misconception, perhaps due to the linear nature of design methods such as the Stanford 5D and the Double Diamond, that the place for prototyping is after you have created your ideas, your new target journey vision and now have something solid to build to test how well it works.

But prototypes are much more useful than that and can be used right through the design process. My advice to students was always "prototype, prototype, prototype". For design students, this should be easy – they are happy to fill a blank piece of paper and visualise something that doesn't yet exist. For others, this is scarier. How do you visualise or prototype your idea, even in the simplest form, in time to find out if people want it or have something to say about how it will work?

One answer is to always have a great design team alongside you, as equally important as your financial manager or technology head, but that doesn't always happen. That's why designers should be a strategic resource that are on hand at every part of your decision-making process and not tucked away in marketing or fired every time there is a slight blip in your sales figures.

Who Are You Testing Prototypes With?

I have emphasised the power of showing ideas to evaluate their value and impact. Does this mean you need to have a constant stream of customers available to test every idea you have every moment of the day?

Knowing when to test with real customers is a skill. When taking over a major development project for a financial institution, I was concerned that there was no picture of the overall product and no testing had been done to check whether it was wanted, desirable or needed by customers. The team visualised the full experience as a clickable prototype on an iPad (no tech platform required), realising that there was still much design to be done but if we didn't know that people wanted the product, we would be wasting our time, and that the insights from the customer research would provide useful feedback in the detailed design.

Having created a compelling mock-up showing the main features, visual design, content, tone of voice and ease of use, all of which delighted the senior managers, we proposed to show it to customers. The reaction was aggressively negative: Managers were screaming at me in the corridors and accusing me of thinking of showing something that had not been "finished" and which would cause reputational damage if shown to potential customers.

Eventually I convinced them of the sense to show the design before it was finished so we could gain insight and validate a product that we were spending a lot of money on building. The results were both positive and insightful and we went on to develop a culture of biweekly customer testing with a small, invited number of potential customers whose input made dramatic improvements to the final product.

So, it's important to show it early enough to learn and implement that learning. But it's also useful to show prototypes even earlier, before you have finalised the brief and requirements of what you might want to develop.

Those Post-its on smartphone paper prototypes and storyboarded scenarios all helped at the very conception of a project to understand what was needed and what was important to the customer in how we delivered it. And even before that, developing storyboards that can be shared with you and your colleagues can bring great insights and stimulate discussions and inputs from across your organisation. Showing ideas to yourselves is a great first step to understanding how your ideas need to be designed, well before you show them to customers or people who will access your service.

The Three Stages of Prototyping: Stage 1 – the Proposition

The most essential stage when creating new ideas that may lead to innovation, or simply fixing a problem, is the proposition. A proposition is the packaging of an idea in terms of the value to the person using it. We take it for granted that the proposition will be good for the organisation in that it is feasible to be made and financially viable. But is the proposition attractive? Will your customer, or person who will benefit from your service, be attracted to it, choose it, and feel the transaction has been valuable? Is it a proposition that will beat the competition, establish brand loyalty and be so compelling that people will return to it again and again and tell their friends about it?

A proposition can be developed through using the design processes of gaining insight and framing problems or opportunities, creating ideas, and populating tools such as the business model canvas – a highly effective template that forces you to consider who you are designing for, what the benefits are to them (which you will have already done if you have redesigned your thinking and followed good design practice), who your partners and resources are, what the activities are that you will undertake and what the revenue streams are. All good for the business. But does anyone want it?

You can test the value of your proposition to your target audience in a few ways:

Make the Advert

As we've seen, an advert is an excellent way to test the proposition and anticipate demand. This is often referred to as "the bus stop sign". If you pass a poster on the side of a bus stop that advertises your concept, what does it look like and what does it say? Developing your advert first has many advantages, not the least of which is that you are forced to consider why people might want it and what aspect of the idea will be most effective in driving demand for it.

A poster is a powerful storytelling device and by sharing a simple poster of your idea, in words and images, you will gain a huge amount of insight, comment and free advice.

Using different channels for your fake advert can yield different results. Instagram adverts can spread the vision quickly but set expectations racing too. "Smoke testing" is a common term in web development where a "fake" website of your proposition is created and people are asked to register if they are interested, thereby creating a pool of potential customers you can use in to research and develop the concept.

My favourite smoke test is FlyingPinata.co, a service that delivers the Mexican Pinata, a papier mâché model of a donkey full of sweets for birthday celebrations, to your door, by drone. It's having a winter break, and has been for several years now, but it got me believing!

These techniques elevate our belief in an idea. No longer is it a paper model, it seems real and we can react and ask how much it will cost or ask how it will be delivered.

Tell the Story

In service design, there is no product, no physical thing to look at. In so many of our decisions and designs, the outputs are complex, and distributed across time. We can't make a model of an experience; we have to tell a story.

Storytelling is a vital part of how we communicate our ideas to ourselves and others, colleagues, associates, customers, people who will benefit from our ideas.

Stories have the advantage of telling us what happens across time when we access or buy or use something. What was our need, how did we find and chose, it, what was it like at first and did we use or access it over time? Did it achieve its objective, were we happy, and what was the impact?

It's the same as in our journey mapping and journey creating – we need to answer all these questions and play them back as a story so that those who might use our outputs can tell us they want it. A simple narrative is essential in showing how the proposition will be discovered, delivered and what will happen along the away.

The story needs to show what the customer will experience, sometimes in detail. What is does not need to tell is your story: why, how, the challenges you have overcome. These are immaterial and will only pollute the insights you get from testing your proposition.

You do not need to describe the technology platform or the training or the new contact centre you have developed or the relationship with your supplier. Everything that is under the "hood" needs to stay there, you just tell the story of what will happen to the person gaining benefit from your concept.

Artifacts

Every year at the various international motor shows, car companies will bring along a new model, usually dripping in gorgeous futuristic styling along with ahead-of-the-curve technology that reflects where they think automobiles will be in 5 years' time. It's a conversation starter that visualises the future in a believable way.

Cars of the future are great examples of a physical artefact that raises expectations and sets out a company's ambition and future strategy. You can hear what people say, measure their excitement and intrigue, perhaps even take early orders for the vehicle (Tesla's sci-fi pick-up truck is a great example).

The white goods manufacturer Whirlpool showed tremendous foresight in producing a vision of the future of washing machines that wasn't all about speech recognition or Bluetooth connectivity when they produced an experimental washing machine that tackled environmental impact. Consisting of a white horizontal platform with a series of buckets connected by trailing green vegetation on the top of the "machine", the cleaning was achieved completely naturally by the water in the machine being filtered by the plants on the top. Each bucket contained clothes soaked in water that filtered through the plants for a week, at the end of which the clothes can be hung up to dry as normal.

The design was shown to consumers and the benefits of a zero energy, no chemicals or detergents method of cleaning was explained. The researchers could ask them what they felt about clothing perhaps not being so brilliant white and maybe not smelling of fragrant detergents but having a completely sanitary and natural process of laundry.

Curious consumers questioned the length of time the washing process took – 1 week seems a long time compared to the one-and-a-half-hour washing cycle of a normal washing machine. This was likely to be the dealbreaker. But the researchers were also armed with the results of a survey into the length of time it takes people from taking off their clothes, leaving them in a laundry pile and then putting them in the washing machine. All of that took, on average, one week. So, the length of current laundry process and the new all-natural one was exactly the same.

At this point the researchers had to admit that the protype was a fake. The ability to filter the water and clean the washing in a week was not currently possible. But the opportunity to create a believable artifact that allowed them to ask new questions and gain insights into attitudes and potential barriers to sustainable washing machine technology was invaluable. This is as close as you can get to a crystal ball. It allowed them to have a dialogue with the future in the present. By simulating in a convincing way a future idea, they learnt of the barriers and the benefits of their vision.[2]

In summary, testing a proposition is not the same as having a hypothesis, though that can and should be tested early too. A proposition is a more complete package, it envisages the value exchange of a service or product as if it exists to find out whether it is desirable and works in a way that people wish it to. It might raise issues or concerns that had not been considered and need addressing earlier rather than later. These could be about sustainability, or the ethical use or security of technology and data, as well as whether people understand the benefit and see that it addresses a real need.

The metric for proposition testing is simple. "Do I want this?" it asks, and in the process validates whether that is true. Then we can move forward with confidence that subsequent decisions, actions and resources are being placed on something that has value and purpose and is not a wild punt with our collective fingers crossed.

---

2 Project F: Our designers featured on the world stage, 2017.

Stage 2 – Features

Once you have understood the value of your concept, business, policy or product or service, you can move to a new level of detail to understand how your ideas should work and what features does it need.

Features are often set by eager business analysts who compile business requirements for a new service. Or perhaps by a product manager who sees an opportunity for a new feature from customer feedback, or because a competitor has added a feature to their product.

Features tend to pile up. Look at your TV remote control. Count how many of the buttons you have ever touched. My guess would be around 10 percent of the total number of buttons. Do you know what the other 90% do?

Understanding what features will be essential and useful and which are completely unnecessary, is the key value in prototyping features. We want to find out what expectations are and what is essential to customer, not our distorted assumptions about what we think is useful and would personally think we would like to use. Remember, we are not the same as the person you are making decisions for and should never assume that they behave like us: We are extremely unrepresentative of the people we design for.

If the purpose of testing our proposition is to create the evidence that "I want this", the prototyping and testing of features is "I want it like this".

The three forms of prototypes described in proposition research are useful for features too. You make a physical artifact that represents anything from a remote control to a hospital ward to emulate and understand where features and functions may be needed. The specific skills of designers can visualise and make real in a variety of rapidly reconfigured ways to test different features.

A handheld product can be quickly shaped in modelling foam and buttons stuck on. A stuck-on button can have a function name such as "On" or "Reset" or an icon which may or may not mean anything to the user, but you will find out pretty quickly!

The speed of prototyping and ability to reformat and retest is a valuable aspect of feature testing. Digital products, written forms and instruction guides can all be mocked up and tested – by yourself, your colleagues, the people who will use and perhaps people who will not use them – you can learn from everyone and sharing ideas is the key point. Someone will give you a good idea when they can engage with how your ideas work. The objective is not just "fake it to understand whether you should make it" but more "fake it to understand how it will work when you've made it".

A banana can be a phone. A box a bank desk. A series of Post-its a depiction of a complex user interface. Digital interfaces can be quickly and realistically mocked up to take people through how something works. As ever, the goal is to listen, to learn, and then redo. If you don't find something wrong or something to learn for the next version, then you haven't asked the right question or you're kidding yourself that people will want the feature on the real thing, they just don't realise it at the moment.

Usability

Luckily, it's quite difficult now to develop a digital experience without using design methods. Digital development teams will usually have UX (user experience) designers who are combining the user interaction design of symbols, words, use of colour and shape with the architecture, navigation, and flow through the digital journey to achieve your goal. It is well understood that digital tools need to be accessible to all, inclusive in ensuring that every user can understand and reach their objective and that the people who create the code are not the same people who can ensure usability, simplicity, and desirability. UX design is a collaborative venture where different people, who may on their own have different motivations, such as velocity of development in an agile team, or a focus on reducing cost of a service, are balanced with those who are motivated by empathy and the desire to ensure that the experience is usable and useful. These aren't often found in the same person, and neither should they be – diversity and collaboration across different skills and expertise is what drives success.

This third stage allows us to test in detail whether a button is understandable, what people expect to happen when they press it and what happens if they're wrong and need to go back. The prototype allows an incredible level of detail to completely reproduce an experience in order to iron out all those wrinkles that we don't see because we are too close to the idea or because we are not the real people who will use it.

A prototype at this point needs to be realistic and needs to be completely designed. The size of every letter, the colour of every button, the flow through the process needs to be as accurate as possible to explore where the weak links may be, the issues and misunderstandings that may prevent your service working and lead to rejection and failure. It's that important, and vital that it is done well, BEFORE you start building the final version.

It's been said very often by very many that the cost of modifying a design is approximately 100 times more if you do it after you have built it than before. It should be obvious that to change something that has been developed, linked to the platforms and systems required, designed and coded or engineered and manufactured, is much more difficult and more expensive in both financial and time terms. Yet, despite this, companies and organisations will skip prototyping and the time to change at an easy stage to ensure they launch as soon as possible. Time is always the goal, be faster, get to market, beat your competitor.

When Orange Mobile launched their Orange Music Player on a Sony Ericsson phone, we had the party, everyone was happy and excited at this strategic win. Except it didn't work. You couldn't download music or play it. They fixed it eventually but at great cost. Needless to say neither Orange Music nor Sony Ericsson made even a tiny dent in the revolution of Apple iPhone and iTunes. I still scratch my head and ask, "Did that really happen?" Yes, it did. Absolute madness.

Useful Exercises

As service design students developed ideas for new probation services, circular economy or digital banking for neurodiversity, it was important to go through all three prototype stages.

1. Whatever your idea, stand back and identify the most important idea, the most critical feature, the big idea. What is the concept that will drive change? What will make the idea more competitive, easier to use, what is the most important motor of change in the idea?

I would then ask students to consider how they could create a prototype that would test that idea. Does it work and bring the required change? Does it sell more, make something easier, change a negative behaviour or bring about a social benefit? How would you prove that main point?

You can use Crazy 8s to generate ideas. You can have a brainstorm. You can prototype the prototype and then you will be able to validate, prove and create the evidence that your idea will work.

2. Create a prototype in 4 different ways:
- A Future Vision – What will your idea look like in 5, or 10 years in the future?
- Fail – How could you prove that it won't work and will fail? What does that experiment look like?
- Physical – Can you create the idea in a purely physical form, even if it's digital?
- Digital – What does it look like in a digital form, even if its physical?

Kiran Dulay, whilst a student on the RCA service design course, worked on her major project with the London Fire Brigade. After a tragic high-rise apartment fire in Grenfell in the west of London, a long enquiry heard tragic evidence of how both residents and firefighters were unaware of the correct course of action and many people died. Kiran wanted to explore how people react in a fire and how did their different behaviours lead to different actions. She couldn't very well use a real fire to recreate or simulate people's behaviour in such a crisis but wanted to use prototypes to gain insight.

Kiran used a digital tool to recreate a physical reality by using the SIMS game. Building an apartment and setting light to it in a digital universe allowed her to populate it with people and firefighters and allow people to run though their thoughts and actions in a moment of such crisis.[3]

The Power of Prototypes

How many start-up ideas would benefit from the use of an artefact that represents the concept in such a believable way that you could do all your future research, market testing, revenue predictions and iron out the problems in advance of spending any development money?

When design students and business students from MBA courses get together, the designers are always amazed that the business students have only considered one idea, and not shown it to customers in an early form to find out what they think. The reaction of the business students is invariably to shift nervously in their seats and tell the designers to get back to doing their PowerPoint slides for them. Which is a pretty good representation of what business thinks designers do, to their own detriment.

We need businesses, organisations and even governments to understand the importance of prototyping in simulating and provoking discussion before delivery. From modelling improbable washing machines to visions of possible automobiles to simulating strategy and policy by using the tools of design to visualise, provide the experience and make the advert so that you can validate or critique your idea, is essential if we are to be successful in answering the challenges of business and society.

They should teach this in business schools, to civil servants and accountants, who should demand to see the prototype and research findings before signing off on development budgets. This is why removing design from our education systems, because of out-of-date perceptions that design is woodworking and domestic science (food science and cooking), is not just unfortunate, it's an expensive and critical failure to prepare us with the skills and tools we need for the future.

Prototyping is at the heart of all design activities, and it should be at the heart of all our activities. The ability to visualise and engage with the consequence of ideas, rapidly and at low cost, is an essential tool for all decision makers.

How to Redesign Thinking to Prototype

Prototyping reduces risks and takes the argument out of the discussion. Prototypes can be extremely simple and yet incredibly informative and valuable to

---

[3] Kiran Duran, www.rcaservicedesign.com/projects/common-ground

your decision-making process. Be creative about how you prototype – what aspect of your riskiest decision can you prototype to find out if the premise for your decision is valid? All it costs is a small amount, time, thought and a little sharing.

Be prepared to be wrong. Challenge your own ideas until you are sure they are right. Let the prototype make your idea better, or lead you to a new one.

How to Use Prototypes as a Designer

Prototypes answer your questions. Do people want this, like that, that works in this way? You can prove things, show the evidence of a prototype that has been shared, learnt from and changed for the better.

Prototyping is possibly one of the most valuable design tools that are accessible to everyone and can help us all move forward with certainty and confidence. The worst that can happen is that you have to tell someone important that their idea might not work, but we can try other things and find out what does work. They'll be grateful in the end.

The same goes for you – be prepared to be wrong, celebrate that and learn. Humility of your ideas and being able to say goodbye to them and hello to new ones is critical and the mark of a great designer. Be that.

Chapter 9
Visions and Stories

> *The most powerful person in the world is the storyteller. The storyteller sets the vision, values, and agenda of an entire generation that is to come.*
> Steve Jobs

If there is one thing designers do, it's to paint a picture of the possible. Something happens when what was just a thought, an idea that has formed in our minds, becomes tangible. It's the value of prototyping, that we can see and touch the idea before it is real. But beyond that, there is a point where the whole story around an idea, the complete experience of it, needs to be told. It stops being a question and becomes an answer. "This is what we will do", the story says, as the future is placed in front of us to look at, marvel, or criticise and then make real.

For someone designing a physical object, such as an architect or a three-dimensional product designer, this moment would be when a model of your proposed design comes out of the model shop, still smelling of paint or glue and as pure in intention as it will ever be seen. A model in this sense is still a fake, but one so perfect that you believe it is capable of working. For a digital designer it is the clickable prototype, where buttons swell and move and take you to the next action. For the service designer it is . . . well, what does a service designer have?

Service designers have stories. Service design outputs are complex and abstract and involve many moving parts. As the model of a new product is accurate on the surface to show you its beauty and a digital experience is accurate in vision and movement, the service design story is an accurate depiction of time. A service design story tells you what happens: before, when the context and situation that requires a solution exists; during, as in what happens and how does it feel for the person using the service; and after, what the impact is and what happens as a result.

You'll recognise that a story is similar in its use of time to the journey map we used to identify problems and opportunities. Both are concerned with the passing of time and taking the point of view of the person who is experiencing the service. Neither is necessarily concerned with how it will work; that is extremely important, but not at this stage. How it will work is a question that will be answered after we understand what the experience will be and why it will be effective. The "how" is always subservient to the "what will happen" in making better decisions. Which will make many uncomfortable, but is where we often go wrong, fascinated as we are by how things work, not how they will feel.

Stories in design are very visual, more like a graphic novel than a book. The combination of images and words brings together the strengths of both modes: We need to plot our story and write out what happens before we illustrate it with the actions of people, the objects and systems that they will touch to achieve their goal and in their context. You might be on a bus whilst you are booking your holiday. You might be in a fire engine when you're meant to read instructions. You might be shopping when you want to know the provenance of materials, social conditions of the plantation workers and carbon footprint of a banana.

Stories allow you to communicate the detail and the intention at each stage of the journey. And when they are told in a way that allows all to agree that they will work, they become powerful tools for driving organisations forward, united by a vision and clarity of purpose and intention. Which is a powerful tool whether you are a CEO, politician or product manager with a desire for positive change.

What Do Stories Look Like?

When the Icelandic-Danish artist Olafur Eliasson wanted to bring attention to the impact of the climate crisis to the leaders attending the United Nations Climate Change COP21 summit in Paris, he arranged 12 hunks of glacial ice from Greenland's Nuuk Fjord outside of Place de Panthéon and invited the global leaders, and citizens everywhere to watch his "doomsday clock" whilst it slowly melted. It was a dramatic method of depicting the impact of increasing climate temperatures and, perhaps in some part because of his intervention, the Paris agreement was successfully reached (though still to be successfully implemented).

When Antony Dunn and Fiona Raby whilst at the RCA began to create objects that challenged our assumptions about technology, it drew our attention to impacts and behaviours that we were hardly aware of. Known as critical and speculative design, Dunn and Raby started a movement to articulate and visualise the unintended consequences of technology and design. Their objects contain compasses that veer wildly off course by the magnetic fields from a mobile phone, or roll away when we try to reach out to them.

In a workshop exploring how to support prisoners when the leave, a series of photos of Lego figures tell the story of how mentors support a prisoner through their transition back to society.

All of these examples show the power of telling stories to visualise data, capture new threats or possible experiences in compelling ways that drive our attention to an issue that needs to be resolved. But for describing future possibilities, our stories need to be different and more detailed. They need to show us what we can do and how it will feel.

Service design stories embrace time and step us through, from the perspective of the person using the service, what they will experience.

The Story of Frank

One example of graphical storyboarding that illustrates the concept of a pension finder is shown in Figure 9.1. To explain what this idea was, a storyboard was generated that captured a person who was close to retirement age who wanted to understand whether they had enough of a pension to allow them to do so. The story then imagined what needed to happen for them to make that decision.

First, we start with Frank. Frank shares many of the features with millions of similar people who will need this service. There may be many other categories who may be older or younger, but this story takes one who is representative of many people with a similar need to understand if they can retire.

The first frame of the storyboard gives this person a name, Frank, and sets out their need and context: approaching a certain age with a question about their future. We now understand the reality of the situation and can identify with the person involved.

The story does not start with the first interaction with the service. It starts with the person and their need. Stories should always start with the problem the service is trying to solve, not the service itself.

In the second frame we see the problem: that he doesn't know where all his pensions are. This is based on data that showed the average person at retirement age has 11 pensions of which 3 are lost. This could have been due to moving house and forgetting to update the pension provider of your new address, or the pension being passed to various other companies over time. As a result, he doesn't know how much pension he will have to live on.

The third frame identifies how Frank will realise that there is a service that could help him. How would he know otherwise? On this frame, a particular channel is shown: a poster at a bus stop.

Of course, other channels may well be used, but in this story we have chosen the channel that Frank is most likely to see. A poster is big, noticeable, and easily seen by Frank so it has advantages over an advert in a magazine or newspaper that he may miss.

The fourth frame describes the job of the poster. It describes the service that solves his need – it suggests that there is a way he can find all of his pensions.

The next frame shows how he can capture the service and find out more – in this case a link or QR code that he can write down, type into his phone or click on. With the rediscovery of the QR code during the pandemic, we have a highly recognisable way of navigating to a digital service through the cameras of our phones.

In these five frames we have created a believable scenario that shows how Frank can start to solve his problem. It doesn't talk about marketing campaigns or apps or make any assumptions about how he will find the service. I have seen

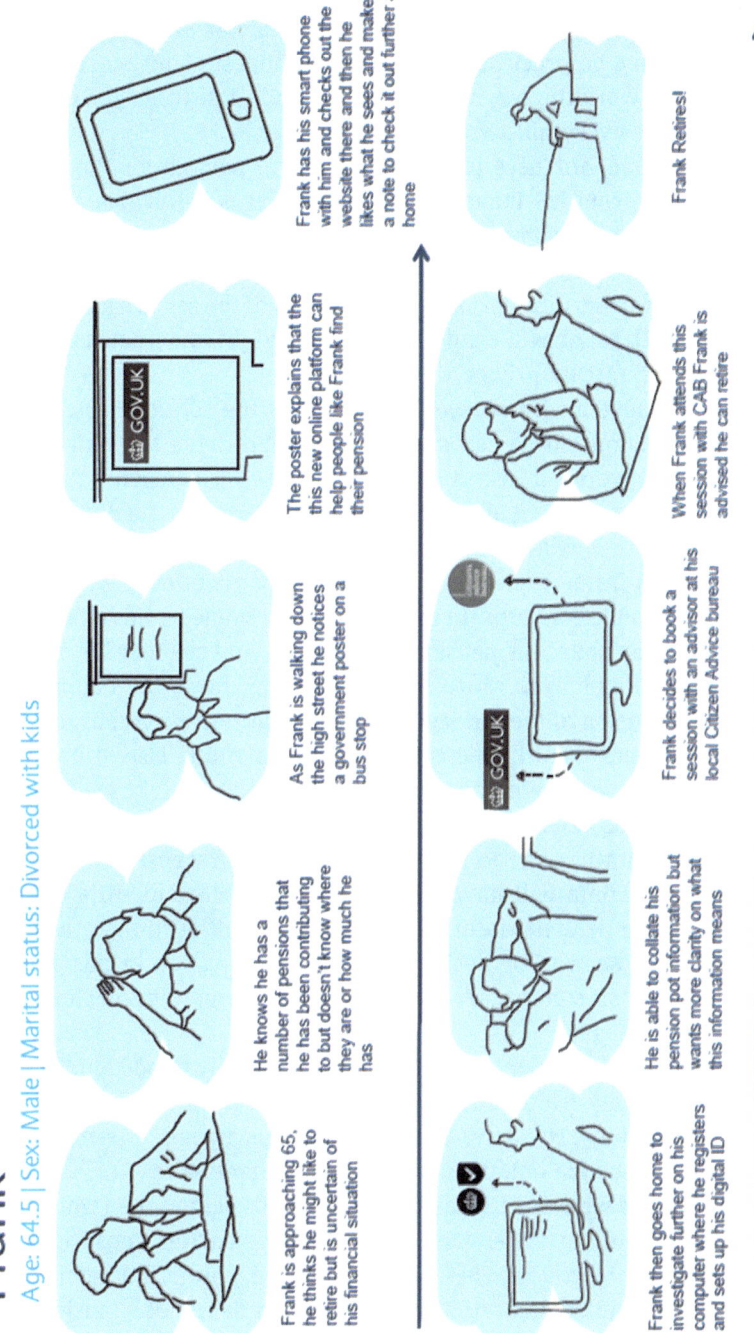

Figure 9.1: Pension Dashboard storyboard.

a lot of presentations that say things like "Frank was delighted to find this useful app whilst browsing the app store". If you'd said an advert on Facebook, I might agree but stories must be practical, believable and honest about when things go wrong or might not work the way we intend. We tend to distrust stories that are too happy and where everything works perfectly.

By the sixth frame, our hero is engaging with the service for the first time when he accesses it from his PC at home. The context is believable as he is an environment that is more comfortable, and he can think about this serious personal financial issue.

The frame also introduces the concept of security of the service and mentions that he sets up his ID. Frank will want his personal and private financial information to be secure and remain private.

Finally, on the seventh frame, we describe what the service does. It brings together all his pensions so he can see what he might have for retirement. It doesn't say how this works, it just says that he can see his pension pots from all his previous employment. But it also raises a new conundrum – he doesn't understand what this means, how much will he have to live on?

So, in the eighth frame Frank choses a feature that is offered where he can book a session with a local advisor. In the penultimate frame he has a face-to-face meeting where he can share his pension information, and see that his combined pension pots will allow him to retire. The final frame shows the happy ending and successful conclusion of the service as Frank enjoys his retirement fishing.

The story describes what happens to Frank and nothing else. It doesn't explain how the service will be delivered but we can immediately see that there will have to be a lot of moving parts to bring this vision to reality. Data will be shared on a platform accessible to lots of organisations. A website that provides secure access to that data will have to be created. A secure identity system is needed to protect the personal information. Advisors will need to be hired and trained. Posters will need to be designed, printed and put up in bus stop billboards. But none of that concerns Frank, he has a problem, finds a solution, and goes fishing.

Of course, how this experience is achieved is immensely important. Every detail needs to be superbly crafted to make sure this will work for Frank, his advisor and all the pension providers. But if the story is wrong, doesn't work or misses something important out, then how it works is irrelevant.

Stories are vital if we want to make sure we are designing the right thing in the right way. They help us understand how to remove barriers, ensure easy access and achieve our objectives. Whether we're making a profit, saving the planet or helping someone think about retirement earlier and be less of a burden on the state, we can evaluate how effective our story will be.

Clear narratives, with a concise and adequately detailed – but not complex – storyline can be a powerful communication tool. A great story will help your colleagues understand what the purpose and context is, which allows them to understand their role and purpose in delivering something better. A story clarifies direction, helps everyone understand the journey they are on, who for and why.

In the 1minute 30 seconds of chief executive attention span, a clear narrative is vital. A story beats any PowerPoint chart in explaining what you want to do to fix a problem, sell a product or deliver a service. It tells us who's got the problem, how they find your solution, use it successfully and bring about a satisfactory outcome for you both. I have seen CEOs' eyes glaze over as slide after slide passes by them. Show them a storyboard and they come alive. They get it, in a rapid and clear way. They can see what is needed to be done and what will be required to deliver it successfully.

Visions

As CEO of Cisco, John Chambers was very keen on vision statements. His rallying cry was "vision, strategy, execution" and he would require every project to have these three elements clearly articulated at the start – he would send it back if they didn't.

When I started as a tutor at the Royal College of Art, I saw many amazing project ideas for services that would do wonderfully important things in innovative ways. But I found myself repeating John Chambers's words and asking students: What is the vision? How are you going to achieve that vision? And what are the actions that will allow you to achieve that vision?

It's a useful and valuable exercise. Many projects are carried out because someone has asked for the project to happen. But if you haven't articulated what the vision, or mission of the project is, and haven't decided how that will be achieved and the actions that will achieve it, then it's difficult and probably a waste of time to continue down that route, just because someone asked you to.

But what do we mean by vision, strategy and execution? How are those terms defined and why are they valuable?

What Are Vision, Strategy and Execution?

We can define each of these simply as:
  Vision and Missions: Describe the outcomes you are trying to achieve.
  Strategy: Define what you will change to achieve this goal.
  Execution: Describe specific actions you will take to make change happen.
  Metric: What will be the measurable outcome?

Visions and Missions: We started this chapter with stories and their importance in helping us understand an issue and how we might solve or create something innovative and new. But stories only exist to describe how we are going to achieve something important. The vision is the "why" to the story's "what".

One of the most famous examples of a vision is John F. Kennedy's speech outlining the programme to land a man on the moon. In that speech, Kennedy mentioned some important details about his vision that made it understandable and realisable, all but at huge economic cost. He said that by the end of the decade, the USA would put a man on the moon and return him safely (sorry, it was to be a man, and it was important that he came back – you could have got there and left him there).

Within that vision statement was enough detail to scale up the project and create a strategy. The strategy was to develop an organisation that could create a device that could escape the Earth's gravitational pull, travel to the moon, land there and return and develop every aspect of the system to design, build and operate to deliver that vision.

There is an apocryphal story that someone asked the janitor at NASA's Mission Control what their job was to which they replied, "putting a man on the moon". It's that clarity of purpose that is so powerful and aligns your organisation to ensure that everyone understands what their purpose is and what success looks like.

For a not-for-profit organisation and charity, the sense of purpose can be strong – find a cure for cancer, or support people with a condition so they can live more comfortably. A vision statement creates a clearer narrative that defines the objective of that purpose. "We will eradicate malaria, globally by 2030" is as powerful of Kennedy's vision to go to the moon. And it focuses everyone's mind on the reason they do what they do.

Another example is where an organisation has a purposeful vision and applies it in many different problems. Final Mile is a team of behavioural economists, scientists and designers who came together to solve problems that conventional practices were not solving. Developing a research lab to understand why behaviours were preventing progress in vaccine roll-out and heathy behaviour that could reduce or prevent diseases such as AIDS in India and Africa, their vision was to solve these difficult-to-solve challenges through a new way of thinking. They have achieved measurable success in improving safety on the railways, improving sanitation, maternal health and young women's relationships. Their vision is that a pragmatic collaboration of different intellectual approaches combined with design methods would create the contextually successful outcomes they wish to achieve, and they can claim to have delivered on that vision.[1]

Strategy is a level down and defines precisely what you need to change to achieve your vision. This might be behavioural, or scientific or political. For our malaria charity, the strategy might be "provide anti-malarial nets to every person who lives where malaria exists". Or it might be "develop a chemical that kills mosquitoes that transmit the disease", or "remove all malaria transmitting mosquitoes". There are different strategies that fit the same vision.

Execution is a description of the specific actions you are going to take. This might be to hire world-leading scientists, build a fabulous laboratory and fund the development over ten years. There are usually lots of execution actions and this is where they are listed.

The interesting thing is that the vision doesn't say how it will be achieved, the strategy doesn't say what you will do specifically, but the execution must be connected to both the strategy and the vision so it is universally agreed that it will deliver the vision of a malarial free world.

The connection across all three statements is vital and ensures that everyone in the organisation is linked to original objective. The janitor is putting a man on the moon just as much as is the Saturn 5 rocket designers, the people at Mission Control and the astronaut who is in the capsule.

At the France Telecom Innovation Centre in Paris, teams would come together at the start of the project and each person was asked to draw what they thought the project they were embarking on was. It was surprising how different their ideas and beliefs were. It was vital at the start of every project that people shared their preconceptions and perceptions to find agreement on what they were doing and for whom. Once that is achieved, life is easy, but if it is ignored, every person is working to a different objective with a different strategy for getting there and a different way of measuring the impact of their work. Setting the vision and strategy right at the start of a project is fundamental to ensure everyone is as creative, active, ingenious and focused on the same objective. Obvious really but amazingly, not always done. With usually disastrous consequences.

Articulating your vision, strategy and execution is a good idea for the largest and smallest activity. What is the reason you are going to the supermarket? Answer: prepare a dinner that will please a friend who is visiting. Strategy? Purchase the ingredients for the meal that will satisfy their dietary requirements and create an enjoyable experience. Execution? Check the recipe and buy the fresh ingredients.

---

[1] Final Mile tackles complex behavioural challenges in public health, financial empowerment, and other issues involving human decisions by creating behavioural science solutions. https://www.thefinalmile.com

For Swachh Bharat Mission health service charity in India, the vision is to reduce the risk to health from defecation in public places – a common occurrence in rural India. Their strategy is to change the behaviour of people and provide clean and accessible toilet facilities for all. Their execution is easy to link to the strategy and includes the manufacture and roll-out of low-cost sanitation. The result was a reduction of 300,000 in diarrheal related deaths in 2019 compared to 2014. When you successfully deliver your vision a through an appropriate strategy and an effective execution, you end up with a measurable impact.[2]

John Chambers soon added a fourth word to his mantra: metrics. How do we measure the impact of our execution actions to confirm that they were delivering on the vision?

We live in a world of KPIs (key performance indicators) and success metrics. It's powerful to clarify exactly how you will measure your success, but it's also often true that the time to achieve success is not necessarily a short one. Some visions will take years to achieve. So how might we know that are actions are having the impact we intend?

Weak Signals

When we take actions, develop new products and services and experiences, there are opportunities to understand what are the weak signals that point to future success.

If you are designing an app to help sustain the mental health of young people, it might take a considerable amount of time before data can be collected to show a beneficial impact of the app. But in the first instance, you can measure how many have downloaded it. This just a very simple and may not be a very helpful measurement but it's a start. Then you can measure how many times it's been opened and used, and measured in the fullness of time. And if there are positive ratings and reviews, you can start to see that your vision is on track.

Measuring such weak signals helps your stakeholders understand that your actions, strategy and approach is working. Putting these four words together is the real power of this approach: a vision you can articulate and share, a strategy that people believe will work, executed actions that make change and measurable impact, even if weak at the start. From going shopping to developing government policy, this mantra works and will sharpen the focus of everyone in the organisation.

---

[2] Swachh Bharat Mission-Grameen works across India to improve sanitation. swachhbharatmission.ddws.gov.in

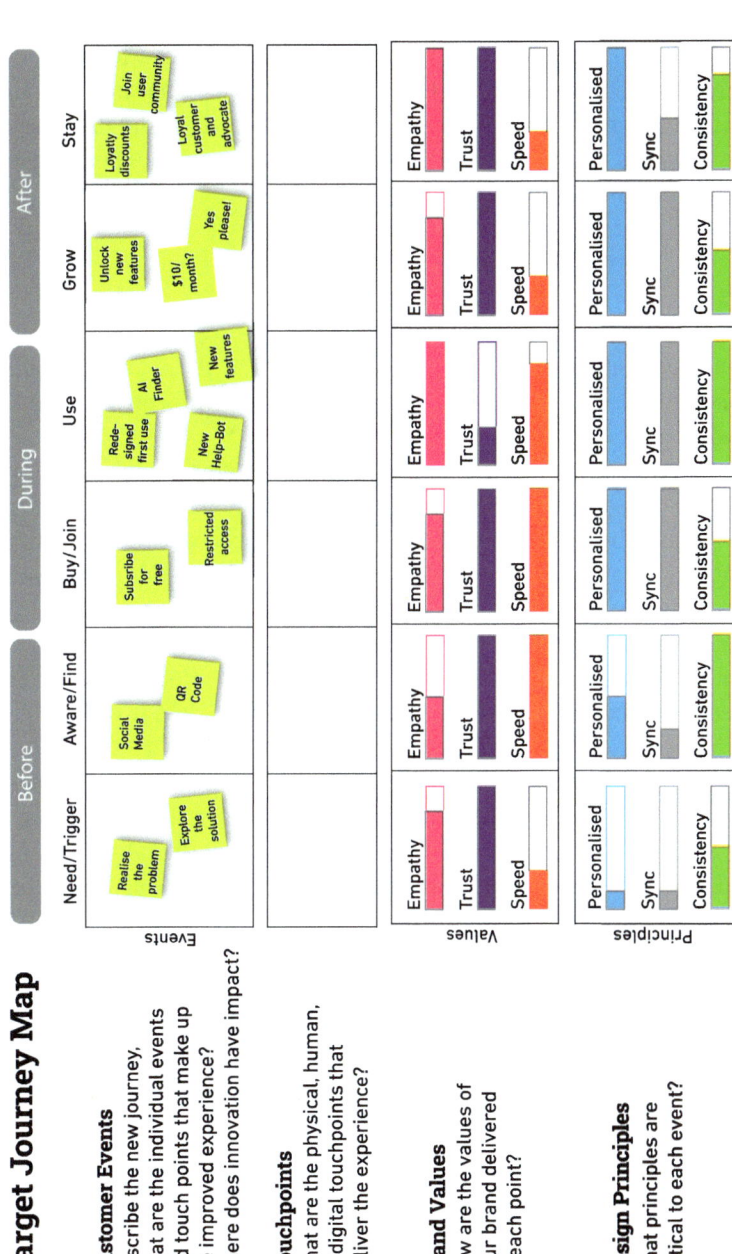

Figure 9.2: Target Visions components.

The power of stories is to show how vision, strategy and execution deliver impact that is measurable. The story is a narrative that shows what happens in this new vision. If you have followed this design path, from insight and discovery through creating solutions and testing their premise, you are now in a position to develop the new journey and from that, the story.

Target Visions

North Stars, moon shots, envisioning, target journeys – all of these are different terms for the creation of a compelling new vision that people will sign up to and collaborate to make real.

Whether our solution is a single idea or a complex systems transformation, we need to represent it as a future story so we can see clearly what our intention is. We do this by reusing the principle of the journey map that we used to identify problems and opportunities and draw on that timeline our alternative, improved future.

Target journey maps (Figure 9.2) fulfil several purposes:

1. Position your solution ideas in the context of time. If your solution is a better signage system, it places the individual idea in the correct time it will be experienced. The result of the signage may be higher sales, or a safe exit or things that happen after the sign in the target journey. This shows us where the success metric is – when someone has found the object they wanted to purchase because the sign showed them where it was. In a digital version of this, a successful button is not measured by when it is pressed, but when the goal is achieved.

    Your solution may not work at all if people can't find it, so awareness, engagement and action have be designed in time around the solution for it to work. This again is where good ideas fail: We forget to design what happens before, and often afterwards. Good ideas are only realised when we design the moments around them. Great innovation regularly fails because the innovators are concentrating so hard on the core idea, they fail to design the customer journey around their innovation, with the result that no one gets to it.

2. When you place your solution in the context of the complete journey, you will see gaps in the journey that need filling. If you have a brilliant new electric vehicle charging station, you need a sign, a link on a Google map, a communication strategy and access at the motorway service station. Your idea needs other ideas to make it work well.

3. In placing the journey across time in the framework of awareness, engagement, transaction, usage, growth and outcome, you allow space underneath to start to identify the elements that are required to achieve the result. You

have room to identity the systems that are required, the elements of your organisation that are required to deliver each part of the journey. And this starts to build up what is called the blueprint that identifies who and what is required to bring the vison to reality.

This aspect of the target journey also allows us to see develop the collaboration required in an organisation to deliver improvement and change. All can see their role and who is responsible for each of the key stages of the journey and all can share an understanding of what the new journey looks like. It's the architect's model and the designer's maquette.

4. Finally, the detailed blow-by-blow depiction of everything that will happen as a series of events that you as a human will go through creates the individual elements of the story you will tell. Your narrative of the events, value and impact of the journey can be delivered to share with others.

It is also a series of events linked together that can be told to others, who can then input and suggest improvements whilst it is still easy to do so. Sharing your target vision with others, from your colleagues to senior managers to customers, is a powerful act of creativity that stimulates new ideas and iterations at a moment where that is cheap and easy. Real-time change after testing an idea will improve your solution before funds and resources are brought in to play. The chance to iterate and rapidly learn – what a great idea! And so easy, all we need to do is think differently, openly and without fear of hearing something that challenges our established view.

"Redesigning thinking" means compiling your best shot and showing it to others with an open invitation to challenge and improve. In a workshop environment, I invite participants to construct their best target vision, then present it to a member of another team working on a different challenge. They are informed about the research into who is going to benefit from the new journey and taken through each of the events that make up the proposed journey. They are forbidden to explain how the journey will be delivered. There is no explanation of the technology platform or details of the organisational changes required, just the elements of the journey as they are experienced. They are then asked to listen to the comments of the new team member. They must not defend their idea or argue with the new team member. They can answer questions as to what happens but must simply take notes of the new suggestions ready to reflect on what they hear before they iterate their journey.

It's a simple and guaranteed method of rapidly improving your target vision and preparing yourself for the potential barriers or misunderstandings that a normal person experiencing your new journey may have.

This simple exercise that can be done at your desk or in your own office simulates the experience of user testing. Formal user testing is with people who are potential customers and will bring their real concerns and contexts. But you can apprehend those by going the through the simple exercise of sharing your ideas early and listening to the feedback, without being defensive or justifying your decisions.

Creating a Target Vision

Using the customer journey framework as the basis for the target vision requires a specific mindset that people can struggle with. The journey you create is the journey of the imaginary person you are designing for. It must tell in all essential details the events and moments along the journey exactly as they will happen. This is NOT the same as listing the process points of the journey. This is where many people struggle.

For example, people see a problem and look to find solutions. In the process of doing so, they discover your and perhaps many other solutions and then investigate them, engage and commit to your solution. So a target journey map that describes this part of the journey as "Maria finds the website and signs up" is unrealistic in that it describes what you want to happen but completely ignores all the steps required for Maria to find, understand, accept and dive into your website.

People really struggle with this and insist on describing what they do to create the journey rather than what happens from Maria's point of view. It's a real shift for some to stop thinking about "how" to describe the "what happens". But it is critically important that whether they are a manager, the CEO or a politician, they see what they are proposing as an experience NOT a system that delivers it. One might liken it to many people designing different door handles without thinking about how people know where the door is, which way it opens and where it leads to.

Engineering Emotion

Describing in detail the events and micro-moments of a journey addresses both functional and contextual issues. We can add to this the emotional resonance of the journey.

Many people look at the brand values on the walls of their offices and feel good. They represent the purpose and behaviour we aspire to in our organisation. But how does your customer feel those brand values in their experience? They don't have signs on the wall, they just have the events and moments, the points they touch or interact with. Who do your values connect and deliver their meaning to then?

In many ways this the most exciting part of engineering an experience. We can list the stuff that people do and engage with, but what is the emotional side of that interaction?

A social housing group I worked with sent me their values in advance of our workshop. Their well-formed brand values were inspiring and were framed as HEART:

Honest
Efficient
Accountable
Respectful
Trustworthy

Lovely. And how do those values become tangible in the experience of their residents?

The target journey map is the moment where we can associate those values to each event in the journey. It's unlikely that every one of those will be applicable to every part of the journey, but we should at least try and understand whether they are or not by considering each one at each point.

So, when creating our new target vision, we have the opportunity to turn it from black and white to colour, from 2D to 3D and apply the emotional values that differentiate your ethos and purpose from others. And if you don't have a well-thought-through set of values, then start thinking of them. What values may be important to a citizen in accessing a service. We usually want to be polite of course, but politeness comes in very different flavours. Are we being supportive, helpful, careful and precautionary? This is the time to dial in emotional context and understand how that supports the success of the outcomes.

How to Use Stories

New ideas, decisions that change or transform what has gone before, delivering innovation, or simply sorting out a mess, require collaboration and agreement from your peers and colleagues, leaders and managers who need to collaborate together to deliver change.

The purpose and value of the story is not simply to share your clever ideas or design processes you have used – they are to create energy for change, move from idea to action, get sign up to the next steps and move forwards in harmony with each other, the person you are designing for and your shared objectives.

The story is a powerful tool if it's done well. It needs to withstand cynicism and doubt, the kicking of its tyres. And it needs to inspire, breathe oxygen into the idea to support it into reality. It needs longevity and to be sustained, though it should never be so inflexible that it can't adapt to changing circumstances. It should represent the North Star, the vision you want to attain to. It should support all the small events and actions along the way and remind everyone of why they are doing it and for whom.

If you don't have a story, what do you have? A set of instructions without a view of the thing you are making. A Lego set without the picture on the cover. A lack of focus and reason, allowing anyone along the way to accidentally, or purposefully, stray and make something different, because they have a hunch or just want to do something differently.

Stories are instruments of leadership. They bring the vision to everyone in a simple and tangible way and remind people every day of why and what they are doing. No story, no vision, purpose or roadmap. Just a load of activities that everyone is expected to work hard at without the fuel of knowing why and what the final destination is.

Stories set ambition. You may not reach the final ambition, and you may have to prioritise parts of the overall vison and possibly never get to the full version. But every change that is needed, every decision that has to be made along the way, can be made in the knowledge of what you are trying to achieve.

One of the most fundamental attributes and values in the design process is that it raises our ambition. It moves us upward from knee-jerk reaction to our competition to a future-proof strategy. It looks at what is around us and asks, how could this be, what could we do? This is not some fancy utopia or fantasy. Design is about what you can do. Why would you replace that with inaction? Why would you not want to share ambition and drive everyone in your organisation to work to create something that is practical, pragmatic and better?

In an age full of medical malpractice, social inequity, environmental crisis, political miscalculation and scientific mistrust, striving to design better to help us achieve better outcomes seems better than the status quo. Stories are the way we show what good looks like. Then, we can start to go there.

Target Visions and Stories for Redesigning Thinkers

1. Don't do anything until you have travelled along the target vision of your idea, checked it and accepted changes that improve it. The value of doing this now, before you commit resources to develop your policy, product or service, will help you hit your objective. You will have the impact you desire and the reduce the cost of discovering potential barriers and hurdles whilst change is cheap.

2. Share the journey with people and get their input, it will always be to your, and your audience's, advantage.

    Ask if the journey communicates your uniqueness, differentiating factors, purpose and ethos. Is this the chance to convert those brand values you commissioned and that are on the walls of meetings rooms and on your intranet into something that your customers actually experience?

3. Tell great stories.

Target Visions for Designers

1. Use the customer journey map to dig deep into the micro-events that will deliver the change you want. Kick the tyres, be realistic and make a believable journey that is convincing in showing how your design is better, will achieve the objectives of the user and the organisation and is believable. Journeys that are too happy are not believable: Make your journey go wrong and work out how to repair it.
2. Don't be afraid to iterate and constantly improve your journey. Understand the motivation and incentive for your target person to go through the journey. This is the engineering of the experience, the bit where everything comes together, and your vision becomes possible.
3. Feel the love. Where can you bring the emotional context and brand values of the organisation into life? How does each part of the journey hit the core values of any design: simple, accessible, clear, inclusive and trustworthy? What other values can be bought to the journey? How do you show security, or empathy, or honesty and accountability in a journey? If necessary, develop the values of the experience as part of the target vision exercise and identify what brand elements or values impact each moment of the journey. Figure 9.2 is designed to stimulate the describing and application of the values at different points of the journey.

Values can be expressed as principles, to be applied when appropriate, with explanations as to where they have impact so others can apply them in a relevant way. Design in colour, design with emotions and values and bring the vison to life.

Examples of Design Principles

Principles can be methods and guidelines. Those used in the UK by Government Digital Services (GDS) are instructions in how to approach the design of a digital service and are aimed as much at managers as designers. The famous first principle, to design for users' needs (not the manager's), is followed by a list of best practice methods to ensure you design appropriately, efficiently, with plenty of evidence and in a way that will create a consistent user experience across many different situations.

Other principles cover sets of values that can be interpreted in a variety of ways but which ensure the core value is present. Some examples might be:

"Getting to Know Me"

How might we recognise and acknowledge customers? What does familiarity look like in a retail store, a surgery or on a website? We are used to personally addressed letters and being named once we have logged into a website. That's more difficult when we walk into a store and might even be slightly disturbing if a store worker knows our name as we walk in the door. But a loyalty system or a pass card can allow acknowledgements, as airlines do when you show your boarding pass as you board and the can identify you as a loyal customer.

This principle generates loyalty and a long-term relationship with a customer. For the customer, it's the feeling we get when we go to a restaurant we have been to before and are acknowledged as we enter. For the restaurant, it's the certainty of repeat business, and a friendly customer.

"Attentive Service"

Do we know the context of a person who is using the service? Do we have data that can be used to anticipate people's needs or circumstances better?

If you contact a company, it might be useful that they can see your recent transactions. If we know your history, or your specific needs, we can predict your preferences. For the customer this can feel special and build the relationship that leads to brand loyalty and for the business, the benefits that brings.

"Celebrating Colleagues"

This is a principle that is aimed at those who deliver service. In many regulated industries such as financial, government and healthcare, there are rules and guidelines to keep customers safe and their personal information secure. Rules of compliance, and risk management limit and restrict the people you talk to in banks or hospitals. Usually, these rules are drafted in a legalistic way by people far from customers and they can negatively impact on the experience we have of those services. For the person you talk to in a bank or government, it can be a minefield of rules that are often changing and difficult to stay ahead of. This can adversely affect a front line service provider's confidence and promote "computer says no" behaviour.

Celebrating colleagues was a principle used in financial services that empowers staff to make decisions that benefit the customer. They have to keep to the rules, but sometime interpretations can be more generous, more empathetic and overcome illogical processes that frustrate. Empowering your staff can make a difference to a customer's appreciation, makes them more loyal and brings happier staff.

These kinds of principles can be interpreted according to different contexts but they provide a golden thread that can be appreciated and lead to better experiences and easier relationships between an organisation and their audiences.

Reasons to Love Us

What might make a human love what you deliver? Is it generous, empathetic, kind or beyond their expectations? This could be a million different things, but the principles encourage us to consider what love might look like. Is there a reason to love what you do?

One of the most famous sets of design principles are those of the product designer Dieter Rams. Rams was the designer of many products for the German company Braun and developed the minimalistic aesthetic with a focus on function. This aesthetic came to represent the brand, and went on to inspire the designer Jony Ive and his team's work at Apple. Although his principles are focused on the physical object, they work across wider contexts too. Think about what it is you do. Is it honest? Does it look good? Is it innovative?

Dieter Rams' 10 Principles of Good Design

1. Good design is innovative
The possibilities for innovation are not, by any means, exhausted. Technological development is always offering new opportunities for innovative design. But innovative design always develops in tandem with innovative technology, and can never be an end in itself.

2. Good design makes a product useful
A product is bought to be used. It has to satisfy certain criteria, not only functional, but also psychological and aesthetic. Good design emphasises the usefulness of a product whilst disregarding meaningless decoration that detracts from its purpose.

3. Good design is aesthetic
The aesthetic quality of a product is integral to its usefulness because products we use every day affect our person and our well-being. But only well-executed objects can be beautiful.

4. Good design makes a product understandable
It clarifies the product's structure. Better still, it can make the product talk. At best, it is self-explanatory.

5. Good design is unobtrusive
Products fulfilling a purpose are like tools. They are neither decorative objects nor works of art. Their design should therefore be both neutral and restrained, to leave room for the user's self-expression.

6. Good design is honest
It does not make a product more innovative, powerful or valuable than it really is. It does not attempt to manipulate the consumer with promises that cannot be kept.

7. Good design is long-lasting
It avoids being fashionable and therefore never appears antiquated. Unlike fashionable design, it lasts many years – even in our throwaway society.

8. Good design is thorough down to the last detail
Nothing must be arbitrary or left to chance. Care and accuracy in the design process show respect towards the consumer.

9. Good design is environmentally friendly
Design makes an important contribution to the preservation of the environment. It conserves resources and minimises physical and visual pollution throughout the lifecycle of the product.

10. Good design is as little design as possible
Less, but better – because it concentrates on the essential aspects, and the products are not burdened with non-essentials. Back to purity, back to simplicity.

These principles cover every aspect of design and are as relevant today as they were when Rams created them in the 1970s.

Dieter Rams' 10 Principles of Good Design — 161

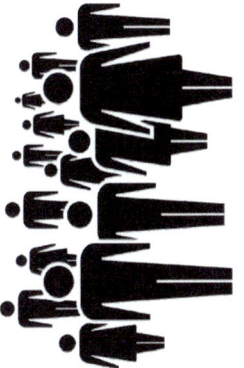

Derek starts to spread the message across his employees and customers and begins to see the **benefits** of sustainable farming. He realises the **consequences** of not making the changes he has made.

"**"**I was a sceptic but green farming has changed my life - and increased my revenue!"

Derek becomes a **green farming ambassador** and innovator. He's on Track to becoming a carbon zero farm.

Derek is sceptical about sustainable farming but gets a report and uses an app that outlines short term and long term changes and incentives

Derek is reaping the benefits of sustainable farming as he grows his customer base, connects with his local community and the network of sustainable farmers.

"I provide my customers with what they want when they want and with the least hassle"

Derek runs the farm he inherited from his Father. On an annual inspection, he is advised that **guidelines are changing**. He's told about the **FARM GREEN** initiative and cash incentives....

Derek uses the platform to track his carbon emissions and is provided with recommendations and community help to reduce his carbon footprint and save money

Figure 9.3: Six-panel storyboard on a virtual whiteboard, RCA Executive Education, Service Design Masterclass.

Creating the Story

We have crafted our journey. We have drawn it in colour with emotion and values and have understood where principles touch each part of the journey. Now let's pull it together to create a narrative we can share with others.

Given the standard unit of CEO attention span of 1 minute 30 seconds and the need to make a compelling case quickly and get to the point, I set workshop participants the task of telling a story in 6 panels. The guidelines are:

1. The first panel is the target customer, business or consumer, citizen, boss or whatever human represents the person you want to take on the journey of your new idea. It also includes the definition of the problem or situation you are designing for – a change in legislation, new technology disruption (with a problem to solve, of course), whatever the context is.
2. The last panel is the happy ending showing the impact, the problem solved, and the new opportunity grasped.
3. Panels 2,3,4 and 5 tell the story of the events, touchpoints, features, interactions and experience of the target human through time. Four panels do not seem much and this is deliberate. If you can't describe the journey in 6 panels, you run the risk of losing your audience. A short, sharp story that tells the story of how things are made better is not the full story, but it sets the scene and captures your audience ready for the detail.

Another important and useful idea is to make an ad for your concept. It's harder than many expect, and you have to boil the idea down to its essence so that they can see the benefit, that it's for them and a call to action in one panel. If you can't sell your ideas with the story and the ad, maybe it's not such a strong idea and you need to run it around again to strengthen it.

I've seen some excellent 6-panel storyboards in workshops. One of my favourites is a panel showing a project taking a climate sceptic farmer and transforming him into an evangelist and enviro-entrepreneur for sustainable farming and rewilding. It was completely believable and brilliantly delivered and would have convinced the hardest CEO (Figure 9.3).

The world is full of stories that show the impact of design. The purpose of the story to share, encourage, inspire and help see that something can be different, is one of the most powerful methods of fostering change in business, society or for the planet.

Dan and Jane Nash of Narativ specialise in developing storytelling around design solutions and have worked extensively with the students at the RCA to develop their ability to tell stories and create compelling narratives. They identify four main components to storytelling, which I think apply to all storytelling but are especially useful for service designers:

- Listening as a part of a research process – working as a team, building relationships with partners and stakeholders, understanding needs, collecting illustrations and case studies.

- Capturing project experience as stories – looking at 4 types of stories that will be useful in different contexts:
  Origin stories: where you and your project come from.
  Milestone stories: the ups and down of the journey.
  Impact stories: what you achieved.
  Future stories: how your story will be told in the future.
- Communicating the process – telling the story in an engaging way so that you inspire and enrol your listener in our story, bringing to life the human journey of the service, for a client, investor, or other stakeholder. They ask you to understand how to tailor your story for different kinds of audiences, to empathise and be sensitive to different mindsets.

Stories are the raw material of service design. Creating believable, compelling, problem solving and inspiring stories can make your vision, strategy and execution come to life and provide the North Star to guide your companions to success.

Chapter 10
The Blueprint for Change

Everybody that's successful lays a blueprint out.
Kevin Hart

At this point in our journey, we have used the design process to create target visions, defined our North Star and set our ambition for positive change that makes our policy, business strategy, organisation goals or social impact objectives clear. But this is just the map, we now have to go on the journey.

Service designer Sarah Drummond, founder of the design agency Snook and now of the School of Good Services design training organisation, developed a view of an organisation as a "Full Stack". Sarah has developed a tool that allows us to see how all the parts of an organisation can come together to impact, negatively or positively, on the experience we have.

In our journey maps and our target journey mapping, we begin to have an awareness of the systems that cause pain, or which work well. The blueprint helps us map all the system elements required to deliver a new or improved service, which is a powerful device to communicate change and stimulate collaboration. But the Full Stack model reminds us that there is even more at play in understanding how an organisation works and comes together to make things happen.

I have seen a great many pictures of icebergs in PowerPoint presentations in my life. The iceberg is of course a great analogy for anything where size and complexity are hidden from view whilst we are only aware of the shiny white part serenely floating on the ocean. But it's an analogy that works and even more so in the Full Stack model.

The model addresses that service design is focused on the part of the journey we see and interact with. In delivering better human journeys, we often find that they are derailed and fail due to the myriads of decisions beneath the surface, political, economic, technological, or cultural. We can imagine a great service design from the user interaction point of view, but if we want to deliver it, we need to work under the waterline to ensure that those myriads of "little accidental decisions", as Sarah describes them, don't do to our iceberg what the iceberg did to the Titanic and sink it.

When we look at the whole iceberg, and how all the constituent parts of a service experience stack up, we can see several levels of strata.

The service itself – all the things we touch and interact with. This is the top line of our target vision or existing customer journey map.

Infrastructure – the elements that enable the service. This could be physical space, digital applications or objects and the way they behave.

The organisation – the way we are organised – if it's in large central clumps or disconnected, differently incentivised units that work against each other, decisions may be difficult to make.

Intention, purpose. Why do we do what we do? Are we protecting our customers, or empowering our citizens. Are we here to make money whatever it takes, or have a social or environmental agenda?

Culture. How are decisions made, what is the role of hierarchy or collaboration and how do individuals perceive their position and purpose.

The Full Stack model reminds us of how organisations are complex but if we don't have a view of how all these are connected and work together, we lose efficiency through added friction, decisions have to made from scratch many times over, people diverge on their sense of purpose and lose energy and organisations struggle and possibly fail.[1]

The Blueprint

A blueprint is a term that refers to a different time and a different process of developing complex structures. Early techniques of sharing an architect's or civil engineer's drawings required a process called dyeline printing, where an ink drawing on transparent tracing paper was fed through a machine with a paper that reacted to ultraviolet light and produced a direct copy of the drawing with a blue tint (and a strong smell of ammonia!).

So, a blueprint is the copy of the drawing you take on site when you are building large structures, or engineering complex forms for manufacturing. It describes the materials, the shapes, the dimensions, the assembly and everything you need to know to build a part of an engine, construct a house or a bridge.

The blueprint is an ancient and forgotten term, as is the graphic representation of a floppy disc to represent saving your file on a digital user interface. But it's purpose in detailing what to do to make something makes it a powerful and extremely useful service design tool of the suite.

A blueprint is not a process map. When we design services, as they are complex and require an organisation-wide approach, we tend to think from an organisational perspective when planning a new activity. That can lead to a process-led way of defining what we need to do.

A blueprint is different, as it combines both the human-centric view with how it will be delivered. We can think of it as a conductor's score, where the notes that each instrument need to play can be seen, but the overall experience is the sound of an orchestra playing a piece of music.

---

[1] https://sarah-drummond.com/full-stack-service-design/

The ability to combine the human element, both the receiver of the experience and the deliverer of the service, with levels of interaction beneath it, across time, demystifies and makes clear what and when the organisation needs to deliver. Which means it can plan, bring together various parts of the organisation to collaborate with a shared view of the purpose of the journey and all the detailed actions they are required to complete it successfully and efficiently.

Without a blueprint, you get anarchy, political disagreement, misunderstanding and mission creep. You get technology tangents (when a developer decides they know better and goes off in a different direction), siloed working and all the things that are common in the everyday life of an organisation. Blueprints create a more coherent, mission-orientated, human-centred, managed and planned approach to improvement, innovation and transformation. Quite useful, don't you think?

At the same time, it's important to remember that the blueprint is a very useful tool, not an output. It's at the end of the second Double Diamond in that it defines precisely what you are going to build now that you have discovered the problem, reframed it, found many potential solutions and prototypes and tested them so you can have confidence you are building the right thing. The design is done, now build it.

The metaphor for a blueprint is more normally a theatre. A theatre has the performance on stage, where the whole experience is played out. We can see the actors and what happens to them. But we also know that there is a backstage, where people change the set, operate the lights and sound effects. And behind that are the builders of the stage props, the writers of the play, etc.

For this reason, you will see that the core structure of a blueprint consists of the events that happen to the person experiencing the service, the actor if you like. The acting takes place on the front stage, where the set and activities all take place. Backstage are the enablers of the service that are unseen, but without which the performance would not be possible.

If we use the metaphor of a restaurant we can see in even more detail how this works. When we walk into the restaurant, we have already decided to go out, chosen the restaurant, booked it and travelled to it. We then go through the door, are met by a real person before taking in the décor, sitting at the table and reading the menu.

The food has been cooked in the kitchens from ingredients that have been grown locally, or supplied by wholesalers who have sourced from around the country or from the other side of the world. All of which must happen for all customers, every night and every day. An amazing feat.

	Aware/Find	Buy/Join	Use	Grow	Stay
The Journey Events The story of the new user journey and all the things that happen at each stage	The service story: context, experiences, solutions and conclusion					
The Touchpoints Everything the user comes into contact with. Places, objects, people, communications & digital	All the points of interaction wih across people, time, place, communications, objects and digital interfaces (apps, web etc)				
Brand and Design Principles How do your brand values and design principles impact the user at each event?	How the user experiences brand vlaues and design principles				
Onstage Actions The actions you need to take at each stage of the journey	All elements required to deliver the experience: training, objects, a physical space, communications, apps and web sites, a call centre.				
Offstage Actions What you have to do to design and deliver a service	Digital software development, supply chains, logistics.				
Support Systems The foundational elements required to deliver a service	Technology platforms, data systems, organisational structures.				
Capability What are the existing elements and what new elements are required?	What is the capability of the organisation to deliver the service?				

Figure 10.1: Blueprint layers of interaction.

The blueprint in detail:

The Story

The top line of a blueprint is what happens to the person experiencing your service. It can be your target customer, a citizen, a business, or several different personas who will go through this journey in different ways. But it is the human first, not the organisation.

The line is marked by the key events that will happen over time. As in the journey mapping version of the tool, you will set out every event across time, starting with the trigger that starts the journey, which is the need identified by your user, or perhaps the opportunity you have attracted them to through your marketing or reputation. It will run through the framework of choosing, engaging, and using as before, marking every transaction but also context, though process, wayfinding or available choice.

I have been in workshops where people really struggle with this and put in place the things that they will make or provide. They will put things like "access website" or "collect data". That's what the organisation is doing but not what is happening to the user of the service. For them it will be more complex. It will be "Rosie is sent a link in an email to register online. She fills in a pre-filled web page and receives an email saying she is logged in." The scenario will be told through drawings, because we know they say much more and are more rapidly understood than if you write a novel to describe what happens in each scene.

The top line is what really happens, with only the minimum reference to how it happens. A customer talks to a person over a video call who sets out the options. The customer spends time considering what to do. The customer then logs back in and sees the details previously discussed. The customer asks for a change in information, etc. Not always the smooth journey; we should be aware of what might need to happen if they change their mind. It's all there, in the "score" of the music we are making.

Here are some of the issues and aspects that we need to consider and design across a typical journey:

Choose:
Trigger – When and why do I need a service?
Find – How and where can I find it?
Choose – What are the factors that I need in order to choose: compare features, price, how does the solution fit my context . . . ?

Join:
Buy/Sign Up – What are the transactional elements and context (am I in a store, on line, talking face to face . . .)?
Receive/Use – How easy is it to complete any onboarding process or register, receive and unpack a product or service . . . ?

Use:
Early use – What is the "out of the box" experience like, is it easy, how easy is it to start to use, what is the usability, accessibility and inclusivity of this service . . . ?
Normal Use – How is the experience over time, does it work as well as I hoped? Does it satisfy my objective and do the job I need it to do?

Grow:
Change – Are their new features, upgrades, things that improve the experience or functionality?
Incident – Failure or an event that impacts the experience – what happens if it goes wrong or breaks, is it repairable, and what does recovery look like?

Stay:
Reconsider – What do I do at the end of the contract or is there new competition that is more innovative or attractive? Am I rewarded for my loyalty?
Leave – What is the end like? What happens when I no longer need the service or I want to leave for another one?

These will be different across each journey so working out your keep moments for your journey is a vital part of designing the top-line target journey.

The Front Stage

Call it interactions, touchpoints, points of engagement, they are all relevant. This line describes all the things that people will touch, hear, see and receive during the journey. They are placed underneath the relevant point in the scenario. They are the components that result in the complete scenario or completed journey and are the elements that enable both user and organisation to achieve their aims.
   Examples of touchpoints are:

An advert on a transit system.
The front door of a retail store.
The layout and signage of an airport.
A salesperson.
A QR code on a billboard.
A notification on your phone.

An email.
A letter.
A website landing page.
A downloadable app.
A motorway signpost.
A mailbox.
A delivery van.
An electric vehicle charger.
A bill.

They are all the things that we see and interact with, providing us with information, helping us navigate, transact, warning us and keeping us safe, or providing useful information and instructions we must follow. They are all individually designed, but are essential components of the total journey experience. If they are inconsistent, at odds with the overall objective or create dissonance, then that one small part of the journey can derail everything. Which frequently happens in real life.

Our journeys through life are, in the main, accidental. As I've said elsewhere, everything is designed, design is not an option, it's just people don't usually realise that their decisions are design. They do not make those decisions consciously or balance between business viability, organisation feasibility and desirability of their proposition. As a result, we get a mess. The UK Track and Trace system, for example.

The blueprint therefore serves an important function: It presents the touchpoints in the context of the overall journey. This allows anyone working on any single part of the overall journey a clear picture of the person, context and reason that everyone is working towards achieving. The alternative is that every person has their own view of the purpose of their part in the overall picture, of the person they are designing for and the objectives they and the organisation are trying to achieve.

Now the app designer can see that the app is being used on a bus, or in an operating theatre and make decisions that will support that person in that context. This contrasts with Agile practice that reduces the experience, for greater efficiency of production, into isolated "use cases". There is a moment when that is the correct approach, but not at the experience design level of the blueprint tool. Placing the event in context and showing its purpose and value is incredibly important and useful.

Every touchpoint has its own micro-journey and design brief. How do we interact with airport signage? What is the before, during and after? What is the process of entering our password to access a function. That can take a while if not done well. There are pitfalls and barriers between every touchpoint and it's when they go wrong, because they haven't been considered or anticipated before it's too late to change, that our world becomes frustrating. We then become angry and may reject the solution that might be brilliant in every other way. The details can and do fell the greatest of ideas.

When London's Terminal 5 opened on its first day, the luggage didn't get processed. Luggage was delayed, missed the correct flights and it took weeks to reconnect owners with the luggage. It was an awful embarrassment that takes a generation to be forgotten. Why did it happen? Because the entrance gates to the staff car park had not been tested and on that first morning no one could get into the airport to service the luggage. Back to experience prototyping, you need to test the start to finish human experience, not just the isolated technical testing. The blueprint allows you to see the key moment of importance and focus on those small events that could break the experience. Unfortunately, it is the broken moment that we remember despite everything else working beautifully.

We tend to think in a very product-focused way that emphasises the touchpoint in isolation and not as part of the big picture. Designers will design a product or a digital interface without concern for how it will be disposed of at the end of its useful life, or how the website copywriting might fit the tone of voice of the marketing campaign. It's rare to find that level of continuity but we really notice when there is inconsistency. At one point in my product design life I designed for SodaStream. They were owned by the chocolate and drink brand Cadbury Schweppes. They made adverts that celebrated the parties you could have with their water-carbonating machine. However, the drinks maker itself was a sinister machine that looked more like a piece of military equipment.

Brand Behaviour and Design Principles

The usual blueprint diagram doesn't show this aspect of the journey, but I think it's an important consideration at this point of the design process and one that deserves to influence the mapping of the touchpoints against the experience events.

It is well understood by businesses, organisations and even governments that brands are an important part of how you are perceived by your audience. A brand is a promise that represents the purpose of an organisation. Whether a food and drink brand, like your favourite fizzy drink or breakfast cereal, or leisure or gym wear, the brand becomes part of your identity, your tribe. Brands build respect and trust and are measurable as a financial asset. If they are damaged in any way, it can be very difficult to rebuild trust and delete the memory of scandal or the stench of bad practice in your supply chain.

To sustain and repeat the values of a brand and to maintain its value in a way that is meaningful and sustainable, we have to understand the behaviour and experience of a brand. A brand is much more than a logo or a marketing campaign. It has to be understood by everyone in an organisation so they can make decisions that reflect the values and expectations of a brand.

We looked earlier at brands such as Orange who went beyond the expected in helping their customers understand how to use their phones. The brand of Apple is present in the logo, but also in the particularly complex radius the corners of their products have (they are not simple quarter circles, they are a series of ellipses that we hardly notice are not exactly circular). But more than that, their brand is seen in the care of the graphical interface, the connectivity of their devices and systems, and how they share a Wi-Fi codeword with a contact who wants to join the same system. Subtle, surprising because we never thought of it, innovation.

The designer Adrian Westaway and Carla Gaggero run the design company Special Projects. Before training as a designer, Adrian trained as a magician. Special Projects use magic as a powerful creative tool that creates solutions that extend beyond our expectations. He celebrates Apple for the Maglite power connector on their original laptops. Walking into a laptop cable of any other manufacturer usually means your valuable laptop is dragged onto the floor. Not the Apple Maglite connector, which is held in magnetically so that if you trip over the cable, the connector just disconnects without dragging the machine with it, so no harm done.

This is a brand value that connects to their marketing message to "think differently". It is present as a way of designing that is embedded into their corporate behaviour – much more powerful and valuable than just a logo of an apple with a bite out of it.

It is now quite common to see the emotional aspect of a brand strapped to a logo and increasingly present as a set of guiding words and principles. The Audi car manufacturer communicates its German engineering tradition in the phrase "vorsprung durch technik", which possibly not that many people know means "lead by technology". A powerful strapline that promises quality and reliability and is experienced through the multiple tactile interactions with the car and long-term reliability.

Brand values are increasingly about the behaviour of the people within the organisation. Barclays Bank created the value framework of Respect, Integrity, Service Excellence and Stewardship, sometimes shown as RISE. These are valuable and commendable values, if they are adhered too. But what do they mean if you are the designer of the Barclays app, or the local branch or a call centre operator? These are more difficult to understand but are just as important to the delivery of a moment and event with a customer as they are about the behaviour of senior management.

But understanding what the experience of a brand value is requires thought and careful design. If you are designing a "respectful" app, that is full of integrity, what does that mean and what does it look like?

Although we think of the blueprint as a framework for showing all the activities that are required to deliver a service, it's easy to forget about the way these activities need to be delivered and to what values and purpose. This is where the

Full Stack approach is not simply the wider picture, the reality above and across the user experience. The purpose and ethos of an organisation and the values it holds need to be present in those events and the way each activity is designed and delivered.

Some of the best blueprints I have seen attach the brand values or design principles that represent those values to the blueprint below the touchpoints so a designer, product manager or technology developer are aware and can see what is important to deliver at each moment of the journey. The values may have a different value, or emphasis, at each point of the journey; there will be times when the values such as seamless, or helpful may be required and others where security and safety are prioritised. Some values will be important to every part of the journey and the blueprint can show what value needs to be emphasised at which point and remind and guide on how the event should be designed, to ensure the values of the organisation are present and not just words on a meeting room wall or in your induction pack on the first day of work, never to be discussed again.

Brands are important and valuable and can differentiate you from others and create lifelong loyalty that has enormous financial value. The blueprint is a point where those values can become tangible and designed into the experience that will be created. Remember that if you don't consider them, then the experience is an accident and your brand values devalued or intangible.

I used the brand of a social housing group earlier. How might those brand values be represented on the blueprint and what would they look like?

You might argue that all these values need to be in very moment, but some will be more important and tangible than in others. Identifying precisely what honesty means in the awareness part of the journey might seem obvious as transparent and authentic marketing or information, but it needs saying and it needs be designed to be a tangible aspect of that part of the journey.

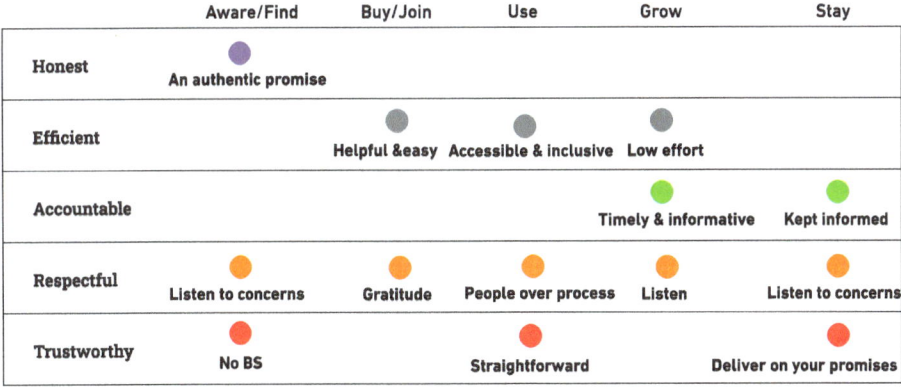

Figure 10.2: Where to deliver different brand values across the customer journey.

The other example of principles for a financial service identified knowing the customer, or exceeding expectations in quality of service. Understanding how your customer data can be useful to the customer rather than just you needs care to design the right experience. This should not be left to chance; your organisation will deliver better results and achieve greater impact by understanding how your brand is meaningful as an experience as well as a promise.

On-Stage Actions

The next layer of the blueprint identifies the actions that are required for each moment of the journey. We've described what a touchpoint is, the actions are what is needed to deliver the experience at the point of contact.

At this point we can identify the people, their roles, the places, the digital touchpoints of app or website and everything that is needed to be constructed, trained and ready for the service to be delivered.

People: The human element of a service, despite the attention given to the digital aspects of service delivery, remain an essential part of the experience of many services. Some examples are:
- Retail shop staff
- Experts in healthcare, finance and law, or in the set-up of technology, or expertise in specific equipment, or in a hotel or luxury experience. The role and ability to give advice tailored to a person's needs remains essential for many services
- Support staff such as call centres

Lou Downe in Good Services argues that if you need a phone number and a person to speak to, the digital aspect of a service has failed. But for some, speaking to a person is a mark of a higher quality of service, and there are still many people who do not have access to internet tools, or do not wish to have them. The point that a digital service such as a chatbot upgrades to a human is a much-discussed battleground and as AI grows in depth and quality, we may well find our needs serviced by digital touchpoints. But that moment has not been reached yet and the most valuable aspect of AI has been in assisting human experts answer other humans' questions consistently, compliantly and accurately.

Places: Touchpoints are often places, shops, cinemas, museums or offices. The design of spaces is often led by architects rather than service designers, but understanding the context and overall service experience leads to better spaces that deliver to the needs of the people who visit them.

Banks have become much more than a queue and a till as the needs of business customers, wealth management or financial advice are integrated into the design and layout of the local bank branch. In the case of the Lloyds Bank flagship store in London, the environmental credentials of the bank are displayed alongside the advisor meeting rooms.[2]

The role of the web and the rise of mobile applications has come to dominate brand experience. Every brand service needs an app, apparently. We've looked at how to challenge that notion but, in many situations, digital can provide valuable access to information and knowledge, tracking past behaviour and supporting many aspects of life. Our technology platforms, websites and apps are vital to service delivery, but they are only part of the total experience, and understanding that not every part of the service comes through the glass of a mobile phone is important to understand.

In defining the technology interaction in the blueprint it's necessary to remember what role the tech is playing. Is it answering a problem, providing a choice or completing a transaction? What is the purpose at each moment? It is not sufficient to say, "access website". It's vital to understand what the value of the technology solution at that point is, and how should it be delivered.

Offstage Actions

As the name implies, this is the stuff that goes on behind the scenes.

People who deliver the service require training, support tools and management processes to ensure they are able and empowered to deliver a service. In the case of call centre and support staff, this will include the digital tools that they require to answer questions or sort problems out.

One problem for governments and organisations everywhere who have support staff talking to people on phones or via chat is the quality of their software. Whereas so much time and effort is spent on ensuring that customer-facing websites and apps are easy and delightful to use, the tools support staff use are usually lowest on the priority for design, yet, as you might expect, have a direct impact on the quality of service the customer receives. How many times have you been on a call to be told that the server has gone down this morning, or there is no access to the information they need. What you don't see is the usually terrible user interface that they are having to deal with, complete with timers telling them to resolve the call within the allotted period or their performance target will be missed.

The blueprint is asking us to make decisions and understand the impact of them. Just because we call this layer "off stage" doesn't mean the consequences and impact of them is hidden. These decisions and inviable systems impact

---

2 Lloyds Bank, Oxford Street Branch: https://www.lloydsbankinggroup.com/who-we-are/sustainability/our-operational-climate-pledges/net-zero-carbon-operations-lloyds-bank-oxford-street

greatly on the service experience and usually get the blame when failure is met. Are they supporting our visions and mission? Are they usable and accessible? Have they been chosen by an expert in IT, or a human-centred designer responsible for the impact and service quality? Understand how these decisions are made and the value against cost issues and your organisation will be more successful and a lot happier.

This section of the blueprint also brings in your suppliers and their supply chains. Do they understand the mission you are on? How is the service fulfilled, i.e., packages delivered, systems maintained over time, external customer-facing touchpoints aligned and quality control carried out? A successful service needs to manage all the elements that allow it to be delivered, sometime those outside or beyond direct control.

Support Systems and Processes

Underneath are the tech platforms, the APIs that connect data together and the collection of data and analysis that brings value to both organisation and user.

Data: Capture the value and purpose of data that creates benefits for both service user and the organisation. Designers are not data experts, and I don't believe that is the role of designers or managers. But designers do know what to ask for and look for in data that will drive improvements, support and ease the burden of users and the organisation. We need to understand how to keep the data we capture safe, model it to inform our decisions and render it into new value – services or business opportunities that bring value and delight to people.

Terrible Tech

At a more fundamental level, it is off stage that we think of the technology platforms on which are built applications and web services, the data and security required around that to store and allow access to. The choice of technology platforms is usually a major cause of service experience disaster. The criteria we use to decide which software systems to provide HR, customer relationship management systems or basic transactions are rarely chosen using the criteria and insight into what problems are required to be solved or their empathy with either customers or staff.

If you want to redesign your thinking, rethink procurement and how and why decisions are made. They are usually, as many governments have found out, disastrous projects, run over time and budget and don't deliver anything of value. In some extreme cases, such as the Post Office Horizon case, thousands of lives, as well as the paltry issue of corporate reputation, are destroyed. And yet we repeat the mistakes every time.

The Capability of the Organisation to Deliver the Service

There are many versions of the blueprint framework and, as with all the tools and framework from service design that I am explaining here, they can be adapted to your context, organisation or service. Critical moments, performance metrics and policies can all be placed on the diagram as they are needed and affect the outcome.

But at this stage, as the blueprint becomes a sprawling size of a room diagram with every action roadmap and enabler identified to bring the service to life, we have to make one final big decision. Can we do it? Do we have the capabilities required to achieve this brilliant new innovative, market-disrupting and winning transformation? Is the concept desirable but also viable and feasible? It's likely we have already asked and answered those questions, but this is where our whole process reaches the tipping point of becoming reality and we need to know that it should be done, can be done and for the right costs for both the organisation and receiver of the benefits.

It is rare to see this on a blueprint, but it is possibly the most important question of all. Designing a new journey, product, service or proposition has to satisfy and balance a lot of criteria, for the business and the user. Having used the blueprint to identify the requirements (in a way that is much more effective and powerful than a requirements specification, by the way), now we can overlay our capability. What road map needs to be influenced by your intentions, who is responsible and is this a project already in play or a new direction, not considered before? Do we have the technology or data available to achieve our aims? Do we need to purchase another company or develop a new capability to match our need?

In balancing the viability and feasibility with the desirability, we start to make some tough decisions. Are we reaching to our new template of ethical technology and sustainable viability perhaps incorporating radical new business models? Do we understand the social impact of our policy decision, business strategy or community project?

The answer may well be "no". We may need to phase our journey to nirvana, or prioritise a part that will have maximum impact from minimum change. We will need to balance cost with the perceived value of a feature, enhancement or journey event that we have created.

At each point we do need to ask ourselves and make difficult decisions on what we can and can't do and this is the normal way of managing decisions, but we can do that against the North Star of our blueprint and desired journey. We can match the value and perceived value of a series of events so we can have a high degree of certainty on what is desirable, viable and feasible. Our decisions will be less opinion, less intuition, less individual but more collaborative, with good data and a clear vision of the mission we are on. Our risk is reduced, our decisions are clearer, we have redesigned our thinking.

I am not surprised that so many service design graduates have told me that the companies that they work for find it such a useful tool. Grounded in journey mapping and a user's eye view of ambition and what good looks like, tracking through time and events from a user's point of view and then overlaying all the activities, touchpoints, system requirements and technology value is a massive undertaking but gives everyone involved clarity and articulation of what needs to happen.

Of course, all of this happens all the time and every day, we just are not aware of the decisions and how they are made and they are not made strategically, with a clear idea of who and what we are designing for. The blueprint just makes tangible, and visible, the decisions we have to make and places those decisions in the service of the people who will use them.

Blueprints show the future – they can be used to make improvements and upgrade a product or service, or they can be used to imagine and prepare to build a completely new one. They give us clarity, are able to identify and explain to any part of the organisation what their role will be and this makes then a powerful tool for collaboration. Collaboration is the main requirement to designing successful outcomes – without collaboration we have the peaks and troughs of everyday disaster which is so much of our world.

Blueprints for Redesigning Your Thinking

The blueprint is your x-ray of who needs to do what and where the action is. It's complex because taking action in an organisation is complex, and it's better to see that complexity than be unaware of it. A blueprint can become a governance document that can guide all your future decisions and prevent people going off-piste and working on their own strategies that will deviate from your journey. Don't throw all your hard work away, the blueprint keeps you on track.

Blueprints for Designers

Impress your clients and colleagues. Map out their future actions and road maps for a better world. Make it real, don't hide difficult stuff, decisions, trade-offs and prioritisation will all need to happen. The blueprint will ensure that change does not derail the vision and the hard work you've done to find the evidence, create the solution and prepare for the massive collaborative effort that is delivery.

Chapter 11
Making Change Happen

> *Design is far too important to be left to designers.*
> Raymond Turner

The impact of change, through a decision or innovation, always demands an understanding of the complexity of systems that are affected by change. Not taking account of the impact on a system is a common reason for failure of innovation or even small improvements to solve a challenge.

Luke Roberts, in his book on systems in education, gives some four definitions of systems and how they work. The four types range from the simple, complicated, chaotic to the complex adaptive, and understanding how they work allows us to understand why things keep happening in the same way, how they are interconnected and a change in one part of the system will have a consequence in another part of the system. Luke makes the distinction often missed between the behaviour of chaotic systems, in the sense of small things effecting bigger system behaviours outcomes over time, whereas in adaptive systems there is a interplay between making change and response to change happening. Understanding the behaviour of a system is critical in our attempts to change a system to allow for a small improvement, or complete transformation.

Luke provides useful examples of the different system types in the context of education. To paraphrase and oversimplify, a simple system is like riding a bike: There is a direct consequence of our action of moving the pedals that stops under our control when we get off. Simple systems in behavioural terms are often a much-repeated ritual, which has a historical legacy and has become embedded in the system. Over time, it may have become unfit for purpose in a world that has changed, and it may now lead to negative consequences, but is so embedded in the culture that it goes unnoticed.

In complicated systems, the parts come together to create a processes and sequences with regularity, but if one part goes wrong, everything stops. Chaotic systems are not really about anarchy, but they are where a small element can, over time, build up to a storm. Chaotic systems like the weather, mean we have familiar types of weather, but we can only predict the probability of the weather changes rather than the certainty of the change.

Complex adaptive systems are the result of feedback loops and regulatory forces that affect networks of interacting points, which we could call people, who are organising and self-managing. A lot of nature works in this way, as do organisations.

These different classifications of systems encompass the totality of elements that are in play in creating the experiences and events we interact with. The components of a system embrace many familiar parts of an organisation, whether in healthcare, financial systems, government services or our local restaurant. Systems are made up by the people who work for an organisation, their roles, motivations and incentives. They are made by the way they work, the tools they use and the platforms those tools work on. Systems are affected by the culture of an organisation or a department and how one action impacts on another. It's why change is often so difficult if you're not starting from scratch (which is the great appeal of a start-up, where you have a blank canvas to develop your idea). There are usually lots of unseen connections that need to dance to a different tune if one part is changed. Systems need to be taken care of, understood and, when possible, used to promote positive change rather than present barriers.

Small Changes for Big Impact

Chris McCormack was a designer at the Helix Centre at St. Mary's Hospital in London, a collaboration between Imperial College and the hospital to identify innovation and improvements in healthcare. Speaking at a conference on the work of the unit, Chris described the difficulties of changing something as complex as a hospital. He pointed out that it takes generations to change the whole system of a hospital, but drew on the experience of the successful UK Olympic cycling squad, who created a gold-medal-winning team through a strategy of perfecting a large number of small improvements that collectively culminated in the competitive edge they needed to be successful.

Chris' solution was to create ripples in the system that collectively effect change. He invited us all to ask the question:

> What's the smallest design that will have the biggest impact? Healthcare is a very complex ecosystem, any big change is likely to fail, so look for the smallest pieces of design that will have the biggest impact. If you want to create change in a large, complex organisation, you need to create ripples that will eventually lead to waves of change. Drop several stones in each pond to generate multiple ripples.

This idea that there is one part of a concept that can create a lever for change without demanding a massive system change is a common thread for designers of services. When systems are complex, identifying and prioritising one aspect of the system that can be easily changed and have a disproportionate large impact is a powerful way to start the chain reaction of change and transformation, without total disruption. Whatever your project, try and identify the minimum design intervention that will provide the largest impact.

Change by Discovery

Working in the world of financial services with Barclays Plc, one of the big four UK banks and over 330 years old, it was impossible to ignore the heritage of complex systems, legacy decisions and process-led culture caused by the forces of compliance to meet strict financial regulation. Despite that historic legacy, Barclays have a tradition of innovation, launching the first cash machines (ATMs) in the UK, developing one of the first mobile banking apps and peer-to-peer cash transfers originally called Pingit – now, of course, an everyday task built into all banking apps.

People often complain about their banks. Things go wrong, people don't understand why things happen or need to have information on charges and costs. They might feel unhappy about how they are treated, and, like every bank, Barclays had their fair share of complaints. In the UK, complaint numbers must be reported and shared with the public, allowing customers transparency when they are choosing a bank. This policy has worked well as it focusses Chief Executive attention on complaint numbers. They don't wish to be seen as worse than their competitors and therefore have incentives to reduce complaints and improve the quality of service they provide.

Barclays had an impressively large and talented design and innovation team who looked to simplify customer processes, especially through the increased use of digital tools. Our job was to redesign the many traditional and cumbersome processes of the bank as well as identify new innovation. Having moved from the digital part of the bank into one of the business units, in the process of establishing a service design resource for Barclays, we started to look at how we could reduce customer complaints. We started by looking at the data, of which there was a huge amount, though often from different sources and sometimes conflicting or differing in how it was categorised.

The data did give a very clear picture, however, of where the biggest problems lay. The largest number of complaints from people were, as with so many organisations, around contacting the bank by telephone and the delays in getting through to a person to discuss their problem or request.

There was a problem though: The call centre data confirmed that the majority of calls were answered within seconds. So why were so many people complaining?

We decided to use the Double Diamond process as a test case to solve this problem and reduce complaints. This involved travelling to the call centre in Liverpool and talking with managers and the call centre operators to discover everything we could about the problems that may cause delays in answering people's calls.

We listened in to customers' calls to understand their issues, the reasons for their call and their levels of frustration or satisfaction. If there was one thing everyone should do in their organisation, it is to listen to the calls of your customers or users, it will be a humbling and revelatory experience. We discovered a lot about the procedures, policies and permissions that call centre operators had to know about and follow. Many problems were well known and could be easily solved, but busy people hadn't got around to it. There was a wealth of insight and knowledge in the operators that gave us loads of ideas on how to improve their customers' quality of service.

We then stumbled on the reason for the delay in answering calls. A bug in the operators' systems meant that when a customer called, the information on that customer that normally appears on their screens, which allows them to immediately see who the customer is and what their previous activity has been, didn't load. However, operators had worked out by trial and error that if they transferred the call to another operator, the customer information did load for them. Calls were being transferred when the information didn't appear, and this was causing the delays as it could be some time in an internal queue before it was answered by the second operator.

This was our "aha" moment. A simple workaround to help the call centre operator understand the customer better was making the wait longer and causing the rise in customer complaints. All we had to do was let the IT team know and they could fix the bug. Except they didn't. They would not admit that there was a bug in the system as they were extremely reluctant to admit that they were at fault. They did not wish for their part of the system to be seen as the cause and in a siloed organisation, with individual performance reporting and incentives, they did not want this black mark on their record. Luckily for them, the bug had not been reported, possibly because the staff were so busy and weren't aware that the call transfer was causing delay and a rise in complaints. The problem was invisible and therefore didn't exist, except for the customers left waiting.

This presented an interesting dilemma, and I began to smell the whiff of internal politics and blame avoidance. Understandably so, but we needed solutions and a reduction of complaints and had to persuade them to admit that the bug existed and that they should take action to resolve it. In the face of their stance, we decided to take a tactical approach. We let it be known that we would move into the call centre and record every instance where the bug appeared over a period of one week, so that we had the evidence to go to management and explain what was required to solve the problem.

I'm delighted to say that the day before we were due to turn up, the IT team moved in and sorted the problem out.

I often say that design is at least 90% politics.

During this project, the experience of collaboration across teams and the opportunity to listen and learn from each other was incredibly valuable. We also discovered that the operators were not particularly keen with some of our more affluent customers who could be quite demanding and more likely to complain, as our data confirmed. Our team devised a training program for a small number of operators where they shared the insights from our research and interviews with different types of customers in the form of personas to help them understand why they were busy or short of time and perhaps a little impatient with their underperforming bank.

Each of the call centre operators who took part in the training was given a plastic golden pineapple, which they proudly displayed on their desks. This had the immediate effect of creating envy in the other operators who demanded to know why they hadn't been given pineapples. They were keen to join the training so they could have one too. A fine example of behavioural science and nudge theory.

Over the next few months, the positive impact of the design process and excellent collaboration across the call centre management and agents lead to some impressive results. Within the first month of our collaboration, complaints had been reduced by 17 percent, which became 60% over the next 12 months, with a 6-point increase in net promotor score (NPS), the favoured measurement of customer satisfaction for most organisations.

This was real, measurable impact that could be shared across the company along with examples of best practice that could be applied to other contexts. No new apps or tech, just making the existing stuff work and helping people be creative about solving their own problems. That's redesigning thinking.

Designing New Lives

Stories are at the heart of service design as we've already discussed. One of the most powerful stories of change by design comes from the service design course at the Royal College of Art.

The tradition of the service design course has been to work closely with organisations large and small, in businesses and the public sector and from government departments to charities on issues that they are trying to solve. Our intention on the course was to prepare the next generation of designers to be ready to effect change and create positive impact wherever they found themselves working.

One particular department which worked closely with students on the course was the UK Ministry of Justice. This ministry is responsible for the judicial system covering the court and prison systems and they approached the course with a simple but very ambitious brief: Could design prevent people who had left prison from returning there?

It is a tragic truth that the rate of recidivism in the UK is around 65%. That is a lot of people and a huge cost, in every sense of the word, to themselves, their families and communities and the government. It costs the country billions of pounds and leads to overcrowded prisons with poor conditions.

Judah Armani was a student on the course having had a previous career in product design and marketing for the music industry. He was also interested in design for social impact – how could design not just design a product or a service for commercial purposes but improve equity in society and support those who are disadvantaged and without the opportunities of others.

Judah volunteered to teach drawing to prisoners at Her Majesty's Prison (HMP) Elmley and was able to get to know and talk to the men and some women who were there. It was his way of researching directly with prisoners to understand what their motivations and ambitions might be. He wanted to learn how they might change their pattern of behaviour away from activities that would put them at risk of returning to prison after release.

Judah had many discussions about skills, ambitions and alternative routes they could take including studying fashion. Many had skills in music: They could rap, play guitar or keyboards, and wrote about their lives and struggles in and out of their prison experiences.

On one occasion, Judah found a cupboard and played guitar whilst recording a rap performance by the artist who would become known as Nathan Somebody. Such was the power and release of that moment that Judah saw a possibility of using creativity and artistry to create an alternative future for themselves.

Prisons have a duty to educate but that education did not well suit the needs of many in prison. Judah proposed an alternative education programme, one that created the space to nurture their musical talent and set up a recording studio to record their music. Judah collaborated with the artists to set up a record label, In House Music, to publish and showcase the music to support a musical career on their return to society. As Judah put it, "it's not a service done to or made for the prisoners, but it's been created *with* and *by* them."

There are now over 60 prisons in the UK with recording facilities and courses in music. There are now 3 in Boston in the US. Over 80% of prisoners still engage with the label after their release from prison and the measured rate of return to prisons for the over 4,500 people who have gone through the programme is under 1%.[1]

It's important to measure the impact of design and the effect of redesigning thinking in real numbers. Reducing recidivism from 65% to under 1% is an incredible achievement and one that Judah and the artists who run In House records have received many accolades. It's one of the most powerful examples of how we can make change happen: working with prison governors and staff, re-

---

[1] Source: Inhouse Records and Royal College of Art.

purposing budgets and bringing the prisoners themselves on a journey to find more positive paths in life.

Judah became the first Head of the Social Impact Challenge Lab for the RCA course, continuing the collaboration with the Ministry of Justice to design and prototype alternative models for the probation system. He led student projects working with those who find themselves homeless through the *Big Issue*, who publish magazines for homeless people to provide a "hand up, not a handout". Judah frames the role of design in society as a "focus on what's strong, not what's wrong".

The rise of service design in government may surprise some, but over the 12 years since the RCA started teaching service design, many of the students have gone on to careers in government departments and local authorities, where they apply a citizen-centric, evidence-led and creative problem-solving design approach to the issues of society.

Designing Policy

Over the last decade, design methods have had significant impact on the development of policy in governments in a number of countries.

The Policy Lab in the UK is a team of diverse specialists using design methods to enhance and humanise the policymaking process for government ministers and civil servants. Taking inspiration from Mind Lab, run by Christian Bason between 2007 and 2014 for the Danish Government, which had a mission to help departments think more innovatively, the UK Policy Lab has sustained a diverse range of government projects of research, problem framing and collaborative policy development across a multitude of areas (Figure 11.1).

Jointly led by Camilla Buchannan and Stephen Bennet, they describe the lab as being at the heart of government and working on some of the UK's most challenging and high-profile areas of policy. "We bring multidisciplinary expertise to help teams understand the present, imagine the future and design ways to achieve the policy impact they intend. Our methods are grounded in evidence, participation and experimentation and draw on diverse perspectives to tackle complexity and build consensus."[2]

With a portfolio of 250 projects, they work mostly with central government policy teams with a mixed portfolio of work as varied as how to expand the numbers of nursery schools, to the future of the subsurface (the systems that lie below ground level, from subway trains to drains). They also work with local authorities, and occasionally international organizations such as the UN, to identify

---

2 Personal interview, September 2024.

how to improve policymaking through design, innovation, and people centred approaches.

The Policy Lab have developed a number of innovative methods and, uniquely, include a team of video ethnographers. They make films about the people who are at the centre of policy development. One example is a film around the "Windrush" generation of migrants to the UK.[3] These were people from the Caribbean isles who answered the call to migrate to the UK after the Second World War to fill much-needed employment opportunities. They later found that their status as UK citizens had not been secured, leading to a loss of their rights to remain in the UK and in some cases, expulsion. Windrush was a national scandal, and the interviews provide powerful and emotional insight, which can be communicated directly to policy makers and civil servants, to help them understand the impact and consequences of policy decisions.

Their methods and practice have helped them develop insights policy makers would not normally have had access to. They help them discover and engage with diverse perspectives and by imagining future trends and the impact of the next generation of technology, policy makers can look beyond current issues.

Through their experience of designing for change, the Lab created a detailed framework of a range of tools for leveraging design and transformation in different contexts and stages of policymaking. It's a master class example of understanding how government works and what levers are available and effective, depending on your role in the process and the context of change.

Camilla Buchannan describes how departments ask: "How can we try a new piece of technology? How can we do something differently? How can we present evidence in alternative ways and gather evidence and alternative ways? How do we get participation, involvement, understanding of people, outside of government, but also for the different parts of policy systems involved in policy development?"

Design is the foundation of their approach, but they do not prescribe a "diet of design and nothing else". They ask how to flip a question round and make it more about designing the best methods for future policymaking, including co-creation and citizen involvement.

In their experience, design becomes more diffuse when it moves into more strategic contexts such as policymaking and needs to interact with other disciplines. The Policy Lab team is made up of a uniquely diverse range of skills from artists to anthropologists that sit on a foundation of design methodology. Perhaps this is the future of design: a starting point of human-centred design methods combined with deeper collaboration across all parts of a system and bringing to-

---

3 Policy Lab Windrush film: https://youtu.be/xEJksQpWkaE?si=kdLtk4F8gfcGIBbM

Styles of government intervention*

Government as a...	Early stage intervention	Framing, piloting and market forming	Scaling, mainstreaming and market building	Acting in mature markets and policy ecosystems
Steward	**Champion** Build a case for change and alliances for action.	**Convening power** Applying government's convening power to draw together expertise.	**Connecting networks** Fostering a process where government, experts and citizens can co-create change.	**Co-producing** Co-deliver by steering different actors from across the system to deliver outcomes.
Leader	**Agenda setting** Build awareness and confidence in new opportunities by providing thought leadership	**Strategy and skills planning** Prepare for changing workforce demands and consequences of change.	**Educating and informing** Ensure regulation is sufficiently agile and permissive to enable innovation.	**Collaborating** Providing platforms for citizens to protect vested rights and interests.
Customer	**Catalyst** Review, identify and prioritise key opportunities with strategic value.	**Standard setting** Develop standards for data collection and presentation.	**Intelligent customer** Utilise public procurement to encourage investment and innovation.	**Consumer, and supply-chain, protection** Protection of consumer rights and upholding of standards.
Provider	**Innovator** Create test beds, sandboxes and trials in real world settings.	**Reformer** Establish legitimacy, harnessing political will for change.	**Service provider** Provide services directly or indirectly through funding and target setting.	**Choice architect** 'Nudging' behaviour so that the default is both attractive and easy.
Funder	**Early adopter** Explore, experiment and trial new opportunities with strategic value.	**Fiscal incentives** Direct finance to stimulate new thinking that can drive future opportunities.	**Grants and subsidies** Incentivise behaviour change through grants or other incentives	**Platform provision** Scale up proven ideas through existing infrastructure and public services.
Regulator	**Encourage voluntary codes** Self-regulation, without legislating, allowing for greater flexibility.	**Governance** Ensure regulation supports the conditions for change and delivers the policy intent.	**Building regulatory environment** Ensure regulation enables the intended policy outcomes.	**Compliance** Support enforcement and harmonise regulatory compliance environment.
Legislator	**Green papers** Publish proposals for discussion with stakeholders and the public.	**White papers & draft bills** Publish proposals for consultation and pre-legislative scrutiny.	**Primary and Secondary Law** Support a bill through parliament and enact legislation	**Amend rules** Statutory Instruments: rules, orders, created by delegated authorities (e.g. Secret. State).

Figure 11.1: Levers at different stages and by stakeholder. Policy Lab and Nesta 2019.

gether diverse skill sets and methods to find pragmatic, easy-to-modify solutions that achieve impact at a societal level.

Policy Design Around the World

In December 2021 United States President Joe Biden announced his executive order titled "Transforming Federal Customer Experience and Service Delivery to Rebuild Trust in Government".

This ambitious document brought customer and citizen experience up the order of government priorities and stated their purpose for "Government must be held accountable for designing and delivering services with a focus on the actual experience of the people whom it is meant to serve", commenting that the public burden of paperwork on the US public exceeded 9 billion hours and referred to a "time tax" on citizens who, when in need of assistance, are confronted by bureaucracy and form filling.

Combining greater use of technology, and of human-centred design approaches to enhance usability and accessibility, the document prescribes a tightly timetabled schedule of improvements in the digital experience of citizens across a wide range of departments. This includes the redesign of the USA.gov website as a centralised "federal front door" from which citizens can navigate to services, benefits and grant programs.

It stands as an invitation to the next generation of designers in the US to step up and into government to help ensure easy access to services and information for all. It is a response to the impact that other international governments' efforts to simplify access and usability of digital services, especially the transformation of the UK government services with the development of Gov.UK.

We have mentioned earlier how the design principles developed by Gov.UK changed the way departments provided digital access to their services. It has been nothing short of transformative to British life through the easing of complex language, accelerated digital access and a more open culture in government.

As Policy Lab have shown, design is more than digital, and there is still a long way for most governments to go in embracing design methods into their everyday activities. The perceptions of design as aesthetic and a luxury commodity still cloud their ability to see it as the problem-solving, risk-reducing, citizen-centred, challenge-busting process that it is. But more and more examples of how design is making change happen are chipping away at old ways of solutionising and "this is the way we do it here" practices that simply don't work for contemporary society.

Organisations such as the UK Design Council have attempted various strategies to champion design in government, from design ministers to departmental design ambassadors. The Gov.UK design team, which at one point was many hundreds of people with research and UX design skills, has been the most effective and from Tokyo to Washington, a combination of digital transformation and policy labs are changing the mindsets of governments and decision makers.

Around the world we see examples of how design is changing mindsets. In Chile, Dr. Nicolas Robelledo, now senior lecturer at the RCA service design course, has shown examples of how policy labs developed closer ties between entrepreneurs and citizens through innovative healthcare solutions. Running a competition-style approach, they were able to rapidly develop prototypes for new healthcare models that went on to be implemented across the nation.

Hilary Cottam in her work at the UK Design Council and her agency Particple pioneered the value of design in connecting policy and people. Her work in creating Southwark Circle, a membership and mutual support group for over 50s living in Southwark, London, showed the way for a new type of social innovation.

From social housing to healthcare, blood transfusion and post office scandals, governments have more reasons than ever to redesign their thinking and embrace more human-centred approaches to the policymaking and delivery of government services.[4]

Organisational Change

As we saw in the pandemic preparedness organisation diagram, the structure of an organisation can play a key role in the effectiveness and inventiveness of its people and purpose. Organisational design can allow people to thrive, inspire and be creative, or it can shut down thinking and close the door to innovation.

Sarah Corney, Head of Digital Experience at CIPD (Chartered Institute for Personal Development), believes that you don't get improvements in customer experience without organisational culture change. Organisations often reject new customer-centred ways of working "as a foreign body rejected by the cultural antibodies in the system".

Organisation development is required to open cultures to a more human-centred approach. This is a collaboration of disciplines including psychology, sociology, anthropology, systems theory, organisational behaviour and management literature. As Sarah describes it, "it is shamelessly humanistic".[5]

The road to a more open culture is unfreezing from past behaviour, not doing change to people but changing with people, group learning, un-learning old ways and having fun!

---

4 Hilary Cottam, *Radical Help: How we can remake the relationships between us and revolutionise the welfare state*, Virago Press, 2018.
5 M. Cheung-Judge and L. Holbeche, *Organisational Development. A practitioner's guide for OD and HR*, Kogan Page, 2015, p. 12.

Design culture is at the heart of facilitating organisational change, if it gets a chance.

Design as an Agitator

The designer and author Mike Monteiro blames design for allowing injustices to happen. In his book *Ruined by Design*, he takes on the complicity of design in working for social media companies who enable appalling examples of social hatred that cause lifelong damage to some, and poor mental health to many. For Mike, design is an act of collusion if you agree to answer a brief that you do not challenge if you believe it may cause harm.

It's a tough call for someone who just needs a job and enjoys making technology helpful and accessible. Is a designer for X as culpable as the CEO when it calls for outrageous acts in the name of freedom of speech?

It's an accusation that could be delivered by just about anyone. We all have probably been part of organisations that did things we don't condone. I wasn't aware the bank I was working for was the largest investor in fossil fuels until there was a demonstration at the entrance lobby.

We all have to make decisions about where we work and what we role we agree to play. For many, working for contentious areas such as for fossil fuel companies is vital to help develop alternative routes for those businesses.

In many areas, design has had a massively benign impact and made positive change happen. Design is not just making things attractive to sell more. Ensuring all have access to the services they need, and can understand them and feel confident in using them is a critical part of an equitable society. Using design to support people to be healthy, manage money, improve their mental health and provide tools for working life is more than just making things attractive.

Take the field of inclusive design. The idea that we should include those with different abilities into the design of the world around us has taken a long time to get there, but there have been huge improvements in integrating the needs of differently abled people with physical or sensorial needs that require different solutions.

The Helen Hamlyn Design Institute has been operating for over 20 years since being set up by two pioneers Roger Coleman and Jeremy Myerson. With a mission to educate designers to consider the needs of older people in society, the institution, now headed up by Rama Gheerawo, embraces neurodiversity, race and gender into its work on creating an inclusive world. Inclusive (universal in the US) design has moved on from the addition of a ramp to an existing building to become a foundational element of every design project.

Inclusive design principes start with the need to design the world for everyone. The wonderful impact of this is that in designing for those with particular requirements, we make the world work for everyone.

An example is the TV remote control. Designed for those who were unable to get up and reach the TV volume or channel changing buttons so they could do so from their wheelchair or hospital bed, it turned out we all wanted one so we could change channels from our sofas.

One of my favourite kitchen products is my Good Grips vegetable scrappers and slicers that were designed for people with arthritis, but are comfortable and easier to use than the traditional potato peeler and much more beautiful.

The lesson of inclusive design is that by designing for all, we all benefit. Our trains and public transport systems have all been improved by high-contrast coloured handrails, step-free platforms and clearer and accessible signage and announcements. Charities, such as institutes for the blind or deaf, play a vital role in effecting wider acknowledgement as well as stimulating better design solutions for those conditions. A number of major banks have run projects with service design students on neurodiversity and removing of gender bias for digital banking apps. These have created innovative new approaches from a starting point of greater empathy and understanding of their customers and their diverse capabilities.

Design Changing the World

Design is bringing change and improving the quality of life across the world. In India design has been traditionally seen as bringing competitive advantage for businesses and a source for innovation in product design. But in answering their particular challenges in insuring supplies of clean water or providing adequate toilet facilities, design teams at the companies Tata and Lever have rethought and redesigned their approach to water treatment machinery and created innovative low-cost nonelectric water filtration systems that are easy to install and operate.

Sanjay Jain, previously head of the National Design Institute of India, sees the trend of design and innovation to solve social problems as a new direction for design in India. "Design in India has evolved significantly, reflecting changes in the economy, societal fabric, technology adoption, and other cultural influences."[6] Through extensive education programmes in over 2,000 design institutes across the country, design has moved from a localised craft-based activity to one that is driving a human-centred approach to digital transformation and government services. Sanjay also points out the impact of digital platforms in India: "Digitiza-

---

6 Personal interview, May 2024.

tion of money through mobile wallets has enabled daily service providers, daily wage workers, and roadside vendors to make the transaction of services easier, accessible and trustworthy. Technology has been wholeheartedly adopted".

Design in China has played a vital role in gaining access to international markets. A multitude of new electric vehicle manufacturers have sprung up using world-class design to capture their own and global markets. Brands such as BYD (Build Your Dreams) are presenting a real challenge to manufacturers in Europe and the US, generating threats of economic sanctions to combat low-cost competition.

But it's worth noting that Chinese companies are exploiting their creativity and fresh approach to bring impressive innovations to global markets ahead of traditional auto manufacturers. Neo, the manufacturer of electric vehicle batteries, have applied a service design approach to reimagine EV battery replacement. They have developed a system to swap batteries out at end of life for rapid replacement and recycling. This is not just a technological and engineering approach, but a total service approach to deliver a ready-to-go system. Whereas more established European battery manufacturers have refined the engineering and looked for performance improvements, Neo have reimagined the solution and created a highly innovative total service experience.

Service design is still an emerging discipline in China, where design is locked into UX and digital development with little advancement into the more strategic and holistic view of design.

The popularity of international design courses with students from China has meant that there are a large number of highly talented and innovative young graduates returning to China with the ambition and energy to work inside businesses and government and develop their ability to innovate their customer experience and outlook. Lin Hu, a designer from China who works in London, feels that design decisions are traditionally made by senior management who are not ready to hear the evidence and insights of research. However, more and more companies are taking a human- and customer-centred approach to sustain success in international markets and stand out from intense competition.

China, with its heritage of manufacturing for the world, is developing a unique approach to service design. China can scale services to a massive level in their own markets and react to the particular challenges in their society of care for an ageing population (over 250 million people in China are over 60) and other issues around rural and urban populations.

Home:Care is a company that provides what the West would call domestic services such as cleaning and house maintenance, alongside care for the elderly in a way rarely seen outside of China. With a strong sense of the basic purpose, service is at the forefront of their business. Their service offer has been developed with both employees and customers, including redesigning of tools they need to carry out their work and the protective clothing required.

In a product-centric world, where services are usually wrapped around the core product, whether it be a car or a financial service product such as a mortgage, it is refreshing and exciting to see service at the centre with touchpoints and products designed around it to be in service to the service itself.

Designing Services in Emerging Economies

Often the challenges and needs of small enterprises in parts of the globe where infrastructures and economic restrictions affect local conditions, design can drive innovation that benefits the wider world.

The lack of physical communication infrastructure in Kenya led a thriving local economy to harness the power of easier to set up and access mobile networks across the country to deliver financial payment solutions. The world's first peer-to-peer mobile payment system came not from technology powerhouse the US but from Kenya in Africa.

Wahu is a social enterprise that provides e-bikes to the thriving gig economy of Ghana. Normally inaccessible to many due to the high prices needed to invest and purchase a bike imported from countries such as China, Wahu takes an alternative approach and provides their bikes through a rental service. That service connects the rider to established delivery networks such as Bolt, which means the rider immediately has access to a source of work that pays for the bike rental and provides a living.

The bikes track activity to prevent them being stolen but, more than that, provides carbon credits as they ride, as well as keeping insurance costs lower. Co-founder Valerie Labi is one of a growing number of female entrepreneurs in Ghana who are redesigning the service and economic models to suit and thrive in the local marketplace.[7]

From sourcing and building products locally to creating innovative and enterprising new business models that are sustainable in every sense, there is much to learn from diverse economies and cultural contexts that will provide the solutions we will all need in the future.

Designing for a Sustainable World

It has been said that approximately 80% of environmental damage is predetermined at the concept design stage.

---

[7] E-bike entrepreneur Valeria Labi: "If I see a problem and I think it can be solved, I follow that thread", *The Guardian*, 30 July 2024.

In inventing, designing and manufacturing the vast amount of stuff that we use on this planet, that's hard to disagree with. As I've mentioned already, I am blamed for the proliferation of remote controls in our house. I try and argue that it's not my fault but Mike Monteiro is not convinced.

The choices designers make can have a massive impact on the environment and are often not always made on the basis of accurate knowledge. It's difficult for a designer to have the scientific knowledge or data required to make the correct decisions: there are gaps in our knowledge systems to assess what is a good or bad material, what will resolve an environmental issue or what will prolong it.

Environmental decisions sometimes feel good, but don't deliver as we intended. Sophie Thomas of the design agency Thomas Matthews is a designer and now investor in environmental innovation. Sophie points out that a single-use reusable "bag for life" tote bag needs to be used a minimum of 131 times for it to have a beneficial environmental impact over a single use plastic bag.

Sophie's company etsaW (waste spelt backwards) was the global first circular-based venture studio with the aim to create, invest in and scale circular economic ideas. "Our interest is to get new circular materials out of waste streams, back into the system for further service. This came from seeing first-hand the real gap where designers want to specify good materials, but don't have the knowledge of where to get those materials from, because there's so much greenwash about materials."

Sophie, along with designer Nat Hunter, shared the role of Head of Design at the Royal Society of Arts (RSA) between 2012 and 2016 and developed, with Innovate UK research funding, one of the first projects identifying what the reality of a circular economy could be. Called The Great Recovery[8] and describing its objective as redesigning the future, the project created a framework that has influenced many and remains relevant today. Focusing on waste and reuse, Sophie, in the introductory video, stated that the work was "an apology for the idiotic design, the unthoughtful briefs and the lack of responsibility to think about the stage of production, the product life". They brought manufacturers, waste recyclers, chemists and, crucially, designers together to engage in how to design for reuse, remanufacture and material recovery. Their four design models of Design for Longevity, Design for Leasing or Service, Design for Reuse in Manufacture and Design for Material Recovery define how we can design for a circular economy and remains valuable and relevant now (Figure 11.2).

Sophie's venture studio etsaW has begun to create a vast AI-driven database of processes and materials that find alternative materials and rediscover knowledge from the past in the use of materials such as hemp and collagen from fish heads to create alternative plastics and other materials.

---

8 The Great Recovery, redesigning the future. http://www.greatrecovery.org.uk

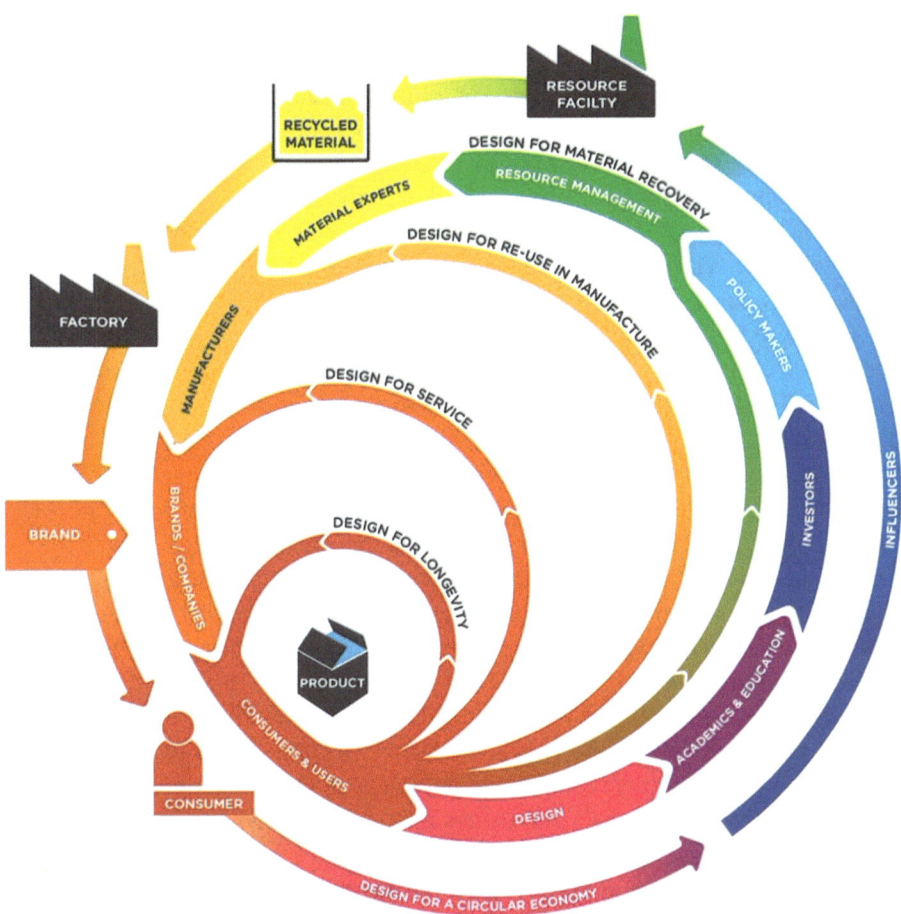

Figure 11.2: Circular economy models from the Great Recovery project.

But the issue is time. "If you think of carbon fibre, it took about 50 years to get from kitchen experiments to be the material specified by Boeing. There's a massive lag of certification testing, scale up and scale out. AI can reduce the sheer amount of tests you need to do because it can run formulas and tell us that, for this particular use, these formulas and materials are the best fit".

Designers are keen to explore new sustainable material, but often lack the technical knowledge or experience of how that material functions or is ready for mass application. For example, seaweed as a potentially excellent alternative to plastic for use in packaging. However, the development of the material is still not at mass scale yet. As Sophie puts it, "it's just not ready."

There are some very successful examples of recycling in high-end materials where the economics are more sustainable. Kevlar is a high-strength polymer used in high-performance yacht sails and body armour, but has a finite shelf life as it degrades over time so its integrity cannot be guaranteed long term. Its ultimate end of life will be incineration – at a huge cost and waste. Through developing the science to reconstitute the resin and fibres and pass the tests required to ensure they are safe, one of etsaW's external start-ups are working on the extraction technology to get reusable Kevlar back into the system, and the economic argument is much more attractive. It's easy to celebrate the specification of more sustainable materials but the adoption of a circular economy needs to overcome the economic arguments against it.

But there has to be a political desire too. Where politicians do not offer support for circularity and regenerative design, it is difficult to drive through new practices. The impact of legislation and producer responsibility that places a cost on materials according to their recyclability and length of life, is forcing manufacturers and designers to think differently. From removing glue in assembly processes to designing for dis-assembly at end of life and recycling waste, new systems, economic models and design practices will make this change happen.

Across commerce and policy and around the world, these examples show us that change is hard, not often desired, but it is possible. Service design is at the heart of change: collecting the evidence, reframing and setting the vision to go forward and engineer the organisation to collaborate and achieve change.

But service design is just a useful tool to achieve an end, an important foundation but part of the picture, not the whole picture. The diversity of skills of the Policy Lab, with the use of innovative tools such as video ethnography, inclusivity, changing business models and values in society and redesigning our thinking to imagine and deliver radical change, for industry and society, is happening, creating ripples and waves of change that are not accidental, not based on power structures or assumptions of others, but with ambition, purpose and pragmatism.

Chapter 12
It's Not Easy

> *Simple can be harder than complex.*
> Steve Jobs

There are many barriers to change. We've looked at levers and inspiring stories of change, but for most, our natural status is quo.

As Ben Terrett, CEO of Public Digital and the Director of Design at the UK Government Digital Service (GDS) describes it: "Change is hard, very hard. People and organisations never want to do it."[1]

But change is difficult to avoid. The cost of stasis, in your product, service, customer experience, or organisation, can hit your profits, your purpose, even your survival. It's not something we can afford to avoid.

Leadership from Within

There are many who are not comfortable with the status quo. They might sense the frustration and dissatisfaction of the people they serve, or listen to the people in their organisation who hear of the problems and the pain of their users. Perhaps they feel the heat of competition, or sense that there are opportunities not being grasped.

They may be leaders in the sense that they are in positions to make decisions and have the power to change direction. But many are not in those positions: They are the beating hearts of organisations, from the coal face of human interaction or responsible for the management for key parts of the systems of an organisation, in that layer between managing their own teams and being managed by those above.

Both large and small organisations, whether a business, a charity or a government department, share the same issues of trying to enhance agency within a system that needs to deliver profit or impact. You are probably working within an atmosphere of competition, lack of resources and investment, restrained by established business practice. Perhaps you are in an industry governed by compliance, regulation and restrictions or a complex ecosystem of external suppliers and partners. You will be affected by all the normal politics and personal relationships that are present in any organisation.

---

[1] Personal interview.

Everything in this book is concerned with making change and understanding our individual roles in making change happen. Herbert Simon believed that we all play a role in designing and shaping the world around us. We are exploring how to uncover the evidence, reason and direction for change. We want to know what will have a positive impact and achieve our purpose. We want to know how to harness our collective creativity to identify how we will generate a positive impact. We want to know how to validate and de-risk our progress. We want to visualise a plan that everyone is both intellectually and emotionally signed up to and can make the right decisions themselves, without micromanagement.

Making sustained progress to deliver the benefits we intend takes leadership from within. This is less to do with presidential behaviour and more to do with diplomacy, persuasion and sharing a collective vision that will carry us over the line.

Our message to the graduates of the service design course at the RCA was to prepare for leadership. That did not mean prepare to be the CEO, though I sincerely hope that will happen now we are well into the second decade of study of service design. This means prepare to lead from within.

For many people in an organisation, this will be a familiar concept. Leadership does not always correlate with positions of power. Leadership can come from within a team – but that is not the same as being assertive and demanding that your point of view is the right one. We must get used to a different concept of leadership.

The context of leadership from within is not easy. By not having positional power, you have to establish respect and earn the right to be listened to and be given permission to facilitate direction. Unfortunately, our perceptions and expectations of leadership are not helpful. The perception of "strong" leaders who direct with absolute certainty that they are right and who demand loyalty rather than be challenged, tend to stick. Those who listen and reflect before making decisions, are often perceived as weak.

Dan Milne and Jane Nash of Narrativ drew a diagram for me to explain different styles of leadership and dialogue inside organisations. Their chart reflects the behaviour of organisations of all sizes (Figure 12.1).

The axis of the diagram is formed from two aspects of leadership: higher or lower energy levels, and whether you are pushing your message out or people are being pulled in. Pushing is with force against an obstacle, whilst pulling is a more natural, shared force. Both contribute to the forces required for change.

It may well be different across different cultures, but for many in business and politics, the two quartiles on the left will be very familiar. Logical Persuasion makes decisions by collating evidence that supports a decision that has been articulated as a logical argument based on facts and data. These facts and this decision cannot be disputed and is therefore perceived as correct. Many of us will feel comfortable in that quarter of the diagram and feel justified and comfortable in our actions, safe from risk of failure, with a sense of responsibility and security.

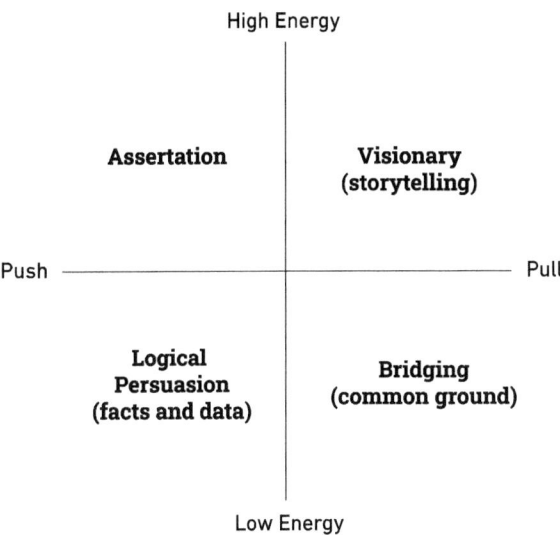

Figure 12.1: Styles of leadership and dialogue.

Assertion matches many people's perception of strong leadership. For both leaders and the led, a feeling of decisiveness feels proper and right. Someone else has made a decision, and that allows us as individuals to follow that path without risk of being questioned or accused of doing the wrong thing. A refusal to deviate and a desire to "see it through to the end" is usually celebrated as strong and decisive leadership.

I think many leaders would agree that it is not necessarily right to be assertive or not deviate and it is good to listen and respond to change. Despite that, many still believe that assertive leadership is the way leaders should behave.

In a rapidly changing world we can also see the benefits of being agile and responsive. We can see the value in listening to others, of including a diverse and even contradictory range of voices within an organisation. Modern leadership does not see it as weak to be reflective and open about how and why decisions are made, or have failed, in order to learn rather than defend.

Common Ground seems a more positive method of making decisions, by bridging differences and agreeing to meet in the middle to removing conflict. It's a low energy way of producing general agreement – arbitration over difficult issues in order to move forward. This might be preferable in contentious and conflicting areas of thought and a good alternative to stalemate and aggressive disagreement, but hardly inspiring and more likely to form a compromise than a powerful call to action.

On the top right quartile, we have Visionary. A vison might be a future possible, a path that illuminates and guides us in a shared direction. Visions are told as stories, not as cold logical facts. The facts can be there, but it's what we decide to use them for that makes the vison interesting and a powerful force for change.

Visions are not fantasies. They are believable, and tangible: You can picture them, and see your role in them. You can understand the value to others and imagine what success will look like. As stories, they are both human and system-focused: They show the human experience and how the system will be configured to deliver that experience. Visions are compelling and pull us along, harnessing our energy to travel along the road to the success.

It's not surprising that we feel more comfortable in a world of facts and logical thinking and feel safer with assertive leadership where someone else has made the decision. However, people who think like designers tend to prefer visions.

The vison is usually the thing that a CEO understands fastest. We can act out our vision, paint pictures and tell stories of future scenarios. Through a story, shown in words and pictures, and delivered with a sense of strategic purpose and pragmatic reality, we bring visions to life.

Visions should be challenged, of course. They need to be supported by the evidence and the facts that are used in their creation. But if we want change to happen, we need leaders to have visons and tell stories that are believable, authentic and inspiring to everyone.

Visions are not just for the ones at the top. They are for us all, to reflect on and use to articulate the future possible. "What does that look like?" "How do they feel?"

Innovation training company Strategyzer create brilliant templates to capture how visions work and where the value exchange lies. The Value Proposition Canvas[2] (Figure 12.2) helps us build pragmatic and tangible value from our ideas. It helps us articulate the functional needs, pain points and opportunities from a human perspective and then identify what actions in a product or service will relieve that pain and deliver the gains.

It's a very useful tool that explains why and how services will have value, but we still need the story to be told. This diagram is a foundation for those who need to see the logic thread. But this is just a tool, it's not a vision that will power change.

People and Change

Leadership within an organisation means working with the people around you who wake up every morning with their own motivations and incentives and characteristics and neurodiverse or typical behaviours and view of what they are doing.

---

2 https://www.strategyzer.com/library/the-value-proposition-canvas

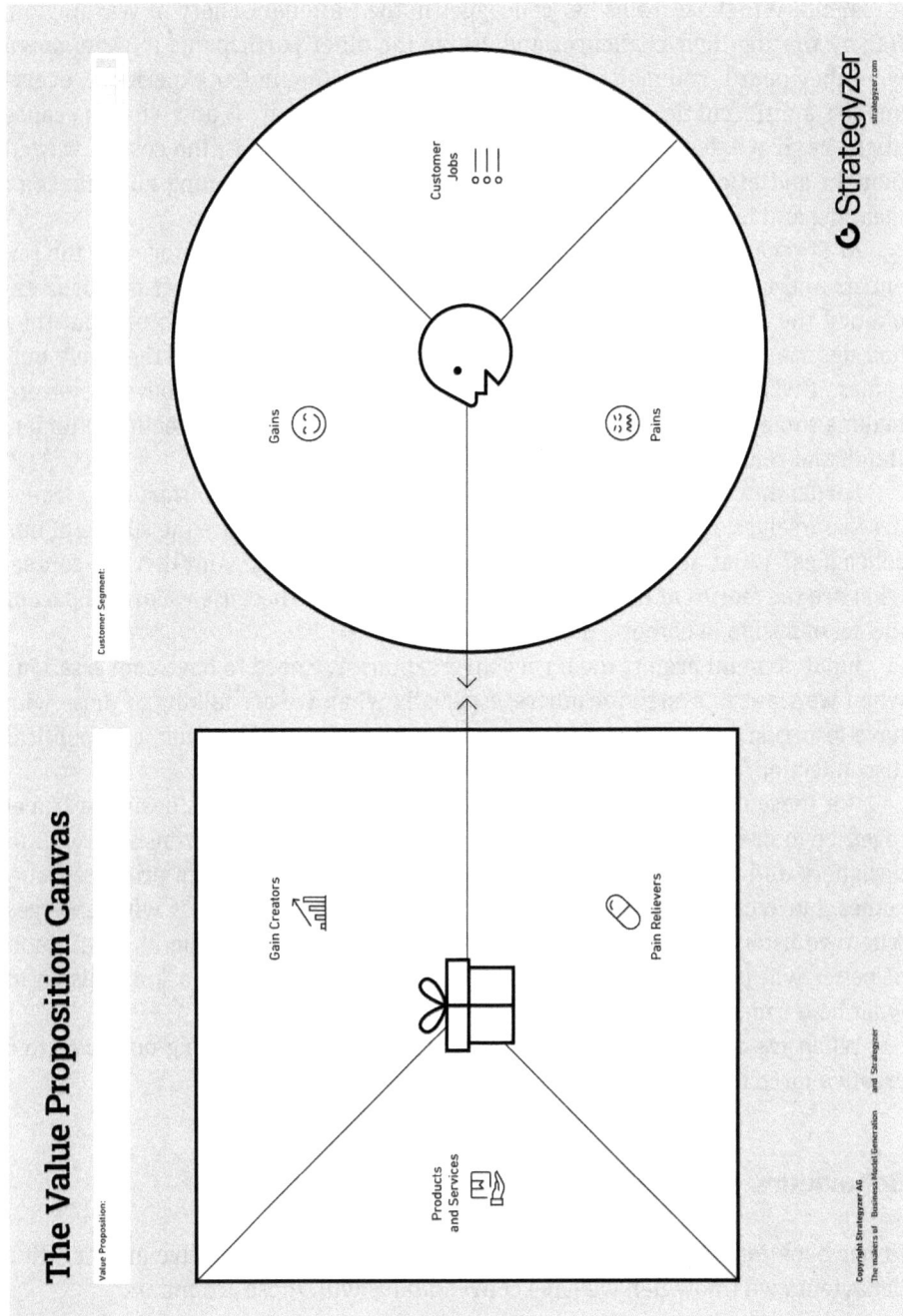

Figure 12.2: The Value Proposition Canvas from Service Design Tool helps capture the benefits and logic of change.

Mendi Wingfield trains her colleagues in the National Gallery in Washington, D.C. by sharing their challenges and asking the other participants to write down what they heard. You may not be surprised to hear that in her experience, everyone has a different description of what the challenge really is and what the cause might be. If we don't rapidly align on what the challenge is, the cost in wasted thought and effort will be high. For her, design is about forming an alliance of meaning and intent at the start, before we start to find solutions.

At France Telecom R&D we developed a practice of bringing together the scientists and designers right at the start of a project. As the project manager explained the concept to be developed, we would produce a sketch of what they had described and asked if this matched their comprehension of the likely outcomes. It was not unusual for half of the room to disagree and believe they were making something completely different to the other half. It's a lot better to understand, and realign that misalignment, early in the process.

Leadership and change start with listening. A good place to start is by listening to ourselves and our colleagues. What's our story? What are the stories of our colleagues? What are the stories of our peers and leaders? And then, of course, what are the stories of the people we are designing for (because we are all part of the act of design, whether a designer or not)?

Judah Armani prefers the term conversations. We need to have conversations when we want to design for others, especially when we are talking to those who have lost trust and confidence in the world, through social, economic or political disconnection.

But these conversations, this knowledge of each other, this desire to travel together to create better outcomes for our business or our citizens, are vital to designers and decision makers alike. We are all trying to make preferred outcomes, but what is preferred, what is better? For Judah, better is what emerges when we listen and, more than that, co-create together. For some, the definition of better will be obvious but we should always be curious and ask and listen to what better means for those we are designing for.

When we are all aligned on our direction, we can then bring our collective creative force to make stuff happen.

Behaviours

In her book *Radical Candor*, Kim Scott looks at the sorts of positive and negative behaviours we find when we have conversations with those around us.[3]

---

[3] Kim Scott, *Radical Candor: How to Get What You Want by Saying What You Mean*, Macmillan Press, 2017.

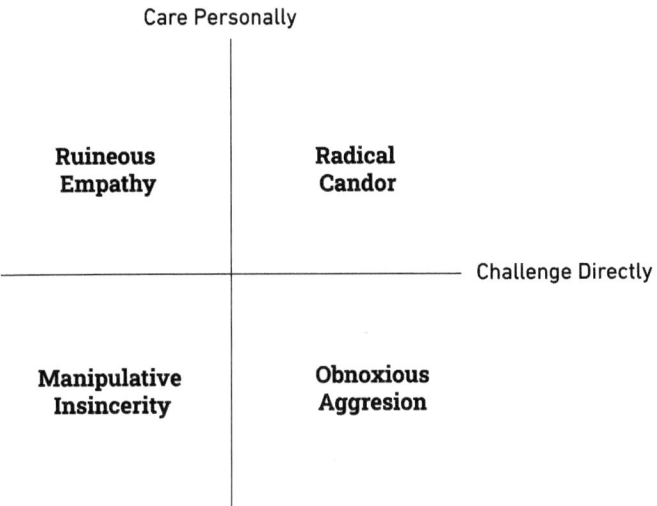

Figure 12.3: Kim Scott's attitudes to change.

This amuses me as it accurately describes the behaviours I've experienced when attempting to make change happen.

Using the axis of personally caring against the ability to challenge, we quickly fall into three problematic behaviours that are not conducive to good collaboration.

Starting on the left, the two categories that we might describe as "weak" are the result of conflict avoidance and an ability to articulate a challenge or a question about what you intend to do.

Manipulative Insincerity is wonderful term for that type of behaviour of people who don't agree with you but don't care enough to challenge you. I shorten this as: "People who you think like you and agree with you, but they really don't. They possibly hate you."

On the same side of non-challenging behaviour, we have Ruinous Empathy. These are people who tell you everything is okay when it isn't. They maybe do like you and want to support you, but they either don't care or are not willing to aggravate the relationship by challenging you so they will simply support you and withhold their beliefs that your path is disastrous. Not helpful.

Much easier to identify, and just as damaging, is Obnoxious Aggression. This is behaviour that conflicts and disapproves with most of your belief system. It might not be personal, but they will really disagree with you, though do not wish to help you or provide feedback that might improve your idea.

This can be scary and damaging behaviour, and is increasingly called out, but it still exists, especially in people who practice with an energetic, push form of assertive leadership. It can be found in many teams and may be caused by fear of losing authority, or individual expertise being challenged, or simply holding an opposing world view. But it is not helpful.

Finally, Kim uses the top right quadrant, which is typically where we define the desired state, to invent the term "Radical Candor". This is where trust and safety allow for behaviour that is honest, not afraid of challenging or being challenged, but personally invested enough in the outcome to bring honesty and authenticity to the conversation.

John Maeda, our most articulate bridge between technology and design, remixed Kim Scott's diagram to reflect his experience developing technology innovation.[4] It's just as revealing, and you may recognise many things as true. For him, the positive right-hand quadrant is Radical Renew, the desire and ability to improve and renew and move forward, together with a shared vison, powerfully and collaboratively.

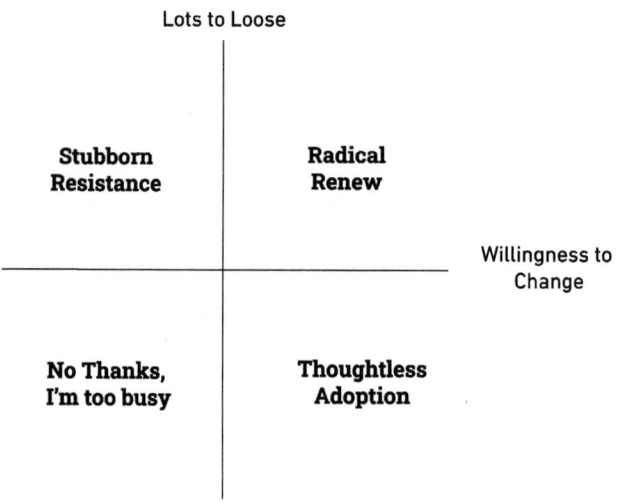

Figure 12.4: John Maeda's attitudes to transformation.

A designer is usually in a minority and suffering from a perception of shallowness, of not having deep relevant knowledge and of not being an expert. The opportunity and role of designers becomes that of facilitators, leaders from within, with well-proven processes and methods and a desire to collectively solve difficult challenges and open up new opportunities.

Andrea Siodmok, in a blog post for the UK Policy Lab,[5] refers to a role developed by US corporates in the 1950s of "Boundary Spanners". This is a term used

---

4 John Maeda blog, 31 March 2019. https://maeda.pm/2019/03/31/radical-renewal-versus-radical-candor/
5 Andrea Siodmok, "From Best Practice to Next Practice", Policy Lab Blog, 24 July 2017.

in social science and science to describe individuals who span across a system to link the organisation "within an innovation system who have, or adopt, the role of linking the organization's internal networks with external sources of information." This is an excellent description of the role of many designers and people who are unconsciously adopting design behaviour.

For the people who use design methods, you need to understand the behaviours of those around you. They may not value your tools and methods and may believe their traditional way of doing things still works.

If asked what advice I wish I'd had as a young designer, it is to understand the reasons for the behaviour of the people around me. Many have disagreed or were uncomfortable with the design approach. It is always better to understand, empathise and then modify behaviour to bring them on the journey, rather than remain in conflict or disagreement. Whether you use a Myers-Briggs personality test or My Creative Type appraisal, understanding and appreciating our differences, on both sides, helps create Radical Candor and Radical Renew.

The head of a design team who had survived often hostile environments described their technique as "resilience and guile". Resilience helps us to not be knocked down and start finding a new job when times are tough but to persevere (I like UK political commentator Alastair Campbell's invented word "persivilience"). Guile is the stratagem, the trick, to outsmart and win over. Two excellent words that every designer needs.

We need to reflect that a designer does not have a divine right to design; it is a responsibility and a privilege. Not everything needs changing; keeping things, building on them rather than changing them, is often the best strategy.

On the other hand, if you don't lead from within and provide the tools and attitudes to help create better solutions, then someone else will. The likelihood is that they will make decisions without forethought, with greater consideration for their organisation than for humans, without properly prototyping or making their decisions tangible and sharing them with others and without any thought of the unintended consequences. Which is what is happening on most days in real life.

Another approach to successful change is to not describe it as design. The poor perception of the role of design is so polluting to many that it can't be overcome and it's better to use another term. Judah Armani describes himself as an educator when working in difficult-to-solve areas in his social design practice. An educator will probably find it easier to engage with a prison governor than if they described themselves as a designer.

But sometimes there are advantages to being labelled as a designer – you have a licence to bring new thoughts, behave in a more maverick style and challenge, partly because you are not taken as seriously as the logical persuaders. On some occasions, working in regulated environments such as financial services, I've been asked to retain the different way of thinking, and not to fall into the same decision-making methods as someone whose job it is to manage huge investment funds. It's the combination of approaches that brings value, specialisms in a vertical expertise combined with expertise in applying and creating value from that specialist knowledge

But this is changing – we have big problems to solve and the methods of processes of designers are increasingly desirable. We must collaborate to develop more sustainable business and reengineer consumption. We need to work together to solve complex social issues and manage the rampage of technology in an ethical and human way to help us envision where we want to go and how to get there. Which brings me to ambition.

Ambition

We seem to have lost our ambition.

In his book *Another World is Possible*, Geoff Mulgan, the co-founder of Demos, one of the first political thinktanks in the UK to gain influence with government, asks why we are so reluctant to create positive visions for the future.

In many parts of the world, we seem to have lost our ability, or perhaps trust, to think ahead, to picture the direction and outcomes we would like. Perhaps, after pandemic and war, and the likelihood of more, we have given up seeing the value in imagining a future that could be blown off course at any time.

In such a climate, we resort to evolution, small changes, triggered by the response to the challenges we see around us. We jump when our competitor jumps, we respond to the current world and ask people what they want now. We don't give them a magic wand to wish for a better future.

One of the greatest contributions of the design process is that through a pragmatic analysis of the current situation, and a creative process of generating new solutions and visualising them to be real enough to evaluate their value, we can move beyond the present. We can raise our ambition, we can show what good and better look like, and how to get there.

To paraphrase a prime minister, where there be cynicism, let there be optimism. Let there be not just hope but a sense of opportunity and of a possible future. Not utopian fantasies, but attractive and pragmatic visons, told as stories, that will drive an organisation forward. We want to give everyone a sense of purpose and reason to get out of bed to work with others to achieve that vision. The methods and principles we are considering here are the architecture that make our ambitions tangible and provide the underlying engineering to make the future happen.

Be ambitious, not reactive. Be responsive, not frozen. Listen, learn and create.

In his book *Centennials: The 12 Habits of Great, Enduring Organisations*, Alex Hill looks at organisations that have been successful for more than a hundred years, in a time when the average lifespan of an S&P 500 company is 15 years. Examining organisations across sport, education, the arts and science, he identifies some key behaviours that have allowed them to retain their core purpose and mission whilst adapting and changing to the world around them.

Institutions such as Sony and Apple have a clear and perpetuating North Star vision that articulates their value and purpose – even in the hard times – that they share, co-create and invest in with their ecosystem partners and suppliers. Steve Jobs' greatest innovations from the Mac, the iPod and the iPhone, have been delivered by extraordinary changes in the practices of their supply chain. He completely reinvented the manufacturing process and materials of how we made personal computers, and did so again every few years.

Resilient and long-lasting organisations think about their future workforce and attract young, and unconventional talent, but they are also stewards of the accumulated skills and experience of their workforce, and ensure their wisdom is heard. They listen to strangers and allow views to be expressed rather than closing their eyes and ears to the changes in the world around them. They ensure their people work collaboratively, sharing different characteristics, to expand their views rather than narrow them.

Looking to the future becomes more urgent when threatened by larger system changes. As the world aims to limit climate change and achieve carbon zero targets, increasing numbers of governments are moving to ban sales of internal combustion engines (ICE) by 2035. The enormous change in strategy and research and development required provoked car manufacturers in 2022 to think to engage in what that future will mean to them.

In 2022 there were 13 years before 2035, and to comprehend the level of change in that period, designers looked backward to 13 years before, 2009, to bring an awareness of how much change happened in an equivalent period.

In 2008, the social media platform Twitter was just beginning take off, the Blackberry was about to be replaced by the iPhone, we still used a printed A-Z map book to navigate London, the Palm Pilot was the first handheld computer and everyone though the future was 3D televisions. Another failing technology push.

Looking to the future was an important part of the strategy of car companies where change was unavoidable. Legislation is proving a powerful lever of change across the globe as manufacturers and services face up to a policy designed to address global challenges, from climate change to social equity and technology.

From car companies to policy makers, design tools allow us to analyse and synthesise possible futures and help us make difficult decisions to ensure we are prepared for the certainty of change. This is one of the ways that design is a strategic tool, not just an end of the process application to ensure desirability. The levels by which organisations consciously integrate design into their decision making mark their maturity: and that can be measured.

A Case Study of a Strategic Approach to Design

They might be more widely celebrated for their engineering and product quality than design, but for Stuttgart-based supplier of technology and services Bosch, user experience and design has become a vital component of their operational business. Manufacturing consumer products from lawnmowers to washing machines, power tools to heat pumps, they also supply electronic components, sensors and electrified power trains for the next generation of cars and solutions for the software defined vehicle.

User experience and design has not been an option for Bosch: Their products have to appeal, fit and combine desirable form with excellent functional performance, and their reputation of engineering excellence has been the focus of their design culture.

Over more than a decade, a centralised team has created a strategic program to further develop design understanding, culture and integration in the whole organization. Judith Pfeiffer, Head of User Experience, and Director of User Experience Enabling Bernd Wiesenauer lead a unique organisation at the headquarters of Bosch that helps to develop design capabilities across every business unit.

The Bosch user experience project started in 2010, within the corporate research team that was at the heart of the Bosch tradition of looking beyond the present and exploring likely future developments and trends. Discussions around the emerging discipline of human machine interface focused on how that could further improve the design of Bosch products. Their initial approach was to work with various external design experts and advisors and to then integrate and further develop the user experience methodology internally. Since 2014 methods of design thinking began to be integrated broadly into the development of their products.

Over the years, user experience at Bosch broadened its focus from where it most obviously had value, on the consumer-facing products, to teams beginning to look at broader customer journeys across different touchpoints.

Like many companies, Bosch has carefully evaluated where designs should sit in the organisation: at the centre, working as a central resource for every business unit, or distributed, integrated into individual business units to work around their particular needs. At Bosch, they had chosen a hybrid approach relatively early: a centralised corporate user experience team and decentralised resources in all business sectors. This is a unique approach, one that fits Bosch's structure in a way that makes sense for them, but may not for other companies. As Judith Pfeiffer puts it: "Companies need to adopt to fit their unique structure, and we had to create a system that was relevant for Bosch, but probably no one else. It is not possible to copy paste an approach onto another company!"[6]

What is unique for Bosch is the range of business activities. Bosch is active in four different business sectors, from white goods and power tools to automotive industry components, energy and building technology as well as industrial technology, with a lot of different brands and subsidiaries in over 60 countries.

In addition, user experience is product-related, journeys are related to consumers, different industries, to other businesses, and also to internal employees, with the internal services and interactions of the organisation itself. So, there are three very distinctive audiences that all require exciting and compelling experiences that fit their context. That is what Bosch has done, by improving the broad definition of UX design to be more relevant and advantageous to consumer, automotive and other industry domains and by learning how design brings additional value to different industries. In doing so, the company has built up a unique knowledge base that can be applied across their different business areas.

Back at the start of the process, success was won by focusing on a series of "lighthouse" projects. Rather than spread thinly across all product lines, lighthouse projects highlighted the value UX could generate in a voluntary, non-mandatory way.

The solution that fits Bosch best is a centralised team, which is quite small for an organisation the size of Bosch, focused on growing the competencies of the individual business units. As a result, and an important metric of their success, the total number of designers at Bosch has grown largely, although the central team has remained almost the same size. There is a clear differentiation between the corporate role of bringing the best knowledge and practice across the company and the operating units mainly carrying out design themselves.

For Bernd Wiesenauer: "One of the main tasks of corporate user experience is to provide the enabling part: training people or supporting them in setting up the organization in order to develop a service approach and develop the professional competencies in the right way. This is something that was and is still really successful."[7]

A particularly successful method Bosch uses across the different business units is also a unique one: Initially called the UX Maturity Model Index, this has now become a Transformation Index, reflecting the increasingly important role design has in Bosch.

The concept of a maturity index that measures design competency has been around since the 2000s when the research company Nielson published a table describing the different levels of adoption of user-led design practices. The table

---

6 Personal interview.
7 Personal interview.

covered various attitudes, the position of user-led designers in the organisation, whether there was budget allocation right up to being an essential part of corporate strategy (Figure 12.5).

Jacob Nielsen, 2006

UX Maturity Stage	Featuring	Time to next stage
1: Hostility	Developers simply don't want to hear about users or thier needs	Up to decades
2: Developer-Centred	Design team relies on its own intuition	2-3 years
3: Skunkworks	Guerilla user research or external usability experts	2-3 years
4: Dedicated Budgets	Usability is planned for	2-3 years
5: Managed	Someone to think about usability across the organisation	6-7 years
6: Systematic Process	Tracking user experience quality	6-7 years
7: Integrated User-Centred Design	Employing usability data to determine what the company should build	~20 years
8: User-Driven Corporation	Usability affects corporate strategy and activities beyond interface design	~40 years

Figure 12.5: Nielsen's original design maturity index, from hostility to corporate strategy.

Bosch created a framework that measures current design activities in a business unit before raising their ambition and navigating to the next level that maps what is required to get to there. Measuring elements such as the level of design in strategy, analysis of designed touchpoints, organisational structure, and management of design are corelated to five levels of maturity through which business units are guided and mentored.

For the last two and a half years, Bosch formed a UX Advisory Board in order to validate the UX Maturity Level Model and to identify trends. This board was supported by the external experts Roberto Verganti, innovation guru and professor at Stockholm School of Economics, Harvard Business School, and Politecnico di Milano, and Gesche Joost, Professor at the Berlin University of Arts, and myself.

For Judith Pfeiffer it's critical to be able to talk about the business value of design. Translating design into business language, bridging the gap between design and user experience and business is crucial.

Design is an integral part of Bosch's strategy for success that will answer the challenges of the future. The tool of building mature capabilities in all business units has become the map to the future. Design will be at the centre of answering the challenge of climate change through materials, technology, services and business models: It will show how the power of AI can be brought to customers, businesses and those who work in Bosch. Design will ensure inclusive and accessible products for all and build stronger and more valuable relationships with the consumers and industrial partners Bosch provides their expertise to.

We may have a perception of Bosch as engineering led, built on the German tradition of engineering excellence. It is certainly that, but it is also a pioneer of how to integrate design tools to ensure it thrives in times that require answers to new global challenges and ensure it continues to deliver economic success and growth. Design is a key driver of their future success.

How to Redesign Your Thinking to Bring Design Into Your Organisation

For organisations who are sceptical about design, you need professionals who can articulate and tell the stories of companies such as Bosch, who convert user experience and design to create value. Design works best with leadership from above and advocates on the ground who enthusiastically deliver expertise across an organisation.

I work with organisations of every type, sharing the tools that we use in service design and inviting people to take control, drive the car and solve the problems they thought they couldn't solve. And they do, again and again. Whether it be a fire station or a luxury hotel, a national financial authority or a social housing trust, a considered approach using design methods can and does transform their thinking and delivers success in whatever way they measure it.

It's counterintuitive but you don't need another expert from your industry: You're that expert. But you do need an expert who will turn your telescope around, view your organisation with x-ray specs, from a customer or citizen's point of view. An expert who will allow you to draw your own conclusions, plans and actions to sort out what you need to do first, and then in the long term. This is not management consultancy, no one's telling you what to do, just how to see and learn.

A 21st century organisation that has not acknowledged that the people who you serve can help you create better, and that design is not handbags and decoration and is a useful tool that allows you to touch and feel the future before you have to commit to it, is an organisation at risk. Talk to people, invest in designers, you don't need many, and don't fire them, they will be your best friends, make you look smart and be successful.

How to Design for Success

If you are a service designer and have experience of working inside organisations, you will be aware that the appreciation of your value and ability to have impact can vary hugely depending on that organisation's purpose and culture.

I've spent most of my career in organisations that didn't want me there, or that I had entered through subterfuge in a Trojan horse. I've always found it better to prove your worth before you shout about what you do. I look for the burning platform and elbow my way to solving it and showing that this stuff works.

Service design is a collaborative occupation, you don't do it on your own. You are always part of a team, working with very different skills and behaviours. It's why we insist that students studying service design work in teams. They usually hate it at first, but learn quickly to enjoy the collaborative creativity and skills blending of a team, which serves them well as preparation for the professional world.

We touched briefly on whether you should be called a designer or hide behind other terminology. Many say that designers should adopt the language of business or policy to be successful. I agree, but I also think that leaders and managers of all types should learn more about design and improve their capability and knowledge of the tools that bring so many epiphanies, solutions and value to their outputs. Eventually, education will help us here but, in the meantime, understand the people you work with, their pride and fears in their own knowledge, respect and facilitate conversations between everyone you meet, and you will increase your chance of success. You do have superpowers, but you don't have to wear the cloak all the time.

Chapter 13
Redesigning Thinking

> *It's not reinventing thinking, it's redesigning thinking!*
> John Bird

From not being able to change the oven clock when the hour changes seasonally to developing a strategy or policy, our processes for making decisions can inflict a range of outcomes from mild consumer frustration to damaging social impact. Incredibly unfair and tragic outcomes can make the headlines, whilst the mystery of and our inability to reduce the pile of remote controls around the TV rarely does, but the unforeseen consequences of technology and the slow-motion impact of climate change are becoming more and more apparent each day.

Yet we rarely question how we make decisions. We cling to established models of leadership and decision making, individual mavericks and pseudo data-driven largely emotional responses to problems, challenges and the opportunities of the world. We think big when we should be thinking of the details and small when we should be thinking strategically and not just pushing down the bulge in the carpet to find another one pop up across the room.

John Bird, founder of the *Big Issue*, has been worried about the way we make decisions for a long time. Having championed the plight of the homeless and developed the street sheet the *Big Issue* to help the homeless by asking others to give them a hand up, not a handout, he has gone on to become a Lord in the UK Parliament. As Lord Bird, he has championed the poor, the disadvantaged and underprivileged and made it his aim to influence policy that reflects those other parts of society who are less well considered or served.

Lord Bird has spoken passionately of his belief that we need to reinvent how we think, to change the way policy is made to take account all aspects of society and create fairer and more equitable outcomes. He used the phrase "reinvent thinking" to describe a new way of taking actions through different criteria that creates better and fairer outcomes.

I was delighted when Lord Bird agreed to visit the service design course at the RCA to view the "work in progress" show of the service design Masters students. They had been developing new ways of providing a helping hand to the homeless for the *Big Issue* in the aftermath of the global pandemic. The business model of the *Big Issue* is to sell the magazine to the seller so they can sell it to people passing on the street for a profit that they keep.

It was a model that worked well in a world where people traditionally had cash in their pocket but during Covid-19 and after there was a big reduction is the use of cash. This threatened their sales, and they had to consider cash-free payments and alternative ways of supporting the vendors.

The students on the course explored various aspects of the positive and negative public perceptions around giving money to people on the street. The transactional process of buying a magazine from a homeless person gives a positive uplift from providing a helping hand. They researched and developed new models of supporting an individual over longer periods of time to provide them with a more sustainable and independent future.

Other students had worked closely with the Ministry of Justice and an organisation, Catch 22, dedicated to supporting prisoners through the probation system after release. The slightest mistake or missed meeting during that process, through a miscommunication or change of venue or delays on public transport, could have massive consequences. People who are well able to return to society and continue with a meaningful life can easily find themselves returned to prison, at great cost, for the rest of their sentence.

Lord Bird saw the powerful presentations of the students' research and the redesigning of processes that created new solutions that could be rapidly prototyped and tested. He saw how design tools could tackle complex challenges with new energy and creativity. When asked what he would like to redesign, he answered "thinking".

It was a powerful statement and one that reflects his desire to find different ways of thinking and making decisions. Starting with people, understanding a problem first and changing your mind if new evidence tells you something different, having an epiphany, admitting you were wrong and celebrating a new truth – his redefining of his objective as redesigning thinking rather than reinventing was a wonderful twist. It affected me very strongly; I often shared his moment of epiphany and was glad that he appreciated the real meaning of design – our conscious consideration of the possible based on an understanding of the present, and then taking action to get there.

Design is an act of shaping the future based on what we currently know, but so is every decision we make that aims to solve a current challenge or create better solutions for the future. Every decision has a consequence and can be seen as an act of design: a conscious decision based on data, information to help us achieve a strategy or higher purpose.

The techniques used to design anything for the people who will use it to their satisfaction and to the purpose of the organisation that is creating it, are laid out here. If you're a service designer student or practitioner, they will be familiar to you. If you are involved in decisions, no matter whether detailed or strategic, then the idea that you should consider who your decisions will impact, how effectively they will be delivered and how they will have the impact you intend, then the methods described here should be extremely relevant and useful. But if that is not the case, then let's consider how they can play a role in our everyday challenges.

Sarah Corney at the Chartered Institute for Personal Development has experience of working with many professional institutions. She has seen that it often takes a considerable amount of time before organisations begin to understand that the users of their information or resources have an experience that needs to be designed. The emphasis is so often on the content material or product that the experience of the user is something many organisations simply don't consider. They don't see it because their own experience is around the challenges and targets of creating the material and they don't walk through the act of navigating, finding, and using their own service. We tend to see and care for the part of the process we are responsible for and rarely look over the fence to see how the whole experience is being linked together and don't live the experience of the people who access our service.

It's an understandable but ultimately highly risky approach. It tends only to get considered when something goes wrong, or when customer satisfaction is measured and scores badly. That can often be the trigger for leaders to realise they are under threat of being responsible and criticised. In that circumstance, organisations rally round the issues, and everyone sets out, with the best of intentions, to use their intuition and knowledge of their systems to identify improvements.

How often do they interview the people who are complaining? How often do they experience the experience of their customers or people who use their service to see what it's like? How often do they make assumptions on how to solve the problem, act on them, before realising they haven't made a difference?

This blind spot in many organisations does represent a major business risk, one that is not touched on in business school. Perhaps it's not seen as a critical issue compared to those perceived as being more important aspects of running a business. When design is taught in business schools, it is for finding innovations that can gain differentiation and business value.

Innovation-hunting start-ups rarely consider the people they are designing for; they are so deep in the day-to-day challenges of raising funds, finding and keeping good staff and running development at breakneck speed. And we wonder why so many start-ups fail.

We are currently living through the rapid rise of generative AI platforms, all of which are terribly designed with difficult-to-find account management and clunky sign-up procedures. We live our lives on virtual meeting platforms, every one of which has a terrible onboarding and set up experience. We create fabulously inventive and innovative resources, services, applications and tools, most of which have significant barriers to adoption that create a high risk of failure.

When we plan for growth, a natural obsession with investors in emerging companies, the established emphasis is on channel growth or talent recruitment. "Hire the smart people, let's add 1,000 new channel outlets!" Rarely do investors look at the customer experience, the barriers to adoption and the human drivers of growth, such as making something people truly value, will purchase and are able to use.

Justin Huang, CEO of Tangshuo Experience Consulting, a designer by training with experience of working in China and for international companies, uses data to create better customer experiences. For him, design methods should not be seen as just a tool for improving the customer experience by removing pain points, but as a delivery mechanism of growth. For him, the value of design is in the emphasis on a company's major assets: its customers. Using data to identify and understand who is using your service (as valuable to a commercial business as a government department) and using the tools to develop good experiences that convert to lifetime value and loyalty, is the key to long term business success. "It's about solutions, not tools, that's where designers go wrong."

If we look at the massive success of Amazon, we can see the evidence of that approach. The personalisation and recommendations engine that is responsible for 35% of Amazon's profits uses your data to provide individual value with a super-efficient frictionless end-to-end experience. Their approach of "working backwards" – starting with the customer first, a revealing comment reflecting that most businesses think of themselves first – is a cultural ethos that runs through the people in the company and everything they do, with hyper enormous profits as a result.

We have been looking at how methods that are used when we design something can be used by everyone to make better decisions. Why are they better? Because they balance the criteria for a decision across internal and externally facing perspectives. They engage with the tension between the financial reality required to sustain an organisation and its activities, the capabilities required to create or act at scale and the human perspective: Do people want it, does it match their need and can they access and use it? If any one of those is out of kilter, then there is a significant risk that your efforts will fail.

This balance is critical if we are trying, as Herbert Simon suggests, to devise "courses of action aimed at changing existing situations into preferred ones".

In the full version of this quote, which is not so often included, he goes onto point out that:

> The intellectual activity that produces material artefacts is no different fundamentally from the one that prescribes remedies for a sick patient or the one that devises a new sales plan for a company or a social welfare policy for a state.[1]

This is the essence of why design is inherent in all our decisions. We are all shaping and forming our world with the decisions we make and we should understand how to balance our criteria. Our decisions need to ensure our financial stability: operate within a sustainable framework; work within organisational and technological capabilities to deliver at scale; and create human value that benefits employees, the people who use the outputs and ensure they benefit society.

---

1 Herbert A. Simon, *The Sciences of the Artificial*, MIT Press (MA), 1969, p. 130.

To redesign the way we make decisions and the way we think, we need to do some key things:

Stop Solutionising

Our constant desire to identify a solution and move rapidly to deliver it, without investing in understanding who has and what is the problem, is a massive risk. When the Design Council created the Double Diamond, and Stanford created the 5D process, they did so because research discovered the problem of acting without thinking and created a really simple way to find the problem and then find the solution.

Listen With Our Eyes

Observing what people do and listening to what they say is not the same as simply asking them a question. The power of listening to frustration, dissatisfaction, or, on the other hand, what they would do and wish for with a magic wand, is extremely revealing and a powerful insight that allows us to experience their nightmares and see their dreams. But observing, experiencing the experience of others, considering all abilities and diversity of culture – these are invaluable insights that are as rich as the most enormous database. AI will undoubtedly help but AI doesn't see customer frustration, or the confusion on a hospital patient's face, or the bit of tape that fixes a problem you never knew they had.

Share Your Ideas Early

It's not clever or good leadership to drive on relentlessly with an idea when you haven't shared it or shown it to the people who will be affected by or will use the idea. Don't hide your work, have the courage to share your decision, your concept, and use the skills of people who can present your idea early and realistically enough that you will have a chance to throw it away, or learn and improve.

Defer Judgement

One of the most difficult parts of a designer's life is quickly putting an idea together and find out it's wrong. I know it's just part of the process, but people tend to see this as a failure rather than what it is: filling a blank piece of paper where others won't or can't, and risking the sharing of it to get a collective opinion and develop/improve it to move towards a better solution. Yet I can't help feeling that I'm being judged by not being immediately correct; I'm at fault.

This is dangerous human behaviour that kills creativity. When an idea is shared, you need to lay down the rules that judgement comes later, when we have considered the possible and have criteria to judge which direction to go in. We continue to base our judgement on intuition and although intuition can be a great driver of creativity, it is not such a good tool for making important decisions that may have considerable impact.

We need to allow ideas to fly before we shoot them down. It's not good to say "we tried that two years ago and it didn't work", or "that's a stupid idea, it will never work". Allow ideas to flourish before you find out whether they are the solution you need.

Engineer Designs, Don't Design Engineering

Engineering genius lies in understanding how to achieve a specification. Design processes define the specification of what needs to be engineered.

That relationship sounds linear but in reality it's not – the relationship needs to be close and collaborative and there is a healthy tension. Healthy or not, collaboration is of the essence to ensure a shared sense of what you are doing, why you are doing it and for whom.

The pioneering course at Imperial College that injects user-centred design methodology into software development processes is always a huge epiphany for the technically gifted students. We can be grateful that the staff at Imperial realised the importance of thinking about humans when designing software. Even more importantly, to think about humans, and the planet, when deciding what you want to design in the first instance.

It doesn't seem rocket science, does it, but it is still amazing that science, technology, start-up companies and investors don't consider human-centred approaches when they are developing their ideas. It should be 101 at business schools and universities, from a basis of understanding the value and power of creativity in solving problems taught in education from an early stage. The objective is not to create designers, but to create design-ready politicians, business leaders and citizens with the creativity to solve the problems and challenges of life.

But more than this, we need to think differently because we have some big issues ahead, and the conventional way political and business leaders make decisions is not good enough for the challenges ahead.

In 2000 the Royal Society of Arts (RSA) research team created a foresight document capturing trends for the next 25 years. They foresaw an ageing population where 50% will be over 50 by 2050; an environmental crisis that would lead to low coastlines flooding regularly and periods of drought followed by heavier rainfall; a radical change to the use of sustainable materials and the ability to recycle and manage waste; a change in workplace practices where technology would allow for more flexible working practices.

We are now amid that prediction and despite the foresight of the problems ahead, we have reacted too late. Businesses are reacting to legislation from global agreements to ward off the worst effects of climate change, at the same time as a cost-of-living crisis caused by rising energy costs, and war and political upheaval that has accelerated the threat to long-established business. As a result, a strategic approach to design has helped new-entry brands from various parts of the world to enter markets with desirable and high-quality auto and consumer products that were traditionally dominated by US and European brands. Heritage brands with generations of loyal customers are under threat and having to rethink every aspect of their business.

With sustainability, the power of consumer perception is enough to threaten organisations that ignore their impact on the environment and are slow to develop new packaging, materials, processes and narratives around environmental practice. They are at risk of being hit hard by consumer impatience and rejection and being forced to make radical changes to packaging, materials and workforce conditions in their supply chain.

We lack the knowledge to know what to do. We've cited that 80% of the damage to the environment is caused at the concept stage of a product. This does not necessarily mean that a designer has been culpable, as so many decisions that we should see as design decisions are done by accountants, or engineers or leaders, often without the conscious consideration of the consequences on the environment or the foresight to consider what happens at the end of a product's life.

Jo McCloed, the author of Ends and the creator of a new design discipline he has termed Endineering has pointed out how little thought we give to what happens at the end of life for a service, object or experience. We are so caught up in the development of new ideas and the marketing and selling of ideas, that we are not interested in what happens afterwards.

For most companies, retaining the stewardship of something they make or provide should be seen as an opportunity to retain a relationship over a whole lifetime. To take responsibility, to care, recycle valuable materials, be proud of reusing and a regenerative approach to manufacturing, could be a powerful customer draw and a reason to reconnect, rather than go back to a web search for a new vacuum cleaner when your old one has broken down.

But of course, it is perhaps more expensive to recycle rather than take out of the ground. It is a change to an established way that all organisations find difficult. Therefore, we have to legislate and set new targets to ensure that everyone comes on the journey.

With the march of AI we have another level of challenge and opportunity. What is the devil's contract between the potential of vast improvements in productivity and efficiency and massive reductions in employment? We have some very important choices to make and if we make them badly, we may decline into civil strife and hardship.

Redesigning our thinking to embrace the potentials of AI means harnessing the power of generative decision making by AI alongside our human creativity. It's why we need to emphasise creativity even more, in education and working life. It is the most essential attribute for a successful organisation that can react creatively, build resilience for the future and create a sense of purpose for the organisation to follow and have at its heart.

Redesigning our thinking means putting people first, in social policy, healthcare, public services and commerce. It means building equity to give everyone a chance to thrive and flourish. It means building new business models that incentivise environmental responsibility, building solutions from an understanding of consumers' behaviour and taking them on the journey. It's means consciously designing our future, rather than letting it be an accident caused by different agendas and motivations.

Every time I think things are getting better (and they often are), I find another example of how stupid the world can be. A banking app that I still can't sign into. The cancelled flight that I can't remove after I've checked in. Online forms that ask for all my details, and then ask them again, when they already have them. A particular favourite worse experience is the software used for university applications and for marking their final degree outputs. Same for booking a dental or medical appointment. They might seem unimportant examples, but they show an underlying lack of empathy for humanity, a belief in the system rather than the user, a technocratic arrogance that we should know how something works, rather than the system knowing how we work. Things that are designed from the service providers benefit, not ours. That end with a flourish of "Have a Nice Day!" and "Would you like to rate your experience?"

For young and old, neurotypical and neurodiverse, this causes a frustration and a dissatisfaction with way things work that is damaging, ultimately to our trust in the world around us and eventually our mental health and ability to flourish.

The Manifesto for Redesigning Thinking

- Thinking human first creates success
- Thinking planet sustains business
- Design your purpose and your people will have passion
- Have a vision of what your purpose looks like

- Observe others' and your own world
- Challenge your own ideas, early
- Creativity is your most important asset
- Build the right thing, in the right way

Product as a starting point	⟶	Human as the starting point
Business anchored in the past	⟶	Radical new sustainable business
Seeing Solutions	⟶	Discovering problems
One idea	⟶	Many ideas

The Consequence of Not Redesigning Our Thinking?

- The continual accidental experience of your products, services and policies
- Continual risk to your organisation through lack of responsiveness to change in consumer and social behaviour
- A continued inability to solve problems
- A continued excessive faith in technology as the solution rather than a contributor to the solution
- A lack of foresight that reduces your ability to prepare for inevitable change

It's a definition of madness that we repeat the same actions even after we have seen that they fail. By that definition, we are certifiably mad and unable to escape from a doom loop of outdated leadership models harnessed to arcane economic models based on one-off transactions that lack long term value or trust and that are massively exposed to the dangers of climate change for supply chains and materials. We risk disconnecting from populations that are disaffected with traditional politics and who are increasingly concerned with identities, social and environmental issues and increasing care for the socially underprivileged and ageing.

The objective of design, with its bias to action, is to place value on the quality of what is around us; to take care that it works so we can all have access; and that all is useful and satisfies our right to have beauty in our lives. It's as important to recognise design in a Chanel perfume bottle as it is in the prison probation service, a visit to the doctor and a government website.

But design, perhaps unfortunately, cannot be of use unless it is invited in. Design requires a conscious request to consciously attend to a failure of design. Leaders have to understand that they are designing, often badly, and that they have a responsibility to design the world and that means hiring people who are capable of collaborating across an organisation and who can champion and represent the user, are curious about individual and cultural difference, share creative ideas without bias or judgement and share an optimism and a desire to make things work better, in every sense of that word.

Increasingly I believe that design should not wait to be asked in. With so many challenges, why should we be waiting to be asked to use the methods and creativity of design. Why should we wait for permission, when everyone else is merrily making poor decisions without thinking of the consequence? Those of you who are designers, and those of you who are changemakers, searching for change and better solutions, should act now. We need to create the visions of what we want, describe the path to a positive future that brings our essential humanity and love for others together. Let's look to the future and do something about it, now.

Chapter 14
The Future's Bright

> *The Future's Bright the Future's Orange*
> Orange advert

Dare we think about the future? What do we think the future will bring? Are we prepared for it?

After a series of regrettably unforeseen and unprepared for events such as global pandemic and war and the creeping but increasingly tangible impact of long-term climate change, there are reasons why some might say that the future is a scary place that is difficult to predict and prepare for.

There is a historical tradition of philosophical visions of the future, the best-known of which is Thomas Moore's *Utopia*, published in 1516, that creates a satirical story of an island where social and political practice are a vision of perfect harmony and good governance. The book serves as a device to imagine what a perfect society might look like in order to both criticise the practices of kings and offer a preferred vision for us all to aspire to.

Given that there are no dress makers in Moore's *Utopia*, as everyone wears the same clothes and people are not allowed to have private possessions, it's not a great place for designers (though I'd like to know who designs the garment everyone wears). But creating visions of the future is what every act of design is – creating an image and a plan to create something that does not exist yet, or to redesign something that does exist, to be better.

Literature has long been the preferred European method of depicting the future. From the novels of Jules Verne to H.G. Wells, stories of science fiction and dystopian visions of a future show a future at risk from alien invasion or amazing technological leaps that will allow us to travel through time.

In the United States, Hollywood and television have been the channels where stories, and our expectations of the future, have been set. The TV series *Star Trek* used devices that flipped open to communicate back to the USS Enterprise. When Motorola developed their first consumer mobile phone, it too flipped open to access the keyboard and screen. When Elliot Noyes, the head of design at IBM, was invited by Stanley Kubrick to design HAL (an acronym of letters one away from IBM), the computer whose misfunction was at the centre of his science fiction film *2001: A Space Odyssey*, Noyes designed a multilayer command centre peopled with operators working at various control desks and screens.[1] Kubrick chose a different design: a single red tinted lens with speech recognition and its own sin-

---
[1] Christopher Frayling's brilliant *The 2001 File: Harry Lange and the Design of the Landmark Science Fiction Film*, Rare Art Press, 2015.

ister character to capture the fear of future technology that might decide it doesn't need humans to control it. "Open the pod-bay doors, HAL".

It's over 20 years since the film *Minority Report* depicted a world of facial recognition and citizen tracking. Gestural hand movements allowed Tom Cruise to operate screens and software. It's increasingly a reality now, though the film didn't predict the bias of facial recognition or in the AI used for trial sentencing. It took MIT researcher Joy Buolamwini to find that and many other examples of bias in algorithms in facial recognition software.[2]

In the 2000s, the European Commission research programme Design for Future Needs, bought together several design organisations across Europe to explore how design could support the development of Foresight at a government level and how this could influence policymaking and decisions based on an understanding of the future. Combining science, technology and social forecasting, Foresight is a policy tool that creates probable scenarios to ensure decisions for the future are resilient and proactive to respond to future challenges and opportunities.

The research reflected on the power of literature and films in setting our expectations and preparing us for the future, but it also found that the outputs of foresight, in reports on the shelves of ministers and government officials, may not be the most inspiring or prescient way of keeping the future in mind when we make decisions.

Design, of course, visualises and creates tangible scenarios of what the future might look like. You can touch the prototype or model and engage with a depiction of a probable or possible future. You can share that vision with others and see what they think, just as Whirlpool did with the washing machine that made us believe that plants could clean our clothes. We can invite a dialogue with our future selves to understand what we think of such scenarios and possibilities.

Speculative Design

In a shared concern of the present and a desire to embrace the future, the designers Tony Dunne and Fiona Raby at the RCA began to use design to make us aware of the invisible influence of technology to ask what would happen if technology behaved in a different way to how we expect.

They made a chair with an embedded compass that would change direction when a mobile phone was close by, making tangible the electromagnetic forces

---

[2] MIT Media Lab and founder of the Algorthmic Justice Lead, Joy Boulamwini's pioneering work can be seen in her TED Talk https://ted.com/talks/joy_buolamwini_how_i_m_fighting_bias_in_algorithms

emanating from our phones. They made a technology creature that would roll away from us when we came close to it. They made objects that might have seemed mad and illogical but the messages they communicated brought awareness of how we might be affected by our changing relationship with technology, to remind us that we may need to be more thoughtful of the consequences.

Morphing into new disciplines of critical design and speculative design, practical tools began to be developed. The Future Cone, that projects the possible, probable and desirable future scenarios. Future Wheels that ask if one thing happens then what will be the consequence, and what will be the next consequence and how to manage that. It asks us to look across 5-, 10- and 25-year horizons, (horizons 1,2 and 3), to project what we know now into the future. We can then then "backcast" to the decisions we make today to ensure we make future proof, or at least future considerate, decisions.

For the designer J. Paul Neely, graduate of the Dunne and Raby course at the RCA, the purpose of creating speculative futures is not to predict the future, but to illuminate it. "It's important to explore the possible, not just the probable, to change our understanding of where things could go and what would be preferable?"[3]

For him, we are too comfortable and satisfied and have too narrow a view of the possible. If you are a product designer, you are happiest designing a product and not extending beyond that. A service perspective shows that even a basic product exists in a service ecosystem of marketing, transaction, out of the box and continual use to end of life.

One of the criticisms of design thinking, where innovative concepts have not all succeeded, as they have not considered the complex systems that impact and prevent innovative ideas from succeeding. Without understanding the complexity of the future, our visions and imagination are likely be ineffective.

Neeley quotes Tony Dunne describing the need for leaders and decision makers to "decouple the near-term needs of their business or government and loosen reality's grip on our minds". We are too obsessed with the challenges directly in front of us to look to the future and construct a plan to make better decisions.[4]

Design tools such as speculative design create their own alternative universes but are increasingly being applied to everyday design projects to ensure we consider the impact of our actions and decisions and avoid unintended consequences. Once again, design methods serve to de-risk our current decisions and ensure they don't do damage to our future selves. This is surely of value to businesses and politicians, and ought to be taught in MBA courses and political theory.

---

[3] Personal interview.
[4] Personal interview.

There are examples where this has been used in policymaking. The Policy Lab worked on the future of autonomous shipping and worked with speculative designer Nina Cutler to develop a set of speculative maritime signalling flags communicating to other vessels the various classes of autonomous, unmanned cargo vessels that may well come to dominate our oceans. In imagining scenarios of vessel malfunction, piracy, when nearby ships are in distress, the requirements of future legislation and regulation can be considered and drawn up.

Raising Our Ambition

There are many reasons why we find it hard to consider the future. It feels a place that will never be reached, that events will knock us off our course and hard work will be worthless. Strategy, foresight and future planning can all seem a luxury, quickly swept aside when more urgent day-to-day challenges take our attention.

Yet every nation-state is built on a vision of its purpose and direction. From the US Declaration of Independence to the French Constitution, the UK policy of free at the point of delivery healthcare at the heart of the National Health Service (NHS) or the Chinese One Belt Initiative, each are powerful visions that provide a template for progress and aspiration. These visions can be prone to danger of becoming frozen and unable to respond to changes – the US Constitution was changed to remove the right to keep slaves, though not guns. But we can see that the impact of sometimes massive social and political ambition can be a unifying and driving force for nation states.

Where are our new ideas? Where are our new visions for the future? Where are the scenarios that depict a path, beyond everyday politics and business concerns, that we can discuss and agree on?

In this time of climate crisis, social dissatisfaction and inequality, economic hardship for many and technological impact on our mental health, you might think that this would be a good time to start thinking about what future we would like. We could then start to make decisions to get us there.

Geoff Mulgan quotes the Chinese proverb "When the wind of change blows, some build walls while others build windmills". He describes the reason for social imagination, the ability to focus on future aspirations, as critically important for us all. A future vision that resonates and whose purpose is agreed on encourages and drives both organisations and societies to own and champion visions of a better future.

If there is one thing of value that the act of designing brings, it is to raise our ambition. So often our ambition is stifled by the current view of the world. CEOs glance at competitors and copy their most recent innovations. As Andrea Siodmok, when she was Head of the Policy Lab in the UK government, put it: "We need to move from best practice to next practice, which looks at the future and asks what might be and what could we do?" Rather than using established archetypes, we need to develop new prototypes that explore and provoke, from which we can learn.

This is a design approach that manages future risk as well as explores new opportunities. It allows us to imagine and contrast a resilient future that is less likely to make the mistakes that litter our past. When we measure against the past and the established, we reduce our ability to look up and ahead and raise our ambition.

When we collectively design something new, whatever its shape, using the methods that we apply when we design a new object or service, it helps us go back to the needs we all have and brings creativity to solve challenges that have not yet been solved and to consider what could be. What would we want to have, with pragmatism and consideration of advancing technology and social change? We have a duty, after all, to those following us not to simply pass on our challenges and the consequences of ill-thought-through decisions.

This might seem like crazy optimism, but we wouldn't have the National Health Service, faults and all, if we hadn't had a vision. We wouldn't have rockets that can land on their bases, policies for removal of fossil fuel vehicles and climate change targets (even if they aren't being reached).

The act of design is an act of defining and articulating our ambition. Not a fantasy, out of reach, but a journey that we can agree we want to go on and can see how we can marshal our resources to achieve it. Of course, events will happen, and competitors will disrupt but that does not reduce the value of a vision of the direction you are traveling and the adjustments you need to make in order to stay on that course.

The success of the GDS design project in redesigning every UK government website was not welcomed by those in the middle of government at the time, but the ease and simplicity of interaction with government, the calm, logical, human-centred words now used on government websites, free (mostly, there is always work to be done) of bureaucratic jargon and acronyms, is a quiet revolution that has had an impact on the whole population. Many of the leaders and designers who came from that project are now working around the world to simplify the bureaucracy and increase ease of access for many other citizens. That vision, and the successful delivery, has changed the world for many.

Optimism, Vision and Pragmatism

I have seen the future and it is the next generation of designers who are energised and have the tools to help us rise to the challenges of the 21st century.

Working with the students at the Royal College of Art service design course for six years taught me optimism. The service design course is still only in its second decade but has attracted students with backgrounds in design, business and social innovation. Many students are not from design backgrounds at all, but share a sense of vision and pragmatism that they want to bring to visualising new solutions for the challenges around us.

The course attracted a diverse range of organisations who wanted to work with the students to develop new thinking around their current challenges, or help them construct visions of new scenarios for emerging futures. Consumer companies such as Adidas, financial service companies including Nat West, Barclays, Lloyds, Visa and Aegon, energy companies, government departments, social enterprises such as the *Big Issue*, and many charities concerned with environmental and social issues, came to the course for inspiration and new ideas.

And they got them. Of course, students on a course don't have the experience of the challenges of change within an organisation, but they have the tools and the creativity to research, discover and create compelling visions of how any of those organisations might do better. They gently, benignly, infect them with raised ambition and a sense of what might be possible.

Here are some examples from the many projects that were generated by the course. All of them were the result of direct engagement with the partnering organisations and with the people who might use and gain benefit, or be affected by the services these organisations were responsible for. They give you a sense of how creativity can generate new possibilities.

Recognising that consumers now align their spending with personal values, students Benedetta Locatelli, Conor McDonald Heffernan and Giulio Ferrato reinvented the traditional receipt into Aethos – the 21st century proof-of-purchase that reveals not just the cost but the social impact behind every transaction, redefining the meaning of values-driven commerce (Figure 14.1). They have made transparent the environmental provenance and social credentials of brands to help consumers make more conscious decisions about what they purchase.

On the surface, their solution is a receipt that shares the price of a purchase, but also the cost: in terms of the environment, CO2 emission, transportation and social impact on employees. By using a blockchain and RFID-tracked supply chain and cross-checking with existing databases to provide a full description of the provenance of the item, they provide transparency to the purchaser.

This is a system-led solution intended to give consumers greater agency over their decisions. Where there is no information, there is no validation or transparency, and this creates a behavioural nudge to brands to share their data rather than be named and shamed for lack of transparency or having something to hide.

You can imagine that if you are a global financial transaction platform looking desperately for innovation in an industry where it's hard to find, you might be interested in this idea. No one asked for it in focus group tests; we can safely say that

Figure 14.1: The 21st Receipt. Giulio Ferrato, Service Designer, Wave HQ. Benedetta Locatelli, Senior Service Designer, EY Seren. Conor Mc Donald Heffernan – Product and Design Lead, Icarus Media Digital.

no product manager ever looked in this direction, but design students searching for innovation and exploiting various technologies that can work to build trust in a brand's activities created something special that makes us imagine: what if?

Another student, Gabriella Mas, wondered during her time playing soccer in Miami, why so much free sports equipment that is donated by the big brands to athletes in sports teams is thrown away every few months when the next delivery comes in. She decided to do something about it and set up a company (re)boot to reuse and recycle discarded sports shirts. Her first collection for Inter Miami CH sold out in a day and she is building her company across other brands and locations. The (re)boot app allows you to scan your recycled shirt and tell you who played in it and its role on the pitch. Did anyone ever ask for that? Time for football clubs the world over to raise their ambition.

I focus on the course I was privileged to lead but in every design course in every design school anywhere in the world students are imagining a better future, with the tools and skills to bring it to life. The amount of creative thinking, pragmatic problem solving and ability to visualise new solutions in the upcoming generation of designers is a fabulous asset we should not ignore. We need this generation of designers, working with social scientists, technologists, and entrepreneurs, more than at any time.

And it's not just design students. I have always been inspired by the younger generation who are working in the corporate environments I have worked in. Post the advent of the FAAMG companies (Meta, Amazon, Apple, Microsoft and Google), who have succeeded though a human-centred design approach with a policy of service innovation, these new graduates, fresh from the world's smartest universities, are eager for creativity. They were attracted to our projects using design to imagine innovative new services and customer experiences. They cared about the needs of their generation that measures success not against competitors of the company they work for, but against the tech leaders Apple and Google. They see that governments are sometimes more innovative than the companies they work for, and vice versa. They are and should be the driving force for innovation, and a more equitable future, where profit and social care are more closely connected.

I fear that their creativity is horribly curtailed by the organisations they work for. This affects us all. The disproportionately high salaries you can earn in financial industries compared to other industries, for example, sucks a generation of our most innovative and exciting minds into routine boring jobs that traps them into a funnel of increasing salaries and bonuses and reduced creativity. This removal of the potential entrepreneurs and innovators into corporate life reduces society's chances to thrive.

I write during a period where the notion of some sort of 'national service' in the military or community service for young people has been rekindled. From the days of the 1950s in the UK, to the Kennedy-founded Peace Corp in the 1960s, and national military service in several countries from Switzerland to Korea, there have been programmes that put aside time for emerging young people to engage in various forms of service before they launch their careers. Imagine a scenario where we provide inducement, or even legislation, to postpone new graduates from working for disproportionately high salaries in the financial services world until they have spent a period using their talents to create the innovative ideas start-ups and services that would reinvigorate our lives. This "National Creative Service" would benefit them and us all and provide a smorgasbord of fabulous investment opportunities for banks to invest in.

Many design colleges already do this. We are familiar with the spin-outs from universities who develop new technologies and innovations that have commercial or societal benefit. At the RCA in London, InnovationRCA supports design-led business to become successful start-ups. Many companies have done so, developing products from new materials, financial management applications, products and services that serve commerce and environmental concerns with ingenuity and commercial value. They won the UK Investment Accelerator of the Year award in 2019 and have a track record that outperforms most MBA schools as well as having over 52% female founders and 34% from ethnic minorities.

As well as creativity at their core, there is a big difference in the way designers arrive at their concepts compared to business school students. Service design students at the RCA are always excited to work with MBA students, but often find that they are asked to use their perceived visual skills to "do the PowerPoint slides". The students returned confused and surprised (and not a little frustrated at the poor understanding of design in the MBA students) that the concepts were untested and unchallenged. Most MBA projects are solutions created without the rigour of analysis that a design student would be expected to show when researching, prototyping and validating which idea they should pursue. To be fair, the design students are no good at business models, or not as good as MBA students anyway.

It is, of course, the collaboration between these skills that is required. MBA students are less likely to be versed in the skills of brainstorming, prototyping, learning from failure at an early stage, as service design students.

It's the same across science and technology. The Designing for Real People course at Imperial was a great example of getting computer software designers to understand, and even collaborate with user-led design methods, with great results and learning. Too much of the world has been designed by technically brilliant people with no understanding of my mum and how confused she is going to be when she tries to change the oven clock.

There is an argument that the separation and increasing detailed specialisation of roles in any organisation has led to less collaboration. The same is true of design. Design used to be product, graphic, interior and fashion disciplines; now there are many diverse specialisations across the digital world of UX, interaction and into services, design ops (operational design) and even service design, which most don't understand at all.

But service design is interesting in that it is holistic and its outputs help define the role and purpose of all other outputs and touchpoints that constitute the experience a person has. It contains tools and outputs that give clarity to everyone in an organisation, setting the vision, locating an individual's role and purpose, defining the actions and encouraging collaboration across the whole organisation to create something consistent and excellent.

This collaboration is what enables organisations such as Design For Good to work across international NGOs to combine local insight with global creativity to create new ideas that help people in difficult circumstances thrive. It allows people to develop the new manufacturing techniques for regenerative manufacturing and provide consumers with the agency to choose better and drive change. It allows for small businesses to identify where they can improve the experience of their business customer and find innovation that is of value to them. It helps citizens collaborate with governments to make policy effective and impactful.

The Future of Design

During my lifetime, design has infiltrated and crept into the cracks, like mercury, of business and policy. A whole new generation of design leaders exists, and can reflect, as a recent EY Seren and RCA report into design in regulated industries quoted, "Most of us have built the digital world as you see it; it was our stubbornness to move things forward that has done a lot of things that have happened in the last 20 years".[5]

Despite the progress that has undoubtedly happened, there remains a gulf between business and design, and, as we often hear, design does need to adopt the language of business and lose it's unhelpful vernacular and preciousness. By the same token, business needs to get a lot smarter about the role of design in strategy, customer centricity, business value, creativity and innovation. It's a two-way discussion that both sides need to have for true and effective collaboration.

But design has come a long way and there is increasing understanding of the benefits of a deeper appreciation of how to design in business and society. Design is there to challenge, to reframe, to explore and reduce risk and although this is counterintuitive to many, many others understand it is not an option and we can do it well, rather than accidentally.

The Design Council Double Diamond (Figure 14.2) has evolved to reflect the complexity and experience of designing for new challenges. Repurposed as a framework for innovation, the Double Diamond sits with principles and methods, engagement and leadership, from a start point of the challenge to be solved. It's an evolution that activates the systems that our design decisions operate within.

AI tools already exist to support this new model. Fuspire is an international innovation team from RCA, Imperial College, and Tsinghua University, focused on design creativity and composed of designers, consultants, and developers. RCA Graduate Aoran Sun created this start-up to develop AI tools to support the Double Diamond (triple diamond in this case) with a focus on gathering inspiration, structured thinking and creative visualisation (Figure 14.3). From broadening research sources to bring in greater diversity, and helping predict outcomes to new scenarios, AI can do more than speed up processes: It will enrich and future proof the design process.

---

5 RCA & EY Seren, "The Strategic Business Function of Design in Regulated Industries", 2024, https://www.leadingdesign.works/report

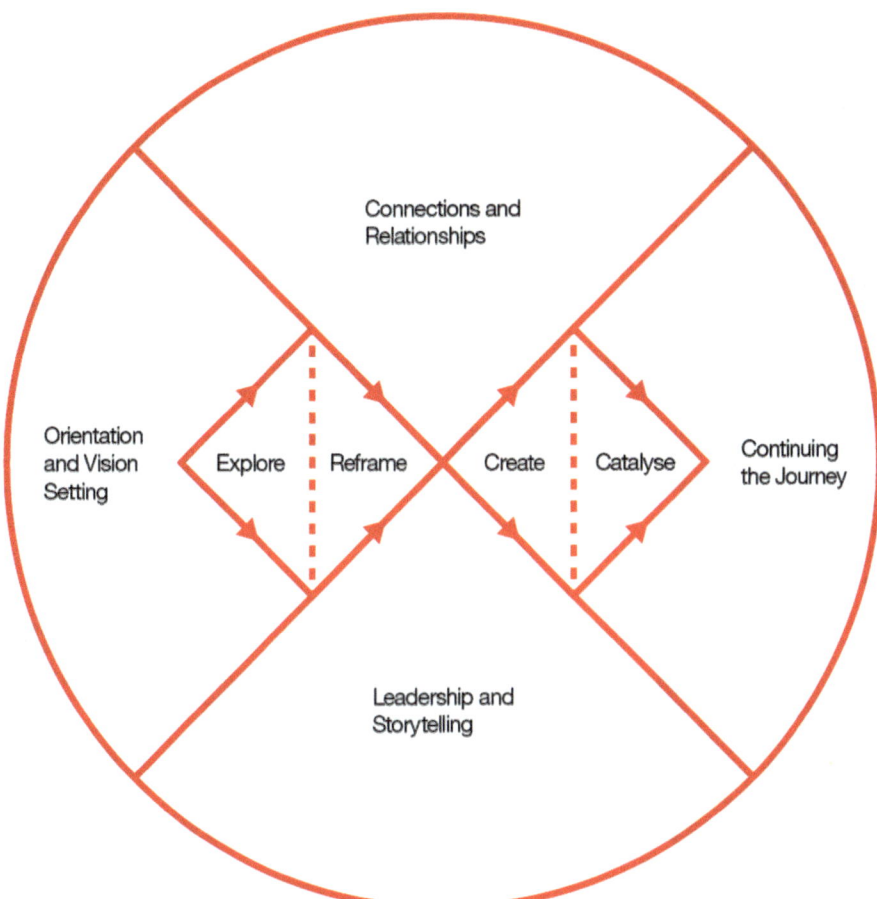

Figure 14.2: Framework for Innovation, Design Council, Creative Commons BY 4 license.

New Territories for Design

There are some new territories for design practice emerging. As design thinking and speculative design have emerged over the past two decades, there are emerging areas and applications of the methods and process of design.

The Fetzer Institute,[6] a US-based philanthropic organisation, with a 500-year mission to explore how we can transform communities and societies in which all

---

6 "At the Fetzer Institute, we believe in the possibility of a loving world: a world where we understand we are all part of one human family and know our lives have purpose. In the world we seek, everyone is committed to courageous compassion and bold love – powerful forces for good in the face of fear, anger, division, and despair." www.fetzer.org

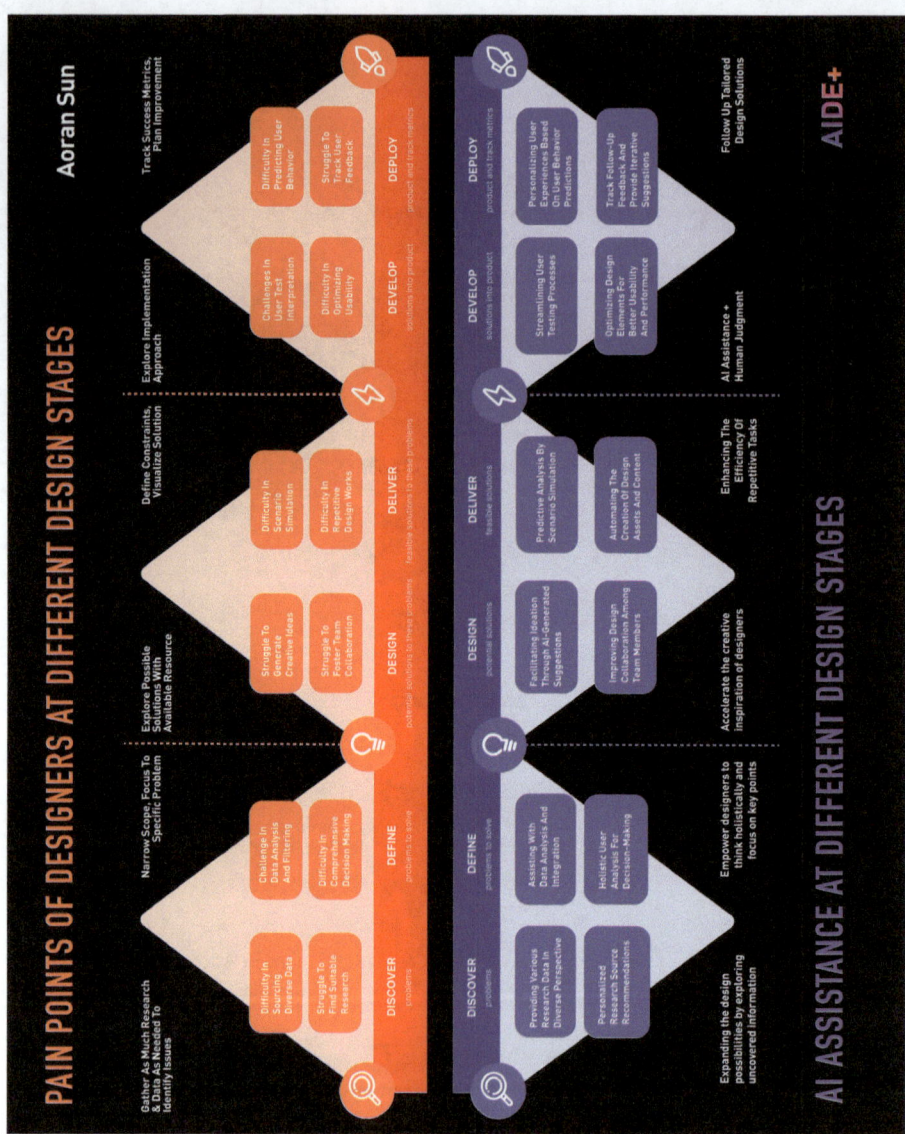

Figure 14.3: Framework AI-supported design process, Aoran Sun, 2023.

people flourish, invited designers to explore how we might design artifacts and rituals and interactions that would encourage a more loving society.

Love is a word that means many different things to different people but understanding how we can be compassionate, tolerant and caring for each other is at the core. Working with a community of designers, Fetzer commissioned a project to use design methods and practice to create new objects, experiences and interactions to foster positive feelings toward each other.

The project captures the bias to action at the heart of design and shows, in a series of prototypes and visions, how design might develop greater kindness to each other, in the workplace or in our communities, or allow us to share stories of love. It provides monuments to love and uses AI to rate our kindness.[7]

It's a start of something interesting – where design can help us envision a new purpose of design, not just to optimise a system or connect humans to the value of technology, commerce or social policy, but one where our behaviour can be affected and changed. Design, which we might define as an act of empathy in designing for and with others, might change how we see our fellow humans, remove some of the conflict, suppress our suspicion and build greater trust between us. If design is anything, it is about configuring processes and systems to suit our real intent and if that can decrease the transactional nature of our relationships and build new ground for empathy and compassion, well, that would be a positive thing.

To stand back and observe the past and present of design is to start to see how it could be more powerfully used to help us have agency over our world, make better decisions, ensure there are equitable benefits without damaging our planetary support system. This is an ambition worth having.

Little by little, design is helping us change the world.

To start at the beginning, design is not something most of us think of being important in the way we make decisions. We might see design as an activity that makes presentable the summation of decisions made for economic, organisational or political reasons. Like marketing, design will sort it out at the end of the process and ensure customers will desire, or encourage a behaviour change for the profit and objectives of an organisation.

But the way we've made decisions has left the 21st world in a dangerous mess. Government policy hasn't prevented obesity, or homelessness, or racial inequality or responded fast enough to the changing climate. The Covid Test and Trace system was an incredibly expensive failure that can be blamed on bad data, cronyism and many things, but we cannot deny that it was fundamentally undesigned.

By undesigned I mean designed accidentally. There was no thought given to humanity and the reality of engagement with populations and the people delivering the service. Of course, there will always be social media-driven madness and extremist political fractures, but that should not stop us considering more carefully and understanding more fully what we are doing when we are responding to challenging and ever-changing futures.

---

7 www.theprojectlove.com

We all design when we make decisions that affect others. And when we make decisions, we should learn from others and use the methods that have been proven to fix systems that don't work well enough and create innovations that will deliver profit, success and positive impacts on people's lives. We need to design to bring joy, bring happiness and fun to our lives.

The vital point here is that design has a bias to action that we all need. This isn't intellectual philosophising about what we should be doing. It's building, and trying out and learning and modifying and finding where success lies.

Weirdly, this is what the military does in times of conflict. The Sherman tank, bastion of the US Army in the D-Day invasion and campaign in Normandy, was unable to go through the hedges of the fields of the Normandy countryside. The forces of necessity forced creativity in the army and having considered many ideas, they saw that they could reuse sharp metal spikes used to defend the territory and weld them onto the front of the tank. A few experiments later, they were ripping through the hedges of Normandy and marching rapidly towards Paris.

The military know well how to collaborate, have a vision, model the reality of the territory and learn through failure before they launch an attack. We seem unable to apply this wonderful use of design methods when not in such a crisis.

Accept we are in a crisis. It's time to stop thinking that design is something to do with handbags and the clothes we use – it is, and very profitably too – but there is so much more of value that we can use.

Enormous Change Is About to Happen

A perfect storm of AI-led technology enablers is about to change everything we know. From peering into screens, we are likely to move to a new generation of devices in glasses and on our bodies that interact with the spaces and services around us. Some problems will go away, some new ones will appear. We need to navigate how much AI we want in our health and education and retain our creativity and life purpose. There are things AI does very well, such as protein folding for treatments for cancer. And things it does not so well, such as replacing human relationships and making decisions without human scrutiny.

We will need to make important decisions about the future – and for that we need to redesign our thinking more than ever. We will need to design legislation to protect jobs and retain our humanity. We will need to design the new interfaces and ways of working to make sure they are equally available and accessible to all.

Lord John Bird comments at the start of this book on how he realised that he had redesigned his life – by recalibrating his actions so he could move out of poverty and crime. John was able "to reflect on the obstacles to my work by approaching it as a Design issue". He realised that redesigning how we think could help him achieve his objective to end poverty. He asks us to "redesign thinking so that we recalibrate our thinking to provide the answers to the most pressing questions of our day."

The methods and tools that design draws on can play a vital part in solving the most pressing questions of the day. It's important to understand that I am not saying that designers or design are the answer to all our problems. But it is too often missing, and needs to be reinstated. We need to collaborate with the social scientists, new technologies and accountants and honour our humanity alongside our economic and scientific capabilities. We need a balanced purpose that will deliver financial and environmental sustainability, use the opportunity of technology ethically and safely and deliver benefits to all in society. Art, science and economics: collaborating together, removing the barriers and misunderstandings between these fundamental building blocks of humanity, this is our opportunity.

We might even love each other a little more.

There is not much time left. We need to raise our ambition and reach higher, embracing these tools across all our skills to redesign our thinking and take better action, now and every day for the future.

Further Reading List

There are many excellent books covering the methods of service design and the reasons and benefits to be gained. Here is a short list for those who want to redesign their thinking and those who are or wish to become designers.

Books for those who want to redesign their thinking

Good Services: How to Design Services That Work, by Lou Downe, 2020, BIS Publishers.
Leading Schools and Sustaining Innovation, How to Think Big and Differently in Complex Systems, by Luke Roberts, 2025, Routledge.
Speculative Futures: Design Approaches to Navigate Change, Foster Resilience, and Co-create the Cities We Need, by Johanna Hoffman, 2022, North Atlantic Books.
Creative Leadership: Born from Design, by Rama Gheerawo, 2022, Lund Humphries and 2024, Penguin.
Another World Is Possible: How to Reignite Social and Political Imagination, by Geoff Mulgan, 2022, Hurst.

Books for those who are or want to be service designers

This is Service Design Doing: Applying Service Design Thinking in the Real World, by Marc Stinkdorn, Markus Edgar Hormess, Adam Lawrence, Jakob Schneider, 2016, O'Reilly.
Your Guide to Blueprinting the Practical Way, by Erika Flowers/Morgan Miller, 2023.
Thinking in Services: Encoding and Expressing Strategy Through Design, by Majid Iqbal, 2018, BIS Publishers.
Society Driven Design, Co-Creating Brighter Futures, by Hoda Judah Armani, 2024, BIS Publishers.
Future Ethics, by Cennydd Bowles, 2018.

Institutions and Organisations

Design Council, www.thedesigncouncil.org
Design Management Institute, (DMI) www.dmi.org
Service Design Network (SDN), www.service-design-network.org
World Design Organisation, wdo.org

List of Figures

Figure 1.1	Pandemic Preparedness and Response Structures in the UK and England, August 2019 – National Archives, Crown Copyright, Covid19.Public-inquiry.uk	9
Figure 2.1	IBM personal computer	19
Figure 4.1	Data research of alternative routes taken by passengers from Waterloo Station to Kings Cross	70
Figure 5.1	The Squiggle, Damien Newman	77
Figure 5.2	The Design Council Double Diamond, revised	79
Figure 5.3	Journey mapping	94
Figure 5.4	The Stanford D-School 5D Design Method	95
Figure 7.1	Theory of Change Canvas, Nicolas Rebolledo 2016, based on Nesta DIY 2014	126
Figure 9.1	Pension Dashboard storyboard	145
Figure 9.2	Target Visions components	151
Figure 9.3	Six-panel storyboard on a virtual whiteboard, RCA Executive Education, Service Design Masterclass	161
Figure 10.1	Blueprint layers of interaction	167
Figure 10.2	Where to deliver different brand values across the customer journey	173
Figure 11.1	Levers at different stages and by stakeholder. Policy Lab and Nesta 2019	187
Figure 11.2	Circular economy models from the Great Recovery project.	195
Figure 12.1	Styles of leadership and dialogue	199
Figure 12.2	The Value Proposition Canvas from Service Design Tool helps capture the benefits and logic of change	201
Figure 12.3	Kim Scott's attitudes to change	203
Figure 12.4	John Maeda's attitudes to transformation	204
Figure 12.5	Nielsen's original design maturity index, from hostility to corporate strategy	210
Figure 14.1	The 21st Receipt. Giulio Ferrato, Service Designer, Wave HQ. Benedetta Locatelli, Senior Service Designer, EY Seren. Conor Mc Donald Heffernan – Product and Design Lead, Icarus Media Digital	229
Figure 14.2	Framework for Innovation, Design Council, Creative Commons BY 4 license	233
Figure 14.3	Framework AI-supported design process, Aoran Sun, 2023	234

https://doi.org/10.1515/9783111397962-017

About the Author

Clive Grinyer is an internationally renowned designer who has led global design teams at Samsung, Cisco, Orange and Barclays, worked at design consultancy IDEO, and was co-founder of the design company Tangerine. Starting as a product designer he has moved across digital, customer experience and service design and was Director of Design for the UK Design Council. As Head of Service Design at the Royal College of Art, he pioneered design as a tool for social impact, shaping how we respond to the environmental crisis and develop life services including financial and healthcare. He is an advisor and delivers executive training to companies including Bosch, the Dorchester Collection of hotels, and the Bank of England. Clive was a trustee of the Royal Society of Arts, Chair of the Design Business Association Effectiveness awards and visiting professor at the Glasgow School of Art. He is currently based in London.

Index

2001: A Space Odyssey 223
4th Industrial Revolution 35
5 Whys 100, 103

affordance 45–46, 68
Airbnb 13, 28, 45
Almere 82–83
Amazon 43, 216, 230
Apple 8, 19, 38, 43, 52, 121, 139, 159, 172, 207, 230
Armani, Judah 74, 112, 184, 202, 205
artifacts 135–137, 234
Arunkundrum, Prakash 31

Barclay, Alex 48
Barclays 62, 172, 181, 228
Beck, Harry 69, 71
Believe Housing 59–61
Biden, Joe 188
Bird, John X, 23, 213–214, 236
Birt, Harriet 97
Blackberry 207
blueprint 18, 125, 153, 165, 167
Bosch 30–31, 208–211
Boundary Spanners 204
Bracken, Mike 12
brainstorming 116, 118, 122–123, 128, 231
brand values 101, 154–155, 157, 172–173
Buolamwini, Joy 224
BYD (Build Your Dreams) 192

Calvert, Margarete 11
Campbell, Alastair 205
card sorting 91
Chambers, John 147, 150
Chartered Institute for Personal Development 189, 214
ChatGPT 9, 47
Chatley, Robert 58
Churchill, Winston 97
Cisco 43, 82, 147
co-creation 28, 32, 73, 89–90, 116, 123–124, 186, 202, 207
co-design 89, 131
Coleman, Roger 190
Conran, Terence 77
Corney, Sarah 189, 214

Cottam, Hilary 189
– Participle 189
– Southwark Circle 189
Coutts, Octavia 67
Crazy 8s 118–121, 128, 139
creativity 6, 11, 18, 27, 32–33, 47, 79, 82–83, 85, 87, 89–90, 99, 102–103, 125, 153, 184, 192, 198, 212, 214, 218, 220–222, 227–228, 230–232, 236
culture 13, 21, 29, 35, 37, 56, 74, 77, 113–115, 133, 165, 179–181, 188–190, 198, 208, 212, 217
Cutler, Nina 226

data 4, 13–14, 17, 19, 24–25, 28–29, 38–39, 41, 43, 45–46, 54, 56–57, 61, 64–67, 69, 72–74, 87, 92–93, 99–100, 103, 106, 113, 136, 143–144, 146, 150, 158, 168, 174, 176–178, 181, 183, 194, 198, 213–214, 216, 228, 235
– qualitative 73–74
– quantitative 64, 72, 74–75
D-Day 236
Demos 206
Design Council 53, 77–80, 111, 188–189, 217, 232–233
Design for Future Needs 224
Design For Good 231
design thinking 208, 225, 233
Designing for Real People 58, 231
Desirability, Feasibility and Viability 20
discovery 37, 57, 73, 81, 85, 88–89, 103, 152, 180–183
Disney 122
Disruptive Innovators Network 61
Double Diamond 53, 79–80, 95, 110–111, 132, 166, 181, 217, 232
Downe, Lou 44, 174
Drummond, Sarah 164
– Full Stack 164
Dulay, Kiran 139
Dunn, Antony 143
Durant, Nick 128

Eiffel Tower 106
Eisermann, Richard 78
Eliasson, Olafur 143
Endineering 219
epiphanies 91–92, 212

ethics 55, 74
European Commission 224
EY Seren 229, 232

features 13, 37–39, 50, 53–54, 56–57, 63, 66, 74, 89, 93, 131, 133, 136–139, 144, 146, 162, 168–169, 177
Ferrato, Giulio 228–229
Final Mile 148
Finisterre 23
foresight 32, 54, 86, 135, 218–219, 221, 224, 226
Fox, Martha Lane 11
France Poste 107
France Telecom R&D 202
Fuspire 232
Future Cone 225

Gaggero, Carla 172
Gheerawo, Rama 190
Google 8, 41–42, 65, 76, 119, 152, 230
Google Glasses 41–42
Gov.UK 11, 52, 188
Government Digital Service (GDS) 11, 158, 197, 227
Grenfell 139
GRiD 51

Hadid, Zaha 106
HAL 223
Hardy, Tom 18–19
Heffernan, Conor McDonald 228–229
Helen Hamlyn Foundation 86
Helix Centre 180
Her Majesty's Prison (HMP) Elmley 184
Hill, Alex 206
Home:Care 192
Horizon 12, 176
How Might We? 100–102, 120
Huang, Justin 216
Hunter, Nat 194

IBM 18–19, 223
ideation 116
IDEO 9, 20, 42, 51, 85, 111, 116–117, 123–124, 131
inclusive design 190–191
InHouse Records 112
Innovation Centre of France Telecom 111
InnovationRCA 230
Internet of Things 35, 43, 65
Ive, Jony 38–39, 159

Jain, Sanjay 191
Jobs, Steve 23, 38–40, 52, 118, 121, 142, 197, 207
Joost, Gesche 210
journey map 54, 58, 92, 100, 135, 142, 152, 154–155, 157, 164, 168, 178

Kamen, Dean 40
Kennedy, John F. 148, 230
King Charles 72
Kubrick, Stanley 223

Labi, Valerie 193
Lin Hu 192
Locatelli, Benedetta 228–229
Logitech 30–31
London Fire Brigade 139
London Transport 66

Maeda, John 106, 204
make the advert 56, 128–129, 134, 140
Marsh, Matt 85
Mas, Gabriella 229
McCloed, Jo 219
McCormack, Chris 180
McKinsey Design Report 32
measure success 103
Milne, Dan 162, 198
Mind Lab 185
minimum viable product 54, 63
Minority Report 224
Moggridge, Bill 9, 51–52, 85
Monterio, Mike 55
Moore, Thomas 223
– Utopia 223
Motorola 36–38, 223
Mulgan, Geof 206
– *Another World is Possible* 206
Mulgan, Geoff 226
My Creative Type 115, 205
Myerson, Jeremy 190

Narrativ 198
Nash, Jane 162, 198
Neely, J. Paul 225
Neo 192
net promotor score (NPS) 183
neurodiversity 114–115, 139, 190–191
Newman, Damien 76–77
Nishizawa, Ryue 82

Nokia 36-38
Norman, Don 45, 68
Noyes, Elliot 223

Obama, Barack 11
One Belt Initiative 226
on-stage sctions 174-175
Orange 36-38, 42, 172
- Wildfire 42
Orange Mobile 139
Osbourne, Ozzy 72

Palm Pilot 207
Pangaia 23
paper prototype 131, 133
Paris agreement 60, 143
Patagonia 23, 30
Pfeiffer, Judith 208, 210
Philips 84
Policy Lab 90, 124, 185-189, 196, 204, 226
- Bennet, Stephen 185
- Buchannan, Camilla 185-186
proposition 21, 31, 37, 56, 110, 133-137, 170, 177
prototype 20, 31-32, 52, 54, 57, 77, 79, 96, 110-111, 125, 127-142, 166, 185, 189, 224, 227, 235

Raby, Fiona 143, 224-225
Radical Candor 202, 204-205
- Manipulative Insincerity 203
- Obnoxious Aggression 203
- Ruinous Empathy 203
Radical Renew 204-205
Rams, Dieter 159
- 10 Principles of Good Design 159
research 16, 28, 46-47, 50-51, 53-55, 61, 66-67, 70, 73-74, 76-77, 79-81, 84-87, 89, 91-92, 98, 110-111, 122, 124-125, 128, 133-134, 137, 140, 148, 153, 163, 183, 185, 189, 192, 194, 207-209, 214, 217-218, 224, 228, 232
- qualitative 61, 74
Robelledo, Dr. Nicolas 189
Roberts, Luke 179
Royal College of Art IX, 24, 61, 70, 107, 147, 183, 228
Royal Society of Arts (RSA) 65, 194, 218
Ruined by Design 55, 190

Schwabb, Karl 35
Scott, Kim 202-204

Segway 40-41
Sejima, Kazuyo 82
Simon, Herbert 8-9, 81, 119, 198, 216
Siodmok, Andrea 79, 204, 226
Social Impact Challenge Lab 185
Sony 207
Special Projects 172
Stanford Design Thinking 95
Stanford D-School 53, 95
Star Trek 223
STEM (science, technology, engineering and maths) 105
storytelling 134-135, 162
Strategyzer 200
Sun, Aoran 232, 234
Suri, Jane Fulton 85
Swachh Bharat Mission 150

Tang, Audrey 12
target journey maps 152, 154-155, 164, 169
Terminal 5 86, 171
Terrett, Ben 197
- Public Digital 197
the Fetzer Institute 233
The Great Recovery 194
The Helen Hamlyn Design Institute 190
the Metaverse 43-45
The Squiggle 77
The Strategic Business Function of Design in Regulated Industries 232
The Value Proposition Canvas 200-201
Thomas, Sophie 194-195
- etsaW 194, 196
Transport for London (TfL) 66, 69-71
Tsinghua University 232
Twitter 207

Uber 14, 28
UK Design Council 16, 53, 77-80, 111, 188-189, 217, 232-233
UK government 7, 12, 52, 188, 226-227
UK Ministry of Justice 183, 185
UK test and trace 8, 13
USA.gov 188
usability 12, 36-39, 51, 58, 97, 138-139, 169, 188
user experience (UX) 30, 48, 52, 54, 57-58, 132, 138, 189, 192, 209, 231
UX Maturity Model Index 209

Vanstone, Chris 79–80
Verganti, Roberto 210
Verne, Jules 223
vision, strategy and execution 147–150, 163

Wahu 193
Wells, H.G. 223
Westaway, Adrian 172

Wheelhouse, Mark 15, 58
Whirlpool 42, 135, 224
Wiesenauer, Bernd 208–209
Wildman, Gill 111, 128
Windrush 186
Wingfield, Mendi 202

Zuckerberg, Mark 44